GRASPING THE HORIZON

JOHN JENKINS AND HIS DESCENDANTS

GRASPING THE HORIZON

JOHN JENKINS AND HIS DESCENDANTS

GARRY MOORE

Copyright © Garry Moore 2021
Cover design, Typesetting: Working Type Studio
(www.workingtype.com.au)

The right of Garry Moore to be identified as the Author of the Work has been asserted in accordance with the Copyright, Designs and Patents Act 1988.

All rights reserved. No part of this publication may be reproduced, stored in a retrieval system, or transmitted in any form or by any means without the prior written permission of the publisher, nor be otherwise circulated in any form of binding or cover other than that in which it is published and without a similar condition being imposed on the subsequent purchaser.

Garry Moore
Grasping the Horizon: John Jennings and his Descendants
ISBN: 978-0-6452041-4-8

Front cover: Frank and Bridget Jenkins in 1902.

Back cover: Swimming cattle across the Murry River in 1887 – a scene reminiscent of the original mob brought across the river by Frank Jenkins in 1847.

Contents

Introduction	1
John Jenkins Senior (1791 — 1886)	5
Early Years	7
Conviction and Transportation	10
First Years in New South Wales	14
A Family Reunited	16
Bong Bong Land	19
Tooyal	22
Berrima House	28
John Jenkins' Later Years	30
Thomas Perrin Surman Jenkins (1812 — 1882)	35
Mary Ann Garner (née Jenkins) (1814 — 1898)	39
John ("Jack") Jenkins Junior and Francis ("Frank") Jenkins	
Jack and Frank Jenkins in Partnership	47
Finding New Land	49
The Wiradjuri War	51
Expansion and Early Years in the Riverina	57
Gold	61
Acquisition of *Yanco* and *Nangus*	63
Partnership Dissolution	66
Jack Jenkins Alone (1816 — 1899)	67
Early Speculative Ventures	69
Hotels	71
Paddle Steamer	73
Middle Years	75
St Paul's Anglican Church, Nangus	76
Legal Troubles	77
Financial Strains	82
Evolving Land Laws	83
Financial Decline	87
Final Days	90

Frank Jenkins Alone (1820 — 1902)   **93**

    Early Years on the Murrumbidgee River   95
    First Marriage and Family   97
    Statesman and *Gol Gol*   *98*
    Wealth and Sorrow   102
    Second Marriage and Family   104
    Further Property Acquisitions   105
    The *Buckingbong* Homestead   107
    Religion   109
    A Further Tragic Loss   110
    Building in Narrandera and Wagga Wagga   111
    The Fruits of Success Coupled
    with More Tragic Losses   115
    Auburn-villa and Still More Tragedy   117
    Third Marriage   118
    Yet More Tragedies   120
    Confronting Selectors   121
    Financial Woes   125
    Industrial Strife   128
    Final Years   130

Elizabeth Jane Williams (née Jenkins) (1818 — 1865)   **137**

    Early Days   139
    Gol Gol   141
    The Lady Augusta   142
    Looking Northwards   146
    Last Days and Descendants   150

Ridley Frederick Williams (1850 — 1922)   **151**

    Early Days in Queensland   153
    The Barrow Creek Cattle Drive   156
    Alice Springs Interlude   169
    Journeying back to *Bierbank*   171
    Ridley Williams on *Bierbank* following the Cattle Drive   178
    Ridley Williams' Last Years   181

Conclusion   **183**

Genealogical Charts   **186**
Maps, Plans and Drawings   **193**
Bibliography   **199**

INTRODUCTION

Over the course of the Nineteenth Century, much of the vast interior of Australia was conquered and occupied by a comparatively small number of men, of predominantly English, Scottish and Irish stock, who were collectively referred to as "squatters". These men, with their herds and herdsmen, sheep and shepherds, rapidly overwhelmed and effectively displaced the original Aboriginal owners of the lands on which they settled. As Margaret Kiddle noted in her magisterial work on the squatters of the Western District of Victoria, *Men of Yesterday*:

> "The avowed purpose of the squatters was to establish themselves in a new country. Nothing could be allowed to stand in its way."[1]

Nineteenth Century squatters were in the main tough and determined men. They needed to be. They not only battled the first Australians for control of the land and exploitation of its resources, they also had to deal with droughts and floods, with great distances to markets and sources of supplies and with boom and bust economic cycles. Perhaps above all, they had to contend with colonial governments.

Relations between squatters and the governments of the Australian colonies were often marked by hostility and conflict. The original squatters were trespassers who occupied their runs "in systematic violation of the law".[2] In time, official recognition of both the inevitability and the economic utility of the spread of pastoral occupation into inland areas led to attempts to regulate that occupation by means of ever more complex licensing and leasing laws.

By the second half of the Nineteenth Century, moves by squatters to secure freehold title to their properties were met by legislation designed to "unlock the land" and open those properties to closer settlement. Squatters were ultimately unsuccessful in using their political power to block the legislative measures. However, they were able to delay and weaken them. Early enactments were not well-drawn. Many squatters were able to successfully manoeuvre their way around and through the laws so as to secure title to most, and sometimes all, of their runs. Some were thereby able to found pastoral dynasties. Many more squatters were far less successful in resisting the attacks on their holdings.

Squatters had varied backgrounds. Some arrived in Australia with both money and social

---

[1] Margaret Kiddle, *Men of Yesterday* (1980), p. 130.
[2] See letter dated 27 October 1837 from Sir James Stephen, the Under-Secretary in the Colonial Office, to the Colonization Commissioners: *Historical Records of Australia* ("*HRA*"), Series I, Vol. 18, p. 684.

status. Others were originally small farmers in their home countries. Still others were convicts transported to Australia who had served their sentences or had been pardoned. Captain Foster Fyans, who served in the 1840s as Commissioner of Crown Lands in the Portland Bay District of New South Wales noted, in an undated letter to Victoria's Lieutenant Governor Charles La Trobe:

> "The squatting population consists of such various classes of persons that it is impossible to speak of it as a body. Many of the squatters are gentlemen, worthy and excellent men, of undoubted character and well connected at home....
>
> Another class of squatters is a kind of shop-boys. A plain man can barely approach them. They have wonderful *sources* of wealth and comfort, with dirty huts and no comfort, but with plenty of pipe-smoking, grumbling and discontent....
>
> Another class consists of old shepherds. I have known this class to grow rich, the master poor, and in time the worthy would become the licensed squatter. I have known many of them to become wealthy, and some who did not forget themselves; but most were out of their places, and it would have been better for the community had they remained shepherds rather than become masters."[3]

In Barry Stone's book *The Squatters*, the author observed that:

> "Squatters were rarely the landless peasants of popular myth. Although all ten of the first free settlers that headed to Bathurst in 1818 were ex-convicts or native-born, the truth is by the 1820s only a small percentage of the white population fitted that description. By 1825, the majority of settlers had come here of their own volition, and with considerably more money than freed convicts could ever hope to acquire. Almost all of those who became squatters were the children of people who had already established a measure of financial independence. Access to capital, that one indispensable requirement for anyone wishing to stock grazing land with sheep and cattle, was all but unattainable for a prospective peasant squatter."[4]

Stone almost certainly overstates his case here. As he himself acknowledges in the above extract from his book, and as what follows in the present work also illustrates, ex-convicts and others who arrived in Australia without money or social status did become squatters. Some were very successful, amassing large holdings and great fortunes. Particularly in the early days of squatting expansion, land was relatively easy to acquire, and herds and flocks could be built up over time.

In this work, I have sought to trace the lives of three generations in a family of squatters.

---

3   See Thomas Bride, *Letters from Victorian Pioneers* (1983), pp. 185, 186 and 187. Presumably, the Victorian politician George Higinbotham had those squatters whose social origins lay in Fyans' second and third classes in mind when he disparaged squatters as a whole as "the wealthy lower order of the community": see *The Age*, Monday, 24 October 1864, p. 5.

4   Barry Stone, *The Squatters* (2019), p. 43.

INTRODUCTION

The patriarch in this family, John Jenkins Snr, started life in New South Wales as an English convict transported to the Colony for life. Attaining his freedom, he ended up as the licensee of a sizable squatting run near Wagga Wagga. In turn, two of his children were able to establish their own substantial runs in the Riverina and elsewhere; and a daughter and her husband successfully ran another large property near the junction of the Murray and Darling Rivers. A number of his grandchildren, for their part, managed to occupy a vast swathe of pastoral land in the south-west of Queensland.

The lives of John Jenkins and his descendants vividly illuminate a number of the major themes which emerge in the history of Australian squatting. As rural pioneers, they were energetic, courageous, enterprising and at times ruthless. They were at the forefront of those who dispossessed the first Australians. They generated and spent great wealth. John's children and grandchildren were challenged in their occupation of their runs by the steps taken by the colonial governments to break the properties up for closer settlement.

In the end, the Jenkins family members were to lose the lands on which they squatted, but not before they had successfully exploited those lands to provide themselves and their families with rich and rewarding lives. The words used by Margaret Kiddle to capture squatters in general may be seen to apply in equal measure to John Jenkins and his descendants:

> "They were men of their time and of their environment. To-day we may judge their purpose selfish but, right or wrong, those who succeeded pursued it with a tenacity which commands admiration. Their success was never accidental. Luck sometimes favoured them but the men of capital who established themselves had the intelligence, many of them the ruthlessness, all the courage, which were the basic qualities necessary for the frontier environment. Over the years, many more were to fail than were to succeed...."[5]

---

5   Kiddle, op. cit., p. 131.

JOHN JENKINS SENIOR

(1791 — 1886)

Early Years

John Jenkins was born in East Malling, Kent a little prior to 22 May 1791. He was christened on that date in St. James the Great's Church in East Malling.[6] At the time of John's birth, East Malling was a small rural village in the Medway River Valley lying some 6 km to the north-west of the Kent County town of Maidstone.[7]

John was the sixth of 12 children born in East Malling to Henry Jenkins and his wife, Mary Jenkins (née King). Henry and Mary were married in St. James the Great's Church on 16 February 1783.[8]

Henry Jenkins was probably born and baptised in East Malling in about 1758.[9] An agricultural worker by occupation, he died in East Malling in September 1844.[10] Mary Jenkins was born in East Malling, being baptised in St. James the Great's Church on 10 January 1763.[11] She died in East Malling and was buried in the churchyard of the latter church on 17 November 1823.[12]

Although Henry Jenkins was almost certainly illiterate and landless, one of Mary Jenkins' great(×3)–granddaughters, Ellen Clark, is on record as asserting that her ancestors had been

---

6   See the page from St. James the Great's *Christening Records* recording the baptism of John Jenkins on 21 May 1791. A copy of this page appears at p. 39 of the Berrima District Historical and Family History Society's file on the Jenkins family (referred to hereafter as "the *Jenkins Family File*"). See also **photo 1**.

7   See the **Medway River Valley Map**.

8   See the *Marr, Aitken, Watts Family Tree — Jenkins, Henry* (http://tinyurl.com/yxchu65f) (at 4 November 2019). John's siblings were:
- Samuel Jenkins, born in 1784.
- Sarah Jenkins, born in 1786.
- Elizabeth Jenkins, born in 1787.
- Henry Jenkins, born in 1788.
- Ann Jenkins, born in 1790.
- Ridley Jenkins, born in 1793.
- Thomas Jenkins, born in 1794.
- Jane Jenkins, born in 1796.
- Charlotte Jenkins, born in 1797.
- William Jenkins, born in 1798.
- Margaret Jenkins, born in 1800.

Ibid.

9   It has been asserted that Henry Jenkins was baptised in St Thomas' Church, Ashton-in-Makerfield, Lancashire in 1759: Ibid. However, this seems unlikely given that Henry was born in Kent some 400 km to the south-east of Ashton-in-Makerfield: see "1841 England Census" at *Public Records Office, England and Wales* ("*PRO*"), HO 107/460/1 at p. 7. (http://tinyurl.com/y9ejvwvl) (at 28 April 2020). Interestingly, a second Henry Jenkins appears to have been christened at Ashton-in-Makerfield on 27 December 1759 and buried 82 years later Hindley, Lancashire (http://tinyurl.com/ybpvad3x and http://tinyurl.com/ybeauxcg) (both at 28 April 2020).

10   See *Free BDM — Henry Jenkins* (http://tinyurl.com/y6987ahs) (at 4 November 2019).

11   See the *Marr, Aitken, Watts Family Tree — King, Mary* (http://tinyurl.com/yyrfo6dv) (at 4 November 2019).

12   See *East Malling Burials, 1570-1924: Mary Jenkins 1823* (http://tinyurl.com/y3jb63ql) (at 4 November 2019).

yeomen, with a known family tree extending back to the Sixteenth Century.[13] As it turns out, it would seem that Ellen Clark's assertions were at least partially correct.

Mary's family can be traced as far back as her great(×11)-grandparents, John and Isabella Kemsley. John Kemsley was born in about 1425 in Bredhurst, a hamlet located between Chatham and Maidstone in Kent. In 1450, Jack Cade led an insurrection of men from Kent, among them yeomen and other men of substance, listing grievances which they attributed to corruption and abuses of power on the part of the government of King Henry VI. The rebels forced their way into London and only agreed to withdraw on a promise of amnesty. Amongst those pardoned for their part in the uprising was a John Kemsley of Bredhurst. He appears likely to have been Mary Jenkins' ancestor.[14]

The Kemsleys apparently once owned considerable lands in Kent around Maidstone.[15] However, there is nothing to suggest that either John Jenkins or his parents inherited any of it.

John Jenkins, like his father, was illiterate, having almost certainly received no formal education.[16] As soon as he was physically able, he probably joined his father, and likely his two older brothers, working as a farm labourer in the area surrounding East Malling.

Life was undoubtedly hard for many rural workers in Kent in the early years of the Nineteenth Century. The English population doubled between 1800 and 1850. Those working the land were swelled after 1815 by soldiers and sailors demobilised following the conclusion of

---

[13] Ellen Clark was a great-great-granddaughter of John Jenkins' elder sister, Elizabeth Clark (née Jenkins). Her assertion regarding her yeomen ancestry was to be found in a biographical note which was read out at her funeral in 2002: see *RootsWeb:AUS-VIC-NE: Clark Family — Wangaratta*, (No. 16) (http://tinyurl.com/tjx2t2d) (at 17 November 2019).

[14] See *Wikipedia — Jack Cade's Rebellion* (http://tinyurl.com/yyc46onf) (at 4 November 2019); the *Marr, Aitken, Watts Family Tree — Kemsley, John (1)* (http://tinyurl.com/ycm5amxx) (at 4 November2109); the *Marr, Aitken, Watts Family Tree — Kemsley, John (2)* (http://tinyurl.com/yysqfjsw) (at 4 November 2019); the *Marr, Aitken, Watts Family Tree — Kemsley, Robert (1)* (http://tinyurl.com/y6073amd) (at 4 November 2019); the *Marr, Aitken, Watts Family Tree — Kemsley, William Gregory* (http://tinyurl.com/yyk5hutf) (at 4 November 2019); the *Marr, Aitken, Watts Family Tree — Kemsley, Robert (2)* (http://tinyurl.com/yxkpzhar) (at 4 November 2019); the *Marr, Aitken, Watts Family Tree — Kemsley, Adam* (http://tinyurl.com/yxoyu77g) (at 4 November 2019); the *Marr, Aitken, Watts Family Tree — Kemsley, Elias* (http://tinyurl.com/y67tetbl) (at 4 November 2019);the *Marr, Aitken, Watts Family Tree — Kemsley, Stephanus* (http://tinyurl.com/yxpfb2dj) (at 4 November 2109); the *Marr, Aitken, Watts Family Tree — Kemsley, Stephen* (http://tinyurl.com/y4oke7zu) (at 4 November 2019); the *Marr, Aitken, Watts Family Tree — Kemsley, Ann* (http://tinyurl.com/y4ylf7v6) (at 4 November 2019); and the *Marr, Aitken, Watts Family Tree — King, Mary* (http://tinyurl./yyrfo6dv) (at 4 November 2019) (at 4 November 2019). See also Colin Thornton-Kemsley, *Kentish Kemsleys and Their Descendants* (1980), pp. 4-8 and 43.

[15] John Kemsley's great-great-great-grandson, Thomas Kemsley, was a yeoman farmer living at Bredhurst. In the 1560s, it seems that he acquired 91 acres (about 37 hectares) of land formerly forming part of *Bredhurst Manor*. By his Will, Thomas devised his *Hemstead* farm near Bredhurst to his eldest son (and Mary Jenkins' direct ancestor), Robert Kemsley. He left his *Gyldrynes* farm at Bredhurst, together with land at Boxley, to his second son, William Kemsley. Further, he left lands at Lidsing and Lighe near Chatham to his youngest son, Adam Kemsley. Finally, he left other lands in the Parishes of Bredhurst, Stockbury and Hartlip to his widow, Joan Kemsley. His Will went on to specify that:

"mye bodye to be buried within the chancel of the Parish church of Bredhurst aforesaid on the north syde of the tombe of one Norwood there lying."

See Thornton-Kemsley, op. cit., p. 7; Roger Crockett, *The Early History of Bredhurst Manor* (2012) (http://tinyurl.com/jtgzunk) (at 4 November 2019); and the *Marr, Aitken, Watts Family Tree — Kemsley Thomas* (http://tinyurl.com/yxeo5rvg) (at 4 November 2019).

In 1495, Isabella Kemsley, the daughter-in-law of John Kemsley Snr, left two pieces of Bredhurst woodland by her Will to her son, John Kemsley Jnr, on condition that he should hold "a drinking" for the local inhabitants each year on the night of All Saints Day. Apparently, this tradition continued in Bredhurst until the Nineteenth Century: see Thornton-Kemsley, op. cit., p. 6; William Ireland, *England's Topography: or a New and Complete History of the County of Kent* (1829), Vol. 3, p. 151 (http://tinyurl.com/zmx5vuh) (at 4 November 2019); and *Wikipedia — Bredhurst* (http://tinyurl.com/hwzuck) (at 2 November 2019). It is interesting to note that there is a Kemsley Street Road still extant in Bredhurst: see **photo 2**.

[16] In "signing" the *Marriage Register* at St. Mary the Virgin's Church, West Malling in 1814, John, like his bride Charlotte Surman, was only able to "make his mark"; that is, sign with an "X": see the page from St. Mary the Virgin's *Marriage Register* recording the marriage of john Jenkins and Charlotte Surman on 16 January 1814 in the *Jenkins Family File*, p. 45.

the Napoleonic Wars. With the final enclosures of common lands, millions of poorer English men and women became wholly dependent on badly paid, and frequently scarce, seasonal labouring jobs for survival. Wages were low and hours long. Many of the landless were forced to become itinerants, often resorting to petty crime in order to sustain themselves.[17] In families like that of Henry and Mary Jenkins, with many mouths to feed, life would have been particularly difficult.

On 16 January 1814, John Jenkins married Charlotte Elizabeth Surman in St. Mary the Virgin's Church, West Malling.[18] Charlotte was born in West Malling and christened in St. Mary the Virgin's Church on 29 May 1789.[19] She was 24 years old when she married: her new husband was 22 years old. Charlotte was the fifth and last child of Francis Surman, a drover when he could find work, and his second wife, Elizabeth Surman (née Doney).[20]

At the time of her marriage to John, Charlotte was the mother of a two year old son, Thomas Perrin Surman, and was pregnant with her second child. Thomas' father, and probably the father of Charlotte's second child, was Thomas Perrin, a carpenter from Wateringbury. Wateringbury is a village some 5 km to the south of West Malling.

Thomas Perrin Surman was born in Wateringbury shortly before 29 January 1812. Soon after his son's birth, Thomas Perrin abandoned Charlotte and the child (presumably to avoid marrying Charlotte) and moved to Milton-next-Gravesend. Charlotte and her son returned to West Malling to live with Charlotte's parents.[21]

Although probably not formally adopted by John Jenkins, Thomas Perrin Surman grew up in his step-father's household and took the name Thomas Perrin Surman Jenkins.[22] A little prior to 27 February 1814, and just over a month after the marriage of John and Charlotte, the latter's second child, a girl, was born. She was christened Mary Ann Jenkins on 27 February 1814. Like those of her subsequent siblings, her baptism took place in St. James the Great's Church, East Malling. John and Charlotte had three more children together. John Jenkins Jnr ("Jack Jenkins") was christened on 6 January 1816, Elizabeth Jane Jenkins on 11 August 1818 and Francis Jenkins ("Frank Jenkins") on 14 January 1820.[23]

---

17   See Carl J. Griffin, "Parish Farms and the Poor Law: A Response to Unemployment in Southern England" in (2011) 59 *Agricultural History Review* 176, at p. 177; James Boyce, *1835: The Founding of Melbourne and the Conquest of Australia* (2011), pp. 32-34; Christine Bean, *From Tradesman to the Poor House (Gransden Family Website)* (http://tinyurl.com/y7z2xkx4) (at 4 November 2019); and Ian McNeill, *In Search of our Colonial Heritage: A Story of John Jenkins and his Family* (an undated manuscript in the possession of the Berrima and District Historical and Family History Society), p. 2.

18   See footnote 16 above and **photo 3**. Another small village in Kent, West Malling lies some 2 km to the west of East Malling.

19   See the page from St. Mary the Virgin's *Christening Records* regarding the baptism of Charlotte Surman on 29 May 1789. A copy of this page appears at p. 30 in the *Jenkins Family File*. Interestingly, the *Christening Record* entry describes Charlotte's father, Francis Surman, as a pauper. See also *Australian Royalty: Charlotte Elizabeth Surman (1789-1869)* (http://tinyurl.com/y9l39tt7) (at 4 November 2019).

20   Ibid.

21   Ibid.

22   See McNeill, op. cit., p. 3.

23   See the *Marr, Aitken, Watts Family Tree — Surman, Charlotte Elizabeth* (http://tinyurl.com/y8zfn83x) (at 5 November 2019); and McNeill, op. cit., p. 3.

Conviction and Transportation

A little over six months after Frank Jenkins' birth, the world of the Jenkins family collapsed. Nothing would ever be the same again. On Thursday, 27 July 1820, John, then 29 years of age, was put on trial before Sir George Wood (a Baron of the Court of Exchequer) and a jury of 12 men at the Kent Summer Assizes held in Maidstone on a charge of burglary. He was charged in company with three others: Thomas Wood, aged 33 years; John Hollands, aged 31 years and Thomas Webster, who was 27 years of age. All four accused were said to be living in East Malling at the time of the trial, although Hollands had apparently lived for a time in the nearby village of Birling.

John Jenkins and his co-accused were presented for trial on an indictment dated 20 May 1820 which read:

> "The Jurors of our Lord the King upon their Oaths present Thomas Wood, late of the Parish of East Malling in the County of Kent, Labourer, John Jenkins, late of the same, Labourer, John Hollands, late of the same, Labourer, and Thomas Webster, late of the same, Labourer –
>
> On the second day of May in the first year of the reign of our Sovereign Lord George the fourth by the Grace of God of the United Kingdom of Great Britain and Ireland Defender of the Faith, about the hour of eleven in the night of the same day with force and arms at the Parish aforesaid in the County aforesaid the dwelling house of Elizabeth King, widow, there situate, feloniously and burglariously did break and enter with intent the goods and chattels in the same dwelling house then and there, being then and there feloniously and burglariously to steal, take and carry away four Beds of the value of twenty pounds, seventeen Blankets of the value of eight pounds, six Counterpanes of the value of six pounds, eight Pillows of the value of four pounds, four Bolsters of the value of five pounds, one pair of Snuffers of the value of two shillings and one Pin Cushion of the value of six pence, of the goods and chattels of the said Elizabeth King in the same dwelling house then and there being found, then and there feloniously and burglariously did steal, take and carry away against the peace of our said Lord the King, his crown and dignity."[24]

It is of interest to note that the victim of the alleged burglary was Elizabeth King, a widow living in East Malling. John Jenkins' mother had of course been born Mary King in East Malling. Thus, it appears highly likely that Elizabeth King would have been related by marriage to John

---

[24] See *PRO*, ASSI, 35/260/2, PFF 790; and the *Marr, Aitken, Watts Family Tree — Jenkins, John* (http://tinyurl.com/y6vxa6ly) (at 5 November 2019). The total value of the stolen goods was accordingly said to be £43.2.6.

Jenkins. One can only assume that if they were related, the relationship was not emotionally close.

The trial of John Jenkins and his three co-accused was seemingly conducted over the course of only one day. Each of the accused pleaded not guilty to the charge and put the Crown to its proof. A total of six witnesses were called for the prosecution. Although a defendant in the early Nineteenth Century in England was entitled to give evidence on his own behalf in a criminal trial, it would appear that John and his co-accused chose to remain silent.[25]

At the conclusion of the trial, the Jury duly found all four accused guilty of the charge on which they had been indicted. The trial judge, Sir George Wood, then sentenced them all:

"to be severally Hanged by the Neck until they be Dead".[26]

The charge on which John Jenkins and his co-accused were convicted was but one of some 220 which, in the early part of the Nineteenth Century, carried the death penalty in England. Most of these offences were concerned with the protection of property. The number and range of capital crimes earned this branch of the legal system the popular title of the *"Bloody Code"*. In 1810, a reforming barrister and member of Parliament, Sir Samuel Romilly, speaking in the House of Commons on capital punishment, observed that there is:

> "no country on the face of the earth in which there [have] been so many different offences according to law to be punished with death as in England."[27]

Perhaps the saving grace of the *Bloody Code* was that most of those miscreants sentenced to death in accordance with its strictures were reprieved. Between 1770 and 1830, some 35,000 death sentences were handed down in England and Wales, with only around 7,000 executions actually being carried out.[28] It was to the great good fortune of John Jenkins and his accomplices that they were fated to join the majority of felons who were reprieved rather than hanged. Shortly after their trial the death sentences of all four were commuted to transportation to New South Wales for life.[29]

On 28 August 1820, John Jenkins, together with Wood, Hollands and Webster, was taken from Maidstone Gaol to the prison hulk *Retribution* moored off Woolwich in the River Thames to await transportation.[30] Life for John and his accomplices on the old Spanish vessel would not have been pleasant. Of life on the *Retribution*, the convict James Hardy Vaux wrote in 1819:

---

25 See Robert Popper, "History and Development of the Accused's Right to Testify" in [1962] *Washington University Law Review* 454, at pp. 454-456.

26 See *PRO*, ASSI, 31/23/95518.

27 See Sir Samuel Romilly, *Parliamentary Debates (Hansard)*, House of Commons, Friday, 9 February 1810, cols. 366-374. See also *Wikipedia — Capital Punishment in the United Kingdom* (http://tinyurl.com/zps5zmh) (at 7 November 2019).

28 Ibid. Soon after John Jenkins' trial and sentence, law reformers began to roll back the number of crimes which automatically carried the death penalty. Thus, the *Judgment of Death Act 1823* (UK) (4 Geo. 4 c. 48) gave judges the power to commute death penalties for crimes other than murder and treason: Ibid.

29 See *PRO*, ASSI, 31/23/95518. It has been estimated that over one-third of all criminals convicted in England between 1788 and 1867 were transported to either New South Wales or Van Diemen's land: see *Wikipedia — Bloody Code* (http://tinyurl.com/y4mql8lf) (at 7 November 2019).

30 See the *National Archives (Home Office — England)*: Convict Prison Hulks: Registers and Letter Books, 1802 — 1849 — John Jenkins (Microfilm, HO9, Roll 5). See also **Drawing of the Retribution**.

> "There were confined in this floating dungeon nearly six hundred men, most of them double-ironed; and the reader may conceive the horrible effects arising from the continual rattling of chains, the filth and vermin naturally produced by such a crowd of miserable inhabitants, the oaths and execrations constantly heard among them; and above all, from the shocking necessity of associating and communicating more or less with so depraved a set of beings. On arriving on board, we were all immediately stripped, and washed in large tubs of water, then, after putting on each a suit of coarse slop-clothing, we were ironed, and sent below, our own clothes being taken from us, and detained till we could sell or otherwise dispose of them, as no person is exempted from the obligation to wear the ship-dress....All former friendships or connexions are dissolved, and a man here will rob his best benefactor, or even mess-mate, of an article worth one half-penny."[31]

From the *Retribution*, Thomas Wood and John Webster were ultimately placed with 139 other transportees on board the convict transport ship *Dick*, which sailed for Sydney on 2 October 1820.[32] For a time thereafter, John Jenkins and John Hollands were left languishing in the *Retribution* off Woolwich.

It would appear that while John Jenkins and John Hollands were being held in chains on board the *Retribution* pending transportation to New South Wales, some consideration was being given by the authorities to further commuting their sentences from transportation for life to transportation for seven years. On learning of this, Sir Henry Hawley of Leybourne Grange, West Malling, a barrister and a visiting magistrate, took umbrage. Writing to the Home Secretary in London, Hawley urged that the sentences of both men remain sentences of transportation for life. Expressing his concern for "the good people of West Malling", he wrote:

> "They [John Jenkins and John Hollands] are, and [have] long been known to have been such desperate bad men, that the neighbourhood have been for some two or three years in a constant alarm for themselves and their property."

Hawley's representations were successful, and the two men's sentences remained those of transportation for life.[33]

---

31 James Hardy Vaux, *Memoirs of James Hardy Vaux* (1819), Vol. 2, Chap. 9. Vaux continued:
"Every morning, at seven o'clock, all the convicts capable of work, or, in fact, all who are capable of getting into the boats, are taken ashore to the Warren, in which the royal arsenal and other public buildings are situated, and are there employed at various kinds of labour, some of them very fatiguing; and while so employed, each gang of sixteen, or twenty men, is watched and directed by a fellow called a guard. These guards are most commonly the lowest class of human beings; wretches devoid of all feeling; ignorant in the extreme, brutal by nature, and rendered tyrannical and cruel by the consciousness of the power they possess; no others, but such as I have described, would hold the situation, their wages being not more than a day-labourer would earn in London. They invariably carry a large and ponderous stick, with which, without the smallest provocation, they will fell an unfortunate convict to the ground, and frequently repeat the blows long after the poor sufferer is insensible... If I was to attempt a full description of the miseries endured in these ships, I could fill a volume...."
Ibid.

32 The *Dick* arrived at Port Jackson on 12 March 1821: see *Convict Records of Australia — Dick voyage to New South Wales, Australia in 1820 with 141 passengers* (http://tinyurl.com/y97ct7p2) (at 8 November 2019).

33 See McNeill, op. cit., p. 3.

John Jenkins and John Hollands may well have been notorious miscreants in the West Malling area as Hawley asserted. However, it is noteworthy that neither had seemingly been convicted of any criminal offence prior to 27 July 1820. It is also interesting to note that on that date, and immediately after their burglary convictions, Hollands and Thomas Wood were further convicted at the Kent Summer Assizes of stealing and killing a sheep belonging to Richard Pye of Birling on 5 May 1820.[34] Presumably, the sheep they killed was eaten. This might suggest that John Jenkins and his three accomplices broke the law because of their desperate financial circumstances in hard times.

In late December 1820, John Jenkins and John Hollands, together with 152 other transportees, were placed on the *Speke*, a 473 ton sailing vessel commanded by Captain Peter McPherson. In the ship's Indents, John Jenkins was described as "a farming man" from East Malling, 27 years of age, 5' 4½" tall and with a florid face, brown hair and grey eyes.[35] On 22 December 1820, the *Speke* left London bound for Sydney. After a voyage of 147 days, and the deaths of two convicts in transit, it arrived at Port Jackson on 18 May 1821.[36]

---

34 See *PRO*, ASSI, 31/23/95518; the *Jenkins Family File*, p. 29; and the *Marr, Aitken, Watts Family Tree — Jenkins, John* (http://tinyurl.com/y6vxa6ly) (at 8 November 2019).

35 See the *Jenkins Family File*, pp. 7 and 27; and the *Marr, Aitken, Watts Family Tree — Jenkins, John* (http://tinyurl.com/y6vxa6ly) (at 8 November 2019).

36 See *Convict Records of Australia — Speke voyage to New South Wales, Australia in 1820 with 156 passengers* (http://tinyurl.com/ya7cazmc) (at 8 November 2019); and Mc Neill, op. cit., pp. 3 and 4. The *Speke* was formerly known as the *Warren Hastings*: see *Wikipedia — Warren Hastings (1789 ship)* (http://tinyurl.com/y72zgums) (at 8 November 2019).

First Years in New South Wales

It is presently unclear where and how John Jenkins spent his early days as a convict in New South Wales. It has been noted that as of September 1821, he was engaged as a convict labourer and messenger, receiving his food from government stores. However, by 1822, and together with John Hollands, he had been assigned by the New South Wales colonial authorities to work for James Atkinson.[37]

James Atkinson lived his short life between 1795 and 1834. He was born on the *Oldbury* estate near Ightham in Kent. In 1820, he immigrated to New South Wales; arriving in Port Jackson on the *Saracen* on 19 May 1820. In July of that year, he succeeded Michael Robinson as Principal Clerk in the Colonial Secretary's Office in Sydney. In July 1821, Atkinson received two Crown Grants of land at Sutton Forest in the County of Argyle. The first, of 800 acres [about 324 hectares], he named *Oldbury* after his father's estate in Kent. He named his second and neighbouring grant of 700 acres [about 283 hectares] *Mereworth*, after a nearby village in Kent.[38]

In July 1822, Atkinson resigned from his government post and moved to a house he had constructed on his *Oldbury* land at Sutton Forest.[39] If John Jenkins and John Hollands had not already preceded Atkinson under supervision to *Oldbury*, then they, and perhaps other assigned convicts, would almost certainly have accompanied Atkinson in his move from Sydney to Sutton Forest in 1822.

In his book, *An Account of the State of Agriculture and Grazing in New South Wales*, Atkinson described the country in the vicinity of his Sutton Forest properties thus:

> "In the country westward of the Blue Mountains, and also in the counties of Argyle and Antrim, are the largest tracts of open forest, where the basis of the soil is granite; this country is thinly covered with trees, of the white and blue gum kinds, and large blocks of granite, of a course texture, and grey colour, are seen lying about the surface. This country, though pleasing to the eye, having a beautiful park-like appearance, is poor and seldom adapted for cultivation; but the soil is light, dry and extremely well suited for sheep grazing, the surface being covered with thin but very nutritive herbage. In the County of Argyle are some small tracts, where whinstone predominates; this is the

---

37 See the *Marr, Aitken, Webb Family Tree — Jenkins, John* (http://tinyurl.com/y6vxa6ly) (at 8 November 2019).

38 See T M Perry, "Atkinson, James (1795-1834)" in *Australian Dictionary of Biography* (http://tinyurl.com/y7mdupxz) (at 8 November 2019); and A V J Parry, "Early History of Moss Vale" in the *Southern Mail*, Friday, 3 December 1948, p. 10. According to Parry, Atkinson's land grants at Sutton Forest were extended to some 2,000 acres [approximately 809 hectares] in October 1822. In December of that year, he was granted a permit to graze a further 4,000 acres [about 1,618 hectares] of land known as *Dittalie* on the right bank of the Wollondilly River, "about one day's journey from *Oldbury*": Ibid.

39 See Perry, op. cit.

finest description of forest land in the country, equally well adapted for grazing or for cultivation; the soil is firm and rich, and the herbage of the most nutritive description."[40]

James Atkinson was regarded both as a progressive farmer and grazier and as a humane master of his assigned convicts. On moving to *Oldbury*, he set about developing his properties. In a Memorial dated 22 August 1826 and addressed to the Secretary of State for the Colonies, Earl Bathurst, by which he sought a further Crown Grant or Grants of land, Atkinson described the improvements which he had by then made to his Sutton Forest lands. He wrote:

> "Your Memorialist humbly represents that, by the employment and expenditure of a very considerable capital, he has erected a house and very extensive buildings upon his land, has brought 150 acres [about 61 hectares] into a complete state of cultivation, has enclosed the principal part of his land, and effected many great and extensive improvements. That in fact he has fulfilled the terms of his Grant to the very letter, and converted what was before a wild and worthless wilderness into a cultivated and highly improved farm, affording constant employment to about 20 convicts, free of every expense to the Crown. That he is in possession of a very extensive stock of cattle, sheep and horses, which his lands have long been insufficient to afford pasturage for, and that he has been compelled to resort to the unoccupied Districts of the interior for their support."[41]

Notwithstanding Sir Henry Hawley's earlier denigration of John Jenkins' character, there is nothing to suggest that the latter misbehaved in any way after his arrival in New South Wales. Presumably, John worked on *Oldbury* to the full satisfaction of Atkinson. Despite their vastly different social origins and circumstances, they may even have become friendly with each other, given that they were roughly the same age and had grown up not far from one another in the Medway River Valley of Kent. Atkinson went so far as to name a small stream which flows through *Oldbury* the "Medway Rivulet"; a name which still stands today. In the event, Atkinson proved to be of great assistance in reuniting John with his wife and children.

---

40   James Atkinson, *An Account of the State of Agriculture and Grazing in New South Wales* (1826), pp. 5-6.
41   See A V J Parry. "Early History of Moss Vale" in the *Southern Mail*, Friday, 3 December 1948, p. 10.

A Family Reunited

John Jenkins' arrest, trial and transportation for life left his wife, Charlotte, and her five young children destitute. It would seem that neither Charlotte's nor John's family was able to provide much by way of assistance. Charlotte and the children were forced to rely for accommodation and sustenance on the Halling Workhouse. Life in the Workhouse would have been spartan and grim. On one occasion at least during this period, the East Malling Vestry Minutes referred to Charlotte as "the Widow Jenkins". She was not, of course, a widow; John's fate would have been well-known in the district. However, she may have been called the Widow Jenkins out of kindness.[42]

On 12 February 1825, James Atkinson departed Sydney on board the *Mangles* on a business trip back to England.[43] He left his younger brother, John Atkinson, in charge of *Oldbury* pending his return.[44]

Whilst in England, James Atkinson made it his business to meet with Charlotte Jenkins, and he did much to help both her and John Hollands' wife to secure government-funded passages for themselves and their children to New South Wales to join their respective husbands and fathers. It would seem that Charlotte was initially reluctant to make the journey. However, by January 1826, she had decided to go; having apparently been convinced by Atkinson that her husband was able to support the family and wanted to have them with him.[45]

Atkinson wrote a number of letters on behalf of both Charlotte and Hollands' wife. One of these letters took the form of character references for both John Jenkins and John Hollands. In it, he stated that both had been in his immediate service for a period of four years, and that "during the whole of that time they conducted themselves in a very regular and industrious manner".[46]

Atkinson further assisted Charlotte Jenkins and Mrs Hollands in petitioning the Home Secretary, Robert Peel, in the matter. He may also have presented Peel with a letter signed by the Governor of New South Wales, Sir Thomas Brisbane, requesting that each of the two families be reunited in New South Wales.[47] Atkinson's efforts were supported by a letter to the Home Secretary from the Halling Parish Council advising that:

---

[42] See McNeill, op. cit., pp. 4-5; and the *Jenkins Family File*, p. 33.

[43] See the *Sydney Gazette and New South Wales Advertiser*, Thursday, 17 February 1825, p. 2.

[44] See A V J Parry, "Early History of Moss Vale" in the *Southern Mail*, Friday, 3 December 1948, p. 10. As to John Atkinson, see the *Southern Highland News*, Monday, 2 May 2011.

[45] See Jennifer Parrott, *For the Moral Good? The Government Scheme to Unite Convicts with their Families 1818-1843* (Master of Humanities Thesis, University of Tasmania, 1994), Appendix 6, pp. xxxii-xxxiii (http://tinyurl.com/dv482zbk) (at 8 November 2019).

[46] See McNeill, op. cit., p. 4.

[47] Ibid.

"the Petitioners and their families are a heavy and increasing burthen to this Parish and that we are perfectly ready to fit them out for the voyage with clothing."

The Parish Council's letter was in turn supported by one from six Justices of the Peace from the County of Kent.[48]

All these representations bore fruit. In August 1826, approval was given for the two wives and their children to sail to New South Wales at government expense.[49] On 8 September 1826, Charlotte, Mrs Hollands and their respective children left England as free passengers on board the *Grenada* bound for Sydney via Hobart. They shared the vessel with some 88 female convicts, who were disembarked in Hobart. The *Grenada*, together with the Jenkins and Hollands family members, arrived in Sydney on 23 January 1827.[50]

On 10 September 1826, two days after the departure of the *Grenada* from Portsmouth, James Atkinson also set sail from England to Australia, leaving on the *Cumberland*.[51] He took with him 30 saxon merino rams and ewes, which he had previously purchased in Saxony; together with a bull, a stallion, sheep dogs, poultry, hop plants and fruit tree and flower cuttings.[52]

Also on board the *Cumberland*, though travelling as one of nine steerage passengers, rather than as a cabin passenger like Atkinson, was John Jenkins' 20 years old nephew, John Clark Jnr.[53] The latter was the eldest child of John Jenkins' older sister, Elizabeth Clark (née Jenkins), and her husband, John Clark Snr. John Clark Jnr grew up with his parents and siblings in the Medway River Valley in close proximity to John Jenkins and his family. Almost certainly, he was primarily motivated to immigrate to Australia by his poor economic prospects in England. However, positive reports regarding life in New South Wales which his family may have received in letters from John Jenkins after the latter's transportation to the Colony could conceivably have played their part. Moreover, it is possible that John Clark Jnr had also met with James Atkinson whilst the latter was assisting Charlotte Jenkins in Kent, and had been encouraged by him to accompany Atkinson to New South Wales on the *Cumberland*.[54]

The *Cumberland* arrived at Port Jackson on 24 January 1827, the day after the arrival of the *Grenada*.[55] Given that the two vessels travelled from England to Australia almost simultaneously, and given James Atkinson's involvement in securing passage to New South Wales for the Jenkins and Hollands families, it seems quite likely that John Clark Jnr joined them

---

48 See Parrott, op. cit., Appendix 6, p. xxxiii.
49 Ibid.
50 See *Wikipedia — Grenada (1810 ship)* (http://tinyurl.com/yxg3upgr) (at 9 November 2019).
51 See "New South Wales — 1828 Census: Householders' Returns" in *New South Wales State Archives and Records* (AONSW: Series 1273, Reels 2506-2507 and 2551-2552).
52 See Charlotte McNeilly, "The Saxon Merino" in the *Molong Argus*, Friday, 5 January 1906, p. 6. Mc Neilly was a daughter of James Atkinson. See also A. V. J. Parry, "Early History of Moss Vale" in the *Southern Mail*, Friday, 3 December 1948, p. 10.
53 See "New South Wales — 1828 Census: Householders' Returns" in *New South Wales State Archives and Records* (AONSW: Series 1273, Reels 2506-2507 and 2551-2552).
54 See the *Sydney Gazette and New South Wales Advertiser*, Thursday, 25 January 1827, p. 3. In any event, with so few passengers on board the *Cumberland*, and on such a long voyage, it seems highly likely that John Clark Jnr and James Atkinson would have become well-acquainted in transit, notwithstanding that the former was a steerage passenger and the latter a cabin passenger.
55 Ibid.

before they all set off in the one party for Sutton Forest. If they did travel together, it would have been a large and slow-moving group. The younger members of the party would probably have assisted Atkinson in managing the saxon merino sheep, the bull, the stallion, the sheep dogs and the poultry he had brought with him from Europe.

After their arrival at *Oldbury* and their reunion with John Jenkins, Charlotte and their children would undoubtedly have lived for a time on that property with John. In all probability, the children would have made themselves useful around *Oldbury*.[56]

---

[56] According to Charlotte McNeilly, James Atkinson's daughter, her father put the Jenkins' youngest child, Frank Jenkins, to work shepherding Atkinson's saxon merino sheep: see Charlotte McNeilly, "The Saxon Merino" in the *Molong Argus*, Friday, 5 January 1906, p. 6.

Bong Bong Land

Later in 1827, Charlotte Jenkins received a Crown Grant of 60 acres [around 25 hectares] of land, probably at or in close proximity to Bong Bong and not far from *Oldbury*. As a free settler, she was entitled to a grant of up to 30 acres [some 12 hectares] in her own right. As she was married, she was entitled to an extra 20 acres [about 8 hectares]; and the fact that she had children entitled her to a further 10 acres [approximately 5 hectares].[57] It is highly likely that James Atkinson assisted in securing the Grant for Charlotte.

The land granted to Charlotte Jenkins was probably open and fairly well-grassed at the time of her Crown Grant due to generations of judicious management by local Aborigines using "firestick farming" techniques.[58] The property may well have resembled British parkland. On a tour of inspection of the Bong Bong area in 1820, New South Wales Governor Lachlan Macquarie was impressed with the lie of the countryside, describing it as:

> "extremely pretty, gentle hills and dales with an extensive rich valley…having a very park-like appearance, being very thinly wooded."[59]

As John Jenkins was still a convict under sentence, he was not permitted to hold title to land in his own right. However, a short time after the Grant to Charlotte, John was re-assigned by the Colonial Government to work the land for her. Again, it seems highly likely that Atkinson was instrumental in securing John's re-assignment.[60]

The 1828 Census conducted in New South Wales revealed that in that year, John Jenkins was indeed working his wife's Bong Bong land. He was almost certainly assisted in doing so by their two younger sons, Jack and Frank Jenkins, and very likely by John's nephew, John Clark Jnr. Together, they had put some 5 acres [around 2 hectares] under cultivation and had cleared a further 5 acres. John Jenkins had also apparently acquired a herd of 30 head of cattle, possibly also with Atkinson's assistance.[61]

The 1828 Census further revealed that the Jenkins' eldest son, Thomas Jenkins, had left

---

57 See *HRA*, Series 1, Vol. 1, p. 14; New South Wales Government State Archives and Records, *Land Grants Guide, 1788-1856: Historical Background* (http://tinyurl.com/y9dnpq8j) (at 9 November 2019); and McNeill, op. cit., p. 6

58 See *Wikipedia — Firestick Farming* (http://tinyurl.com/tfqrc54).

59 See Lachlan Macquarie, *Lachlan Macquarie, Governor of New South Wales: Journals of his tours in New South Wales and Van Diemen's Land 1810-1822* (1956), p. 146 (18 October 1820); and Bill Gammage, *The Biggest Estate on Earth: How Aborigines Made Australia* (2011), p. 62-63.

60 See McNeill, op. cit., p. 6.

61 See "New South Wales — 1828 Census: Householders' Returns" in *New South Wales State Archives and Records* (AONSW: Series 1273, Reels 2506-2507 and 2551-2552).

his parents' home and was working for William Ryrie on the latter's *Arnprior* grazing property near Braidwood. The Jenkins' younger daughter, Elizabeth Jenkins, was employed as a servant by James Atkinson at *Oldbury*. Thomas was 16 years old at the time, and Elizabeth all of 10 years of age.[62]

At the time of the 1828 Census, the Jenkins' older daughter, Mary Jenkins, was living in the family home which had been constructed on her mother's land. Presumably, she was assisting Charlotte with the discharge of household duties. If so, this state of affairs did not last long. On 29 June 1829, Mary married James Garner, an ex-convict and a local farmer. It would appear that the marriage was conducted in the Jenkins' home by an itinerant Anglican minister. Mary was 15 years of age at the time of her marriage, and her husband was around 20 years old.[63]

The lives of John and Charlotte Jenkins' sons and daughters will be explored in detail below.

The Jenkins family undoubtedly prospered on Charlotte Jenkins' Bong Bong land. John proved to be both a hard worker and, like his two younger sons, entrepreneurial. On 5 August 1829, he was granted a Ticket of Leave.[64] This allowed him a form of conditional parole. Holders of Tickets of Leave were authorised to live and seek their own employment within a specified district, but not to leave it without the permission of the Colonial Government or that of the resident magistrate in the district concerned.[65] In John's case, the district to which he was restricted was Sutton Forest.

By the early 1830s, John was both ready and keen to expand his family's pastoral land holdings. However, his options in that regard were somewhat constrained.

On 5 September 1826, Governor Sir Ralph Darling of New South Wales issued an Order at the direction of Earl Bathurst, the Secretary of State for the Colonies, limiting land settlement in the Colony to a defined area surrounding Sydney. On 14 October 1829, the Governor promulgated a further Order which extended this defined area so as to encompass a total of 19 counties; with the area so encompassed extending from Murrurundie in the north, to Cowra in the west and Batemans Bay in the south. The outer boundary of the 19 counties, taken as a whole, was known as the *"Limits of Location"*. Sutton Forest, and with it Bong Bong, was located in one of the 19 counties, that of Camden.[66]

On 19 January 1831, the new Secretary of State for the Colonies, Viscount Goderich, instructed Darling that there were to be no more free grants of land within the *Limits of Location*. All unalienated land within those limits was to be subject to disposition by auction.[67]

These colonial measures relating to land settlement and disposition narrowed John Jenkins' opportunities to acquire new pastoral land. He likely lacked the money in his own right to

---

62 Ibid; and McNeill, op. cit., pp. 3 and 6.
63 See the *Marr, Aitken, Watts Family Tree — Jenkins, Mary* (http://tinyurl.com/y9ekyfez) (at 9 November 2019).
64 See the *Jenkins Family File*, p. 37.
65 See *Wikipedia — Ticket of Leave* (http://tinyurl.com/y8ouhjwp) (at 9 November 2019).
66 See "Land Grants Guide, 1788-1856: Historical Background" in *New South Wales Government State Archives and Records* (http://tinyurl.com/y9dnpq8j) (at 9 November 2019); and *Wikipedia — Nineteen Counties* (http://tinyurl.com/y9pany9e) (at 9 November 2019).
67 See "Land Grants Guide, 1788-1856: Historical Background" in *New South Wales Government State Archives and Records* (http://tinyurl.com/y9dnpq8j) (at 9 November 2019).

purchase land at auction within the 19 counties. As the holder of a Ticket of Leave, and without title to land in his own name, he would almost certainly not have been regarded by lenders as a good credit risk. John's solution was to seek land to the south-west of Sutton Forest beyond the *Limits of Location*.

Tooyal

John would have been well aware that there was excellent grazing land to the south and west of the *Limits of Location*. In 1824, Hamilton Hume and William Hovell had located good pastoral country during their exploratory expedition to Port Phillip Bay.[68] On his return to Sydney following his 1830 expedition down the Murrumbidgee River to the Murray River and thence on to the sea, Charles Sturt spoke and wrote effusively of the rich lands he had traversed along the Murrumbidgee.[69]

Following in the footsteps of Hume and Hovell, Europeans began to occupy squatting runs to the south-west of the 19 counties and beyond the *Limits of Location*. By 1829, Henry O'Brien had occupied the *Jugiong* run, William Warby had taken up *Mingay*, Henry Stuckey had settled on *Tumblong* and the latter's brother, Peter Stuckey, had occupied *Willie Ploma*.[70] All of these runs were situated, broadly speaking, in the area near present-day Gundagai where the Murrumbidgee River leaves the foothills of the Snowy Mountains.

The years 1832 and 1833 saw an explosion of European settlement down the Murrumbidgee River Valley to the west of the Gundagai area. By the end of 1832, James and William Macarthur had occupied the *Nangus* run, Charles Thompson had taken up both the *Oura* and *Eunonyhareenyha* runs and George Best had settled on the *Wagga Wagga* run.[71]

In 1832, male members of the Jenkins family were among the first to occupy pastoral land along the Murrumbidgee; squatting on a run which they named *Tooyal*.[72] The run was located on the right bank of the River, to the west of the Malebo Hill and some 15 km to the west of present-day Wagga Wagga.[73] *Tooyal* initially covered an area of approximately 25,600

---

[68] In this context, it is interesting to note that in early October 1824, Hume and Hovell had eaten breakfast with James Atkinson at *Oldbury* soon after the commencement of their expedition. More significantly, they again visited *Oldbury* on their return journey in January 1825: see Robert Macklin, *Hamilton Hume: Our Greatest Explorer* (2016), pp. 89 and 123.

[69] See H. J. Gibbney, "Sturt, Charles (1795-1869)" in *Australian Dictionary of Biography* (http://tinyurl.com/3qhcu76) (at 9 November 2019); and McNeill, op. cit., p. 7. It would seem that whilst travelling on this expedition, Sturt may have had occasion to visit *Ploughed Ground*, the small farm then owned by John Jenkins' son-in-law, James Garner: see Charles Sturt, *Two Expeditions Into The Interior Of Southern Australia* (1834), Vol. 1, Preliminary Chapter, p. xxxviii).

[70] See *Wikipedia — Gundagai* (http://tinyurl.com/mybx35s) (at 9 November 2019). The word "squatter" was initially used to describe a pastoralist in unauthorised occupation of land. Stephen Roberts observed:

"the word was first used in Van Diemen's Land — in the twenties there emerged a class of what might be termed frontiersmen, 'bushrangers', or ex-convicts — shingle splitters, or small cultivators who gathered flocks both by legal and illegal means. These people were known as 'squatters' — even in the twenties, and their holdings were termed 'runs' — a most convenient depot for stolen sheep."

Stephen Roberts, *History of Australian Land Settlement* (1924), p. 175.

[71] See James Gormly, "Exploration and Settlement on the Murray and Murrumbidgee" in (1906) 2(2) *Journal of the Australian Historical Society* 34, at p. 39.

[72] Ibid. According to James Baylis, the name "Tooyal" was seemingly derived from the Wiradjuri word "Toyeo", meaning the jag of a spear: see James Baylis, "The Murrumbidgee and Wagga Wagga" in (1927) 13(4) *Journal and Proceedings of the Royal Historical Society* 253, at p. 254.

[73] See **photo 4**. The original *Tooyal* run is now crossed by the Old Narrandera Road.

acres [approximately 10,360 hectares].[74] By 1865, the run had grown to 49,920 acres [about 20,202 hectares].[75]

It has been suggested that because his movements as the holder of a Ticket of Leave were restricted to the Sutton Forest District, John Jenkins dispatched his two sons, Jack and Frank Jenkins, south-westwards to find and take up land in the Murrumbidgee River Valley on his behalf.[76] Whilst this is possible, it seems more likely that in view of their ages, the two boys were in fact accompanied by their father.[77] Jack Jenkins would have been about 16 years of age at the time of this venture and his brother Frank only 12 years old. While John may have sought official permission to accompany his sons, there would appear to be no record of such permission being either granted or sought. Nonetheless, he could well have accompanied them surreptitiously and without official permission.

Whether or not John accompanied his sons to claim the *Tooyal* run, two things seem certain. In the first place, the run was initially managed by Jack and Frank Jenkins on behalf of their father. At least in the early 1830s, the latter appears to have been still living on his wife's property at Bong Bong. Secondly, the Jenkins family commenced their occupation of *Tooyal* as trespassers.

Although the occupation of land by squatters beyond the *Limits of Location* in the years immediately following 1829 was unlawful, it was very soon recognised by the Colonial Government in Sydney that it would be almost impossible to evict all of the trespassers. In a dispatch to Viscount Goderich, the Secretary of State for the Colonies, on 17 February 1831 in relation to the permeability of the *Limits of Location*, Darling noted that:

> "precise boundaries [are] being established, beyond which settlers are not allowed to receive grants or to lease land; but it is impossible to prevent their sending their cattle to graze beyond these limits."[78]

Yet the Colonial Government was loathe to recognise the squatters' entitlement to runs outside the 19 Counties. By an Act of the Governor in Council promulgated on 1 September 1833, newly appointed Commissioners of Crown Lands were armed with authority to "warn off" all trespassers on Crown lands beyond the *Limits of Location*.[79] On 4 July 1834, Darling's

---

74 J. F. Campbell, *'Squatting' on Crown Lands in New South Wales* (1968), p. 50.

75 See John Vann, *The Squatting Directory for New South Wales* (1865), p. 69. As Vann noted, *Tooyal* had passed out of Jenkins' hand by 1865.

76 Thus, it was asserted anonymously in the *Southern Highland News* on 14 April 2014 that:
"In 1832 John extended his family holdings south into the Murrumbidgee area sending his sons, aged only 12 and 15, to run a station there.
Why did he have to send his sons?
John only had his ticket of leave at this time and was therefore forbidden to leave the Berrima district."
See Anon., "Focus on the lives of Berrima individuals; Part 2" in the *Southern Highland News*, Monday, 14 April 2014. See also Anon., "Census 'snapshot' of Berrima 1841" in (July, 2014) 463 *Berrima District Historical and Family History Society* 1, at p. 6 (http://tinyurl.com/sdc7jql) (at 5 April 2020)

77 See Gammage, *Narrandera Shire*, op. cit., p. 38; and McNeill, op. cit., p. 7.

78 See Campbell, op. cit., p. 5.

79 See *Act for Protecting the Crown Lands of this Colony from Encroachment, Intrusion and Trespass 1833* (NSW); and the *New South Wales Government Gazette* (No. 80), Wednesday, 11 September 1833, p. 356.

successor as Governor of New South Wales, Sir Richard Bourke, wrote in a dispatch to the new Secretary of State for the Colonies, Thomas Spring Rice:

> "I would observe that it is not beyond the southern boundary alone that flocks and herds of the colonists have wandered for suitable pastures. They are numerous to the south-west along the bank of the Murrumbidgee….These unauthorised occupations must not, however, be permitted to continue so long as to create any title to the land in the occupier."[80]

It soon became clear that squatters were not amenable to being "warned off" their runs, and in 1836, the Colonial Government bowed to the inevitable. The 1833 Act was repealed. By the terms of the repealing Act, squatters were given permission to apply to the Colonial Secretary in Sydney for licences to depasture vacant Crown lands beyond the *Limits of Location*. Such licences were made conditional on the applicants first securing Certificates of Good Character from their nearest Justices of the Peace or Commissioners of Crown Lands, and on payment of flat annual licence fees of £10 irrespective of the size of the runs.[81]

The legislative changes of 1836 were an acknowledgment that the eviction of squatters from their runs beyond the *Limits of Location* was not only impractical but also economically undesirable. In a dispatch dated 19 December 1840 from Governor Sir George Gipps to Lord John Russell, the Secretary of State for the Colonies, Gipps stated in oft-quoted words:

> "As well might it be attempted to confine the Arabs of the desert within a circle, traced upon their sands, as to confine the Graziers or Wool-growers of New South Wales within any bounds that can possibly be assigned to them, and as certainly as the Arabs would be starved, so also would the flocks and herds of New South Wales if they were so confined, and the prosperity of the Colony be at an end."[82]

On 28 February 1832, John Jenkins' Ticket of Leave was varied so as to enable him to live and work in the Inverary District.[83] It is not presently known why John sought and obtained the variation. Inverary was and remains a rural area some 20 km to the south of present-day Marulan, and around 90 km to the north-east of Canberra. It was located within the *Limits of Location* in the County of Argyle, and therefore would not have given John free access to *Tooyal*. However, an Inverary base may have improved John's unsanctioned access to Tooyal, as stock routes heading to the west then passed through and close by the District. Again, it

---

80   See Campbell, op. cit., p. 6.
81   See *Act to Restrain the Unauthorised Occupation of Crown Lands 1836* (NSW); and the *New South Wales Government Gazette* (No. 242), Wednesday, 5 October 1836, p. 745. See also the *New South Wales Government Gazette* (No. 254), Wednesday, 21 December 1836, p. 376.
82   See dispatch dated 19 December 1840 from Sir George Gipps to Lord John Russell: *HRA*, Series 1, Vol. 21, p. 127.
83   The variation was authorised by the Colonial Secretary in a letter dated 28 February 1832 (No. 32/171) and noted on John's original Ticket of Leave: see the *Marr, Aitken, Watts Family Tree — Jenkins, John* (http://tinyurl.com/y6vxa6ly) (at 10 November 2019).

may be that John applied for the variation in order to work for a time on David Reid's *Inverary Park* pastoral property.[84] However, this is pure speculation.

The year 1832 also witnessed a second marriage in the Jenkins family. On 11 June 1832, John and Charlotte's younger daughter, Elizabeth Jenkins, married Henry Thomas Williams, another ex-convict and transportee. This marriage was celebrated by the Reverend John Vincent in the newly constructed and dedicated All Saints Church at Sutton Forest near the bride's parents' home. Elizabeth was 13 years of age at the time of her marriage.[85] Her husband was likely about 29 years old.

As stated above, in the early years of the Jenkins' occupation of *Tooyal*, it would appear that the run was largely managed by Jack and Frank Jenkins.[86] However, the two brothers, as will be seen below, soon came to have squatting interests which extended well beyond *Tooyal*. By 1843, their brother-in-law, Henry Williams, was on record as managing the run.[87]

Who worked for whom according to law in the Jenkins family during the 1830s appears to have been somewhat fluid. It would seem that by early 1836, John Jenkins was no longer legally assigned to work for his wife, Charlotte. He had apparently been re-assigned to work for his son, Jack Jenkins. According to Bill Gammage, Jack stated in support of an application for a depasturing licence with respect to *Tooyal* for his father early in 1837:

> "My father is a Ticket of Leave holder…. I purchased two hundred head of cattle from my father about eighteen months ago at one pound a head….My father has been in my service for the past eight months."[88]

In reality, by the time of this application John Jenkins was no longer the holder of a Ticket of leave. As will be seen below, he received a conditional pardon from the Colonial Government in September 1836.[89]

John's application for a depasturing licence was initially refused because Justices of the Peace at Yass refused to supply him with a Certificate of Good Character, as he was said to be "not known" in the district. However, a licence was subsequently granted after Evelyn Sturt, the younger brother of Charles Sturt and then the Commissioner of Crown Lands for the Murrumbidgee District, assured the Justices on 12 September 1837 that John "bears good character amongst the neighbouring settlers", and that he had a wife, three sons, 500 head of cattle and eight horses.[90]

---

84 See Charles Bateson, "Reid, David (1777-1840)" in *Australian Dictionary of Biography* (http://tinyurl.com/y7gblxem) (at 10 November 2019).

85 See the *Marr, Aitken, Watts Family Tree — Jenkins, Elizabeth* (http://tinyurl.com/y3popqa4) (at 10 November 2019); the *Marr, Aitken, Watts Family Tree — Williams, Henry Thomas* (http://tinyurl.com/y4x6qkja) (at 10 November 2019); and *Ancestry — Henry Thomas Williams* (http://tinyurl.com/y3j3yom9) (at 10 November 2019). See also **photo 5**.

86 See Gammage, *Narrandera Shire*, op. cit., p. 38; and p. 23 above.

87 See *New South Wales State Archives and Records* (AONSW Reel 2748).

88 See Gammage, *Narrandera Shire*, op. cit., p. 38.

89 See p. 26 below.

90 See "Colonial Secretary: Letters from Commissioners of Crown Lands" in *New South Wales State Archives and Records* (AONSW, 4/2348.2); Sherry Morris, *Wagga Wagga: A History* (1999), p. 20; and Campbell, op. cit., p. 22. The depasturing

Whatever the precise legal relationships were within his family, it seems clear that John Jenkins always regarded the *Tooyal* run as his own. It is of interest to note that by 1837, the 30 head of cattle which had been in John's possession in 1828 had grown to 500 head.[91] He might properly be seen as one of those squatters who succeeded with a small amount of capital and a large amount of ability combined with good fortune.

In or about 1833, the Jenkins family were joined for a time at their Bong Bong home by John's older sister, Elizabeth Clark (née Jenkins); together with her husband, John Clark Snr, and at least two of the Clarks' sons, William and George Clark. A third son, Richard Clark, probably also accompanied them.[92]

It might be recalled that the Clarks' eldest son, John Clark Jnr, had earlier arrived in New South Wales as a free immigrant on board the *Cumberland* on 27 January 1827. He had then gone to live with his uncle and aunt and their family at Bong Bong.[93] Letters possibly written by John Clark Jnr from Bong Bong to his parents back in Kent may have contributed to his own family's subsequent decision to emigrate Australia.

In the event, the Clark family probably did not remain long at Bong Bong before moving south-west towards the Yass Plains.[94] Nonetheless, there is extant evidence suggesting continuing contact between the two families after the Clarks moved away from the Jenkins family.[95]

On 11 May 1836, John was provided with a new Ticket of Leave. This one, issued in lieu of his original Ticket of Leave, entitled him to live and work in the Yass District.[96] It is something of a mystery as to why he was issued with the new Ticket of Leave. It seems likely that John was drawn for a time by work or pursuit of some other economic advantage to the Yass District. That he was physically present in the Yass District in early 1837 is attested by the fact that he had at that time unsuccessfully sought a Certificate of Good Character from the Yass Justices of the Peace.[97]

In any event, John's new Ticket of Leave was to have a short lifespan. On 8 September 1836, he received a conditional pardon from the Crown.[98] This entitled him to move freely about

---

licence was apparently granted to John in November 1837: see Tim Sherratt, *SRNSW-Index, Data, Depasturing Licences, CSV* (http://tinyurl.com/qtw9no7) (at 12 November 2019).

91 See p. 19 above.

92 The precise timing and other details surrounding the Clark family members' voyage from England to New South Wales have yet to be ascertained. However, in a letter to Martha Clark, John Clark Jnr's widow, dated 1 December 1865, Richard Clark wrote:
"It is now 32 years since I left old England."
See (2008) 12(1) *Snodland Historical Society Newsletter*, p. 3 (http://tinyurl.com/j26229j) (at 10 November 2019).

93 See p. 17–18 above.

94 A short biographical newspaper article in 1993 dealing with William Clark observed that he was 23 years old when his family settled in Yass: see the *Wangaratta Chronicle*, Monday, 4 January 1993, p. 21. If accurate, this would mean that William and his family arrived in Yass less than a year after first landing in New South Wales, given that William was born in 1809.

95 Ridley William Jenkins, the fourth child of Frank Jenkins and his first wife, Rebecca, died in Melbourne in December 1866. He was buried in John Clark Jnr's grave (Grave 201, Church of England Compartment F) in the Melbourne General Cemetery.

96 See the *Jenkins Family File*, p. 38.

97 See p. 25 above. When John was ultimately granted a depasturing licence for *Tooyal* in November 1837, he was said to be a resident of Yass: see Tim Sherratt, *SRNSW-Index, Data, Depasturing Licences, CSV* (http://tinyurl.com/qtw9no7) (at 12 November 2019).

98 See the *Jenkins Family File*, p. 38; and the *Marr, Aitken, Watts Family Tree — Jenkins, John* (http://tinyurl.com/y6vxa6ly) (at 11 November 2019)

the Colony, but he could not return to the United Kingdom. Finally, on 1 December 1838, John was granted an absolute pardon.[99] By then, he presumably had no intention of returning to England. His children were establishing their own families in New South Wales, and he himself was clearly doing much better in the Colony than he could reasonably aspire to be doing in England.

---

99 See McNeill, op. cit., p. 7.

Berrima House

Shortly prior to 1829, the New South Wales Colonial Government decided to lay out a town at or near to Bong Bong to serve as the administrative and commercial centre for the County of Camden. However in 1829, the nearby site of Berrima was selected for the new town in lieu of Bong Bong by the New South Wales Surveyor General, Thomas Mitchell, whilst he was visiting the area to plan the route for a new road alignment to replace the old Argyle Road alignment of the road from Sydney. The old road alignment had proven to be unsatisfactory due to a steep hill climb over the Mittagong Range and a wide crossing of the Wingecarribee River at Bong Bong. The chosen site for the new town was situated some 8 km to the north-west of Bong Bong. On Mitchell's instructions, Robert Hoddle surveyed the new town site in 1830. His town plan was approved by the Government in 1831, and land sales and the construction of public buildings commenced soon afterwards.[100]

On 20 April 1835, Thomas Horton James, a wealthy Sydney merchant and landowner, purchased a vacant lot fronting Jellore Street in the new township of Berrima from the Colonial Government for £8.6.8.[101] In the same year, James caused a two-storey random coursed stone dwelling house to be constructed on the lot. Now known as *Berrima House*, it is reputed to be the first such house to have been built in Berrima.[102] It has also been asserted that the house was constructed for James by John Jenkins.[103]

At least one local Berrima historian has forcefully questioned whether John Jenkins, in fact, built *Berrima House*. In *Unravelling the Story of Berrima in 1841*, Chris Thompson wrote:

> "It is difficult to see why [Thomas] Horton James would employ John Jenkins, a Ticket of

---

100 See *New South Wales Office of Environment and Heritage — Berrima House* (http://tinyurl.com/yaxzhq8c) (at 11 November 2019); and *Wikipedia — Berrima, New South Wales* (http://tinyurl.com/y94mcnun) (at 11 November 2019).

101 See the *Jenkins Family File*, p. 6. The allotment purchased by James was Lot 3 of Section 5, DP 758095. The current street address for the lot is 19 Jellore Street, Berrima: see *New South Wales Office of Environment and Heritage — Berrima House* (http://tinyurl.com/yaxzhq8c) (at 11 November 2019).

102 Ibid. *Berrima House* was listed on the New South Wales State Heritage Register on 2 April 1999: see *Wikipedia — Berrima House* (http://tinyurl.com/ycrq286a) (at 11 November 2019). According to one of John's descendants, Edwin Jenkins, *Berrima House* was:
> "built of sandstone, quarried close to the site, with dressed stone quoins. The house was the traditional 'four up/four down' room house. The heights of the door openings are approximately 6 4 (190 cm), which indicates the height of the average person in the early 1800s as compared to the present day. The original flagged verandah is supported by six timber columns with barge board in a charming Georgian style. It has a simple and narrow boarded staircase and had twelve-pane windows, six-panel doors, simple timber fireplace surrounds with built in cupboards either side — all made from the local stringybark timber. Gone are the detached kitchen, wood shed, stables, laundry and earth-closet lavatory which were positioned along the eastern side of the backyard. The half acre block runs down to the Wingecarribee River."

See the *Marr, Aitken, Watts Family Tree — Jenkins, John* (http://tinyurl.com/y6vxa6ly) (at 13 November 2019). See also the **Historic Berrima Plan** and **photo 6**.

103 See McNeill, op. cit., p. 8.

Leave farmer/labourer, who in 1835 was resident in Inverary District, to build a home for him, especially given the probable number of builders in the township associated with the building of the gaol and courthouse."[104]

However, John's son-in-law, James Garner, is on record as claiming, in a letter to his mother dated 4 July 1841, that John had built "a fine house" in Berrima.[105] Even if John was not the builder engaged by Thomas James to build *Berrima House*, it is of course possible that he could have played a substantial part in its construction; as by working as a builder's labourer for the contracted builder.

Whilst there may be some doubt regarding John's involvement in the construction of *Berrima House*, there is no doubt but that he purchased the property on 27 April 1841 from John Atkinson for £30.[106] John's original name for *Berrima House* was apparently *Square-View*.[107]

---

[104] Chris Thompson, "No. 11 of Berrima 1841 — John Jenkins, Jellore Street" in *The 36 Households: Harper's Mansion, Berrima* (http://tinyurl.com/y3azfpw2) (at 11 November 2019). As to Thompson's assertion that John Jenkins was resident in the Inverary District at the time when *Berrima House* was being built, see pp. 24–25 above.

[105] See the *Jenkins Family File*, pp. 3-4.

[106] It might be recalled that John Atkinson was the younger brother of James Atkinson, and that John Jenkins had been assigned to the latter after his arrival in New South Wales: see p. 14 above. John Atkinson had purchased *Berrima House* from a Joseph Sly on 14 June 1838. Sly had in turn purchased the property from its original owner, Thomas James, on 14 October 1837: see the *Jenkins Family File*, p. 6. *Berrima House* remained in the possession of Jenkins family members until 1965, when it was sold to the Wrightson family: see the *Marr, Aitken, Watts Family Tree — Jenkins, John* (http://tinyurl.com/y6vxa6ly) (at 13 November 2019).

[107] See McNeill, op. cit., p. 9.

John Jenkins' Later Years

On 17 August 1841, Jack Jenkins married Maria Ray, a 19 years old Australian-born farmer's daughter from Airds, near present-day Campbelltown. The marriage was solemnised in St. Peter's Anglican Church at Campbelltown.[108] Shortly afterwards, on 30 August 1841, the Jenkins' eldest child, Thomas Jenkins, was also married. His bride was a Jane Dunstan. Jane had been born in Bath, England, and was around 21 years of age at the time of the wedding. Thomas was 29 years old. The marriage was conducted according to Anglican rites "at Sutton Forest", very likely in All Saints Church.[109]

Following his acquisition of *Square-View* in 1841, both John and Charlotte Jenkins made it their principal home for the balance of their respective lives. From time to time, it also became home to a number of their relatives, including at least one of their grandchildren.[110] In a letter to his mother, the Jenkins' son-in-law, James Garner, wrote from Berrima on 4 July 1841:

> "My dear mother, I have not forgot your instructions of educating my children. At present I have my oldest daughter at a respectable school in Berrima, her name is Charlotte, living with her grandfather. Her age is 10 years, and she is beginning to write....
>
> My dear mother, I am going to leave this part to farm a station close to my wife's father's on the Murrumbidgee as my stock is increasing. I have not sufficient run for them in this part of the country. My brother in laws they are getting on well, all send their kind love to you. They have got 800 head of cattle of their own, about 30 breeding mares. As for me, I have got at present 140 breeding cattle, 9 mares and one horse. My wife has received no fortune as yet. All I have got is by my own industry. My father in law says at his death he will divide his stock equally amongst his children. He has got 2 sons and 2 daughters, excluding my wife. He is now living in Berrima and has built a fine house. You can direct all your letters to him to be forwarded to me. His name is Mr. John Jenkins. Direct to him at Berrima, County Camden, New South Wales, to be forwarded to me."[111]

During the many years in which John and Charlotte Jenkins lived at *Square-View*, it no doubt

---

108 See the *Marr, Aitken, Watts Family Tree — Jenkins, John* (http://tinyurl.com/ya5ohz7a) (at 11 November 2019); McNeill, op. cit., p. 9; and **photos 7** and **8**.

109 See the *Marr, Aitken, Webb Family Tree — Jenkins, Thomas Perrin Surman* (http://tinyurl.com/y796tfl4) (at 11 November 2019); and **photo 9**.

110 See Thompson, op. cit.; and the *Jenkins Family File*, p. 2.

111 See the *Jenkins Family File*, pp. 3-4. James Garner was clearly in error in his numbering of John Jenkins' children. In fact, he had three sons if his de facto stepson is counted. Further, although John did have two daughters, one of these was James Garner's own wife, Mary Garner (née Jenkins).

received many visitors. It has been alleged that the bushranger, Ben Hall, slept the night on a wooden settee on the building's verandah in 1864. Although this assertion has had wide currency, it has not been verified.[112]

Whilst principally based at his *Square-View* home in Berrima after its acquisition in 1841, John no doubt spent significant periods of time on his *Tooyal* run. He had been granted a depasturing licence for the run in his own name in September 1837.[113] This was renewed annually, at least until 1845.[114] John was clearly a successful pastoralist. He was probably also an astute businessman. He likely acquired interests of different kinds in New South Wales pastoral properties in addition to *Tooyal*.[115] No doubt assisted to a significant degree in the early years by his sons and sons-in-law, he probably made much money during his long life. In turn, he probably rendered valuable assistance to his sons and sons-in-law as they made their respective ways in life.

On 23 August 1842, the last of John's children, Frank Jenkins, married Rebecca Charlotte Higgins in St. John's Catholic Church at Campbelltown. The second child of a Campbelltown farmer and his wife, Rebecca was just shy of 16 years of age at the time of the marriage, having been born shortly before 4 July 1826.[116] Frank was 22 years old when he married Rebecca.[117]

John Jenkins lived a very long life. The latter part of that life appears to have been largely uneventful. However, it was sadly marked by the deaths of many members of his immediate family. At least nine of his grandchildren predeceased him. Two of these nine grandchildren were the children of John's middle son, Jack Jenkins.[118] The remaining seven were the children of his youngest son, Frank Jenkins.[119] Rebecca Jenkins, Frank Jenkins' first wife, died in childbirth on 20 June 1856; with her child being stillborn.[120]

On 16 August 1869, John's wife of 55 years, Charlotte, died at the family home, *Square-View*, in Berrima. Her cause of death was given on her Death Certificate as "senile decay".[121] Aged 80 years old at the time of her death, Charlotte was said in a family death notice published in the *Sydney Morning Herald* to have been "much lamented by a large circle of relatives and friends".[122] Years later, an anonymous man, who wrote under the pseudonym "Old Tom" and who apparently knew both John and Charlotte, referred to the latter in his "Reminiscences"

---

112 See *New South Wales Office of Environment and heritage — Berrima House* (http://tinyurl.com/yaxzhq8c) (at 11 November 2019); and *The Canberra Times*, Friday, 12 April 1985, p. 22.

113 See p. 25 above.

114 See the *Marr, Aitken, Watts Family Tree — Jenkins, John* (http://tinyurl.com/y6vxa6ly) (at 12 November 2019).

115 On dates as yet unascertained, John appears to have purchased 60 acres of freehold land from a George Rattray for £15, and another more substantial landholding from a James Richardson of Yass for £500. The precise location of each of these properties is not presently known: see the *Jenkins Family File*, p. 6. The land so acquired from either Rattray or Richardson, or perhaps another property licensed for a time in John's name, may well have been called *Lonyon*: see the *Marr, Aitken, Watts Family Tree — Jenkins, John* (http://tinyurl.com/y6vxa6ly) (at 13 November 2019); and Tim Sherratt, *SRNSW-Indexes, Data, Depasturing Licenses, CSV* (http://tinyurl.com/qtw9no7) (at 13 November 2019).

116 See the *Marr, Aitken, Watts Family Tree — Higgins, Rebecca Charlotte* (http://tinyurl.com/r4tmd9e) (at 12 November 2019).

117 See the *Marr, Aitken, Watts Family Tree — Jenkins, Francis* (http://tinyurl.com/ydhcm5k2) (at 12 November 2019). See also **photo 10**.

118 See the *Marr, Aitken, Watts Family Tree — Jenkins, John* (http://tinyurl.com/ya5ohz7a) (at 13 November 2019).

119 See the *Marr, Aitken, Watts Family Tree — Jenkins, Francis* (http://tinyurl.com/ydhcm5k2) (at 13 November 2019).

120 See the *Marr, Aitken, Webb Family Tree — Higgins, Rebecca Charlotte* (http://tinyurl.com/r4tmd9e) (at 13 November 2019).

121 See the *Marr, Aitken, Watts Family Tree — Surman, Charlotte Elizabeth* (http://tinyurl.com/y8zfn83x) (at 13 November 2109); and the *Jenkins Family File*, p. 42.

122 See the *Sydney Morning Herald*, Friday, 20 August 1869, p. 1.

published on 26 March 1902 in the *Scrutineer and Berrima District Press* as "the kindest old nurse that ever lived". He also wrote that Charlotte was known (presumably in later life and in and around Berrima) as "Granny".[123] On 23 August 1869, Charlotte was buried in the churchyard of Christ Church at Bong Bong.[124]

John's son-in-law, Henry Williams, died in Adelaide on 12 March 1879.[125] His son by informal adoption, Thomas Jenkins, died on 22 December 1882.[126]

On 25 August 1886, John Jenkins himself died at *Square-View*. According to his Death Certificate, the cause of his death was "characteristic decay".[127] Presumably, this simply referred to the effects of old age. John was apparently not the subject of any obituary.[128] He was 97 years old when he died.

John was buried in the Berrima General Cemetery after an Anglican funeral service. It is interesting to note that according to one of his descendants, a Mrs. Baxter, he had stored his coffin for some time before his death under the stairs at *Square-View*.[129] John's horizontal gravestone bears the following inscription:

'Sacred

to the Memory of

John Jenkins

who departed this life

25th August 1886

Aged 97 years

Third son of the late

Henery Jenkins

of East Malling, West Kent,

England

Eternal process moving on

From state to state the spirit walks

And these are but the shattered stalks

---

123 See the *Scrutineer and Berrima District Press*, Wednesday, 26 March 1902, p. 2.

124 See the *Marr, Aitken, Watts Family Tree — Surman, Charlotte Elizabeth* (http://tinyurl.com/y8zfn83x) (at 13 November 2019). This Anglican church was constructed and consecrated in 1845. Charlotte was buried in the same grave as her daughter-in-law, Rebecca Jenkins, and Rebecca's eldest son, who had been named Francis Jenkins after his father. The younger Francis Jenkins had drowned in the Murrumbidgee River when 8 years old in 1853: see the *Marr, Aitken, Watts Family Tree — Jenkins, Francis* (http://tinyurl.com/ybnw7zam) (at 13 November 2019); and McNeill, op. cit., pp. 11 and 12.

125 See the *Marr, Aitken, Watts Family Tree — Williams, Henry Thomas* (http://tinyurl.com/y4x6qkja) (at 13 November 2019).

126 See the *Marr, Aitken, Watts Family Tree — Jenkins, Thomas Perrin Surman* (http://tinyurl.com/y796tfl4) (at 14 November 2019).

127 See the *Jenkins Family* File, p. 41; and the *Marr, Aitken, Watts Family Tree — Jenkins, John* (http://tinyurl.com/y6vxa6ly) (at 14 November 2019).

128 There were, however, two published family death notices: see the *Sydney Morning Herald*, Thursday, 26 August 1886, p. 1; and the *Sydney Mail and New South Wales Advertiser*, Saturday, 4 September 1886, p. 516.

129 As Mrs. Baxter has also noted, the practice of storing one's coffin at home before death was evidently not uncommon at the time of John's death. Should a death occur during a time when transport and communication were difficult, coffins could be hard to come by when needed: see the *Marr, Aitken, Watts Family Tree — Jenkins, John* (http://tinyurl.com/y6vxa6ly) (at 14 November 2019). John lies buried in the General Section of the Berrima General Cemetery in Row 7, Plot 2. See **photo 11**.

Of ruin'd chrysalis of one"[130]

Some measure of John Jenkins' character may be gleaned from the following account taken from "Old Tom's" "Reminiscences" published in the *Scrutineer and Berrima District Press* on 26 March 1902:

> "Old Jack was a terrible swearer, his oaths being quite unique. 'Old Tom' remembers when Atkinson kept a flour mill at Oldbury. It was a custom of 'old daddy' Jenkins to buy his wheat and take it to the mill to be ground; on one occasion the horse jibbed and would not draw the few bags, so 'daddy', after the usual accompaniment of oaths, told the horse he would disgrace him, and he took him out and pulled the dray and wheat to the mill himself. Jenkins and George Williamson found Captain Allman and his daughter when they were lost. Allman was the second police magistrate at Berrima, and his usual custom was, with his daughter, to take walks down the Berrima river. On this occasion they were lost for several days and the whole district was out looking for them: when found by Jenkins and Williamson they were in the last stages of exhaustion. 'Old Tom' remembers the bringing home and the hurrahs that welcomed the lucky finders."[131]

This account arguably captures John's public-spiritedness and bush skills, together with his mercurial temper; a trait he apparently shared with his second son, Jack Jenkins.

After the hard scrabble of life in the Medway River Valley of his youth, his near-death experiences in the clutches of British justice and the radical dislocation associated with his transportation to New South Wales, John Jenkinson went on to establish himself as a respected and successful citizen in his new home. In New South Wales as an early squatter, he acquired extensive pastoral lands and significant wealth. In part of yeoman stock, he was certainly living the life of a yeoman in his later years. By the time of his death, he was the patriarch of a large and widespread family. A number of his descendants also led colourful lives, and some of those lives will be addressed below.

---

130 The inscription on John's grave is now virtually illegible. The poetic epitaph inscribed on his tombstone is transcribed from Canto 82 of Alfred Lord Tennyson's *In Memoriam A. H. A.*

131 See the *Scrutineer and Berrima Free Press*, Wednesday, 26 March 1902, p. 2. See also the *Bowral Free Press*, Saturday, 19 April 1902, p. 4. It may well be that John either acquired or extended his repertoire of "unique" and frequently used oaths whilst incarcerated on board the convict hulk *Retribution* in the Thames River in 1820 while awaiting transportation to New South Wales: see pp. 11-12 above. As to Atkinson's flour mill on *Oldbury*, see *Wikipedia — Oldbury Farm* (http://tinyurl.com/vzlpjdn) (at 14 November 2019).

THOMAS PERRIN SURMAN JENKINS
(1812 — 1882)

As mentioned above, the eldest child in John and Charlotte Jenkins' family was Thomas Perrin Surman Jenkins. Thomas was born to Charlotte Surman (as she then was) in Wateringbury, Kent shortly prior to 29 January 1812 — almost two years before Charlotte's marriage to John Jenkins on 1814. As his first two names indicate, the infant's father appears to have been Thomas Perrin, a carpenter from Wateringbury. Not long after Thomas Jenkins' birth, his father abandoned both Charlotte and the child and moved to Milton-next-Gravesend on the lower Thames River with a Sarah Singyard. There, he was probably employed as a ship's carpenter in the Gravesend Naval Dockyard during the latter stages of the Napoleonic Wars. On 18 November 1813, he married Sarah at Plaxtol, Kent.[132]

Although he was probably never formally adopted by John Jenkins, Thomas Jenkins grew up in his step-father's household, and was given and retained the surname of Jenkins. In late 1826 and early 1827, he accompanied his mother and siblings to Sydney on board the *Grenada*, and then from Sydney to *Oldbury* at Sutton Forest.

Thomas was 15 years old when he arrived in New South Wales. He likely worked during his first year or so in the Colony as a labourer on James Atkinson's *Oldbury* property, and on his mother's 60 acres in or near to Bong Bong. However, by the time of the 1828 New South Wales Census, Thomas had left his family's home. He was recorded in that Census as living and working on William Ryrie's *Arnprior* grazing property near Braidwood.[133]

As also mentioned above, Thomas married Jane Dunstan on 30 August 1841; most likely at John and Charlotte Jenkins' Bong Bong property. Jane had been born in 1820 at Bath in Somerset. At the time of her marriage to Thomas, she was living in or near Berrima. The marriage was performed by the Reverend George Vidal according to the rites of the Church of England. Between 1842 and 1867, Thomas and Jane Jenkins had a total of 14 children; two of whom seemingly died in infancy.[134]

Shortly after his marriage to Jane, Thomas moved with his wife to *Buckingbong*, the squatting run near present-day Narrandera, then occupied by his two younger half-brothers,

Jack and Frank Jenkins. It has been said by some who knew him that Thomas was "a bit simple". If true, this may account for the fact that he apparently did not participate as a partner in any of Jack's and Frank's pastoral pursuits. Thomas lived and worked on *Buckingbong*, and on his half-brothers' adjacent *Gillenbah* run, until his death on 23 December 1882.[135]

---

132   See *Australian Royalty — Charlotte Elizabeth Surman 1789-1865* (http://tinyurl.com/y9l39tt7) (at 14 November 2019). See also p. 9 above.

133   See "New South Wales — 1828 Census: Householders' Returns" in *New South Wales State Archives and Records* (AONSW: Series 1273, Reels 2506-2507 and 2551-2552).

134   See *New South Wales Register of Births, Deaths and Marriages — Marriages: Thomas Jenkins and Jane Dunstan* (Vol. 25C, No. 467). Both Thomas and Jane marked the Marriage Register with an "X", indicating that they were unable to otherwise sign their own names: Ibid. See also *My Heritage — Thomas Jenkins* (http://tinyurl.com/sva4hee) (at 14 November 2019); *Ancestry: Stokes Family Tree — Thomas Perrin Surman Jenkins* (http://tinyurl.com/yyz89ncq) (at 14 November 2019); and p. 30 above.

135   See the *Marr, Aitken, Watts Family Tree — Jenkins, Thomas Perrin Surman* (http://tinyurl.com/y796tfl4) (at 14 November

According to Ian McNeill, he also bought and sold land on his own behalf.[136] Following his death, he was buried in the small graveyard on *Buckingbong*.[137] It would appear that Jane Jenkins died on or about 6 July 1895, either on *Buckingbong* or in Narrandera.[138]

2019); and *Ancestry: Stokes Family Tree — Jenkins, Thomas Perrin Surman* (http://tinyurl.com/yyz89ncq) (at 14 November 2019). See also footnote 407 on p. 112 below.

136 See McNeill, op. cit., p. 9.
137 Ibid. See also **photo 12**.
138 See *Ancestry: Stokes Family Tree — Jane Dunsdon* (http://tinyurl.com/tgr2o7d) (at 14 November 2019).

MARY ANN GARNER (née JENKINS)
(1814 — 1898)

Charlotte Surman was heavily pregnant with her second child when she married John Jenkins on 16 January 1814. The child was born shortly prior to 20 March 1814, and christened as Mary Ann Jenkins on that date in St. James the Great's Church, East Malling in Kent.[139] The identity of Mary's father remains opaque. He may have been Thomas Perrin, the apparent father of Charlotte Surman's first child, Thomas Perrin Surman Jenkins. It is also possible that John Jenkins was Mary's father. He was identified as such in her baptismal record. However, as Charlotte was married to John at the time of Mary's birth, that record cannot be taken to be definitive with respect to paternity. In any event, Mary, like her older brother Thomas, was raised as the child of both John and Charlotte Jenkins.

Like her older brother or half-brother and her other siblings, Mary Jenkins travelled from England to New South Wales with her mother on board the *Grenada*. The family arrived in Sydney on 23 January 1827; proceeding from there to *Oldbury* at Sutton Forest to be reunited with John Jenkins.[140]

As mentioned above, at the time of the 1828 New South Wales Census, Mary was living on her mother's property at or near to Bong Bong, and was probably assisting her mother with domestic duties.[141] However, about a year later, on 29 June 1829, she finally left her parents' home when she married James Garner. Mary was 15 years of age at the time of her marriage. Her new husband was around 26 years old.[142]

James Garner was born in Bedford, Bedfordshire shortly prior to 13 February 1803; the child of William and Joanna Garner. On 14 March 1822, James was convicted in company with three other men after a trial conducted during the Bedford Assizes in that year. On 16 July 1822, his father, William Garner, was also convicted after a Quarter Sessions trial in Bedford. James and his father were each sentenced to be transported to New South Wales for a term of seven years.[143] The offences committed by James and William remain unascertained, as does the question of whether the offence or offences committed by the son was or were in any way related to that or those committed by the father. The two Garners arrived in Sydney on board the convict transport ship *Princess Royal* on 9 March 1823.[144]

James Garner's early years as a convict in New South Wales appear to have been far from pleasant. In a letter dated 3 January 1839, which he addressed to his mother and siblings in England from his home to the south of Bong Bong, James wrote:

---

139 See the *Marr, Aitken, Watts Family Tree — Jenkins, Mary Ann* (http://tinyurl.com/y9ekyfez) (at 15 November 2019).
140 See pp. 17–18 above.
141 See p. 20 above.
142 Ibid.
143 See the *Marr, Aitken, Watts Family Tree — Garner, James* (http://tinyurl.com/y8ruqna5) (at 15 November 2019).
144 See *Convict Records of Australia — James Garner* (http://tinyurl.com/yd585zsk) (at 15 November 2019); *Convict Records of Australia — William Garner* (http://tinyurl.com/y7bppbg2) (at 15 November 2019); and McNeill, op. cit., p. 8.

"I cannot explain to you the hard usage I have received in this country after my coming. First I was given out to a master and only stopped with him 6 months, and I got took to Court for taking a few oranges and received a punishment of 50 lashes and sentenced 12 [months?] to a punishment gang. And obliged afterwards to serve the remainder of my sentence in government. During the time in my gang I was obliged to starve myself half the week. We got our rations on Saturday which only served me half the week and remainder obliged to go without. Had no ways or means to get a morsel. My ration was 10½ lb. coarse wheat meal and 7 lb. meat, very bad, which was my week's ration. God knows my suffering while in government afterwards. Until I served three years, I got promoted to Deputy Overseer at 6d. a day with rations. In 9 months afterwards I got promoted to Principal Overseer by good conduct at 1/-. In 6 months afterwards I got promoted again to 2/- per day in charge of 140 men with three deputies under me."[145]

On 7 April 1829, James was granted his Certificate of Freedom.[146]

After attaining his freedom, James acquired pastoral land to the south of Bong Bong. He called the property *Ploughed Ground*.[147] Following his marriage to Mary Jenkins, he took his new wife to live with him at *Ploughed Ground*.

James proved to be a reasonably successful grazier in his own right. In his January 1839 letter to his mother and siblings, he wrote:

"When I got free, I had some money which put me in the way of taking on a farm, and from that to this time I have got on well, thanks be to God, as I shall tell you. At this present time I have 20 working oxen, 12 head of horses mostly breeding mares value £40 to £50. I have 100 and odd breeding horn cattle. I have sold lately 9 bullocks which brought me £59.10.-. I have at present a very good prospect of getting on in this country."[148]

It would appear that James Garner did "get on" in Colonial New South Wales. In about 1841, he purchased the depasturing licence rights to the *Ulong* run from James Devlin.[149] Situated on the right bank of the Murrumbidgee River, this run of some 21,000 acres [about 8,500 hectares]

---

145 See the *Jenkins Family File*, pp. 2-3. In the same letter to his mother and siblings, James also advised that:
"[M]y father has been dead 11 years from the cause of hard treatment. He died at a place called Parramatta in the hospital."
Ibid.

146 See the *Marr, Aitken, Watts Family Tree — Garner, James* (http://tinyurl.com/y8ruqna5) (at 15 November 2019).

147 Charles Sturt may well have travelled near to, or even visited, James Garner's property during Sturt's 1829-1830 expedition tracing the Darling and lower Murray Rivers. Sturt wrote of the geology of the Yass Plains to the south of Bong Bong as follows:
"[S]and-stone again forms the basis of the country to a considerable distance beyond Bong-bong. At a small farm called Ploughed Ground, it is again traversed by a dike of whinstone, and a rich but isolated spot is thus passed over."
Charles Sturt, *Two Expeditions Into The Interior Of Southern Australia* (1834), Vol. 1, Preliminary Chapter, p.xxxviii. It appears that the terrain at *Ploughed Ground* was naturally corrugated. James Garner probably named the property as he did because it resembled land which had been ploughed. See also pp. 14–15 above.

148 See the *Jenkins Family File*, pp. 2-3. In a subsequent letter to his mother dated 4 July 1841, James noted:
"I have got at present 140 breeding cattle, 9 mares and one horse."
See the *Jenkins Family File*, pp. 3-4.

149 See Gammage, *Narrandera Shire*, op. cit., pp. 40 and 46.

lay around 40 km to the north-east of the location of present-day Narrandera. However, he was not to hold *Ulong* for long.

In 1847, an Imperial Order in Council empowered the New South Wales Government to grant leases of up to 14 years in duration of "unsettled" lands beyond the *Limits of Location*. Section 11 of the Order in Council of 1847 stated, in part, that:

> "All occupants of Crown Lands who have been in licensed occupation of the same for at least one year at the time of this Order in Council shall come into effect are to be entitled to demand leases of their respective runs under the present regulations within six months from the date of the publication of this Order in Council by the Governor or other officer administering the government of the said colony but not afterwards...."

Section 12 of the Order in Council of 1847 went on to provide that if the licensee of such a run failed to make demand for a lease of the run within the specified period of six months following the publication of the Order, then the grant of a lease of the run could be put out to tender, and a lease granted to the highest tenderer.[150]

Apparently in ignorance of the Order in Council of 1847, James Garner failed to make a demand for a lease of *Ulong* within the six months window of opportunity available to him under section 11 of the Order. Seizing his chance, a Sydney-based squatter, James Flood, successfully tendered for a lease of the run. Enraged, James Garner then assaulted Flood. A resulting action brought against James by Flood was seemingly settled out of Court.[151]

After losing *Ulong* to James Flood, and apparently disposing of his *Ploughed Ground* property, James Garner acquired the *Gap Inn* and surrounding pastoral land at Jerrawa near Yass. The *Gap Inn* was situated on what was then the main road from Sydney to Yass and apparently enjoyed a flourishing trade.[152] He subsequently also acquired the *Walgrove* pastoral property to the south-east of Yass.

Mary and James Garner had four children in all. The eldest, and only daughter, Charlotte Elizabeth Garner, was born on about 26 December 1830.[153] In his letter to his mother dated 4 July 1841, James observed with respect to his children:

> "My dear mother, I have not forgot your instructions of educating my children. At present I have my oldest daughter at a respectable school in Berrima. Her name is Charlotte, living with her grandfather. Her age is 10 years, she is beginning to write. John, James and Francis is being teached at my own place. Respectable schoolmaster and they are doing very well."[154]

---

150 See the *Port Phillip Gazette and Settlers' Journal*, Saturday, 14 August 1847, p. 1. See also pp. 83–84 below.
151 See Gammage, *Narrandera Shire*, p. 47. See also footnote 407 on p. 112 below.
152 See the *Sydney Mail*, Wednesday, 23 February 1921, p. 17.
153 See *My Heritage — George Merriman, 1820-1860*, (http://tinyurl.com/ycozudp7) (at 15 November 2019).
154 See the *Jenkins Family File*, pp. 3-4.

On 1 October 1844, Mary and James' daughter, Charlotte Garner, married George Merriman. Charlotte was not quite 14 years old when she married her husband. George was 24 years of age.[155] In 1865, their son, George Merriman Jnr, founded the *Ravensworth* merino stud farm near Yass.[156] It would seem that one of Charlotte Merriman's uncles, Frank Jenkins, provided his great nephew with a flock of ewes from Frank's *Buckingbong* run. These formed part of the initial breeding stock at *Ravensworth*.[157] In 1903, a portion of the *Ravensworth* property was excised to become the *Merryville* merino stud farm. On George Merriman Jnr's death in 1915, *Merryville* passed into the hands of one of his sons, being one of Mary Garner's great-grandsons, Walter Merriman. Walter Merriman was knighted in 1954 for his services to the wool industry.[158]

On 18 August 1860, James Garner died at his home on Walgrove.[159] Mary Garner survived her late husband by almost 38 years. By 1884, she was apparently living at Berrima in her father's home, *Square-View*. On 8 November 1884, Mary executed he last Will. By it, she gave a life interest in the *Gap Inn* and 180 adjoining acres of pastoral land to her daughter, Charlotte; with the remainder interest in those properties being vested in Mary's youngest child, Francis Garner. Mary devised a further 100 acres of nearby land to Charlotte absolutely. Finally, she left the unspecified residue of her estate to Francis.[160]

It would appear that Mary Garner's middle son, James Garner Jnr, was excluded from benefitting under the provisions of her Will by virtue of having died before its execution.[161] It is not presently known why her eldest son, John Garner, was not provided with a share of

---

155   See *Wikitree — George Merriman (1820-1860)* http://tinyurl.com/sua7o3o) (at 15 November 2019). The son of transported convicts, George Merriman was the younger brother of James Merriman. The latter had a varied career as a cooper, a whaler, a publican, a ship owner and the founder of the pearl-shell industry in the Torres Strait. Elected to the Sydney City Council in 1867, he served as Lord Mayor of Sydney in 1873, 1877 and 1878. James Merriman was elected to the New South Wales Legislative Assembly in 1877. He died in 1883: see G. J. Abbott, "Merriman, James (1816-1883)" in *Australian Dictionary of Biography* (http://tinyurl.com/qn3p5nd) (at 15 November 2019).

156   See *Merryville Stud — History* (http://tinyurl.com/y7a3olck) (at 15 November 2019).

157   See McNeill, op. cit., p. 8.

158   See *Merryville Stud — History* (http://tinyurl.com/y7a3olck) (at 15 November 2019); G. P. Walsh, "Merriman, Sir Walter Thomas (1882-1972)" in *Australian Dictionary of Biography* (http://tinyurl.com/w98td9z) (at 15 November 2019); and Mc Neill, op. cit., p .8.

159   See the *Marr, Aitken, Watts Family Tree — Garner, James* (http://tinyurl.com/y8ruqna5) (at 16 November 2019). James' obituary, published in the *Yass Courier* on Wednesday, 22 August 1860, read as follows:

  "We regret to announce the death of Mr. James Garner of Walgrove, an old resident of this district. The deceased formerly occupied a large squattage on the Murrumbidgee River, where he devoted his attention to the breeding of cattle. Since disposing of this property he resided at the Gap, and subsequently at Walgrove, near Yass, at which place he died at eight o'clock on Saturday morning last. The deceased had been for some time in bad health, and an attack of influenza hurried him to the grave. His remains were interred yesterday in the Church of England cemetery, and were followed to their last resting place by a long cavalcade consisting of his relatives, friends and neighbours."

160   See the *Marr, Aitken, Watts Family Tree — Jenkins, Mary Ann* (http://tinyurl.com/y9ekyfez) (at 16 November 2019). In Mary's Will, she referred to her daughter Charlotte as "Charlotte Margules". Charlotte's first husband, George Merriman Snr, died at Kiandra on 3 November 1860: see *Wikitree — George Merriman (1820-1860)* (http://tinyurl.com/sua7o3o) (at 16 November 2019). At the time of his death, he was almost certainly separated from Charlotte; with Charlotte probably living with a Louis Edward Margules. Charlotte and Louis' first child, Louis Margules Jnr, was born on 24 April 1860 — over seven months prior to George Merriman's death. It would appear that Charlotte and Louis Margules Snr were married in 1861: see *Wikitree — Charlotte Elizabeth Gardner (1830-1896)* (http://tinyurl.com/y6wxlkqo) (at 16 November 2019); *Wikitree — Louis Edward A. Margules (1819-1896)* (http://tinyurl.com/yazcwqbk) (at 16 November 2019); and *Wikitree — Louis Margules (1860-1949)* (http://tinyurl.com/y9gmvczl) (at 16 November 2019). It would also seem that Charlotte and Louis Margules were managing the *Gap Inn* at the time Mary Garner executed her Will.

161   See *New South Wales Register of Births, Deaths and Marriages — Deaths: Mary Ann Garner* (1898/6329).

his mother's bounty. It may be that they were estranged. On the other hand, Mary or her late husband may have made inter vivos provision for John prior to 1884.

Mary Garner died on 26 May 1898. Her Death Certificate indicated that she died at Narrandera.[162] However, it is highly likely that she was living immediately prior to her death on her brother Frank Jenkins' *Buckingbong* run, a short distance to the east of Narrandera.

Probate of Mary's Will was granted in the Supreme Court of New South Wales on 27 October 1898.[163] Although the Will divided Mary's estate between her daughter, Charlotte, and her youngest son, Francis, Charlotte predeceased her mother; dying on 9 April 1896.[164] The estate accordingly passed in its entirety to Francis Garner.

---

162 See the *Marr, Aitken, Watts Family Tree — Jenkins, Mary Ann* (http://tinyurl.com/y9ekyfez) (at 16 November 2019).
163 See the *Marr, Aitken, Watts Family Tree — Jenkins, Mary Ann* (http://tinyurl.com/y9ekyfez) (at 16 November 2019).
164 See *Wikitree — Charlotte Elizabeth Gardner (1830-1896)* (http://tinyurl.com/y6wxlkqo) (at 16 November 2019).

JACK JENKINS and FRANK JENKINS
JACK and FRANK JENKINS in PARTNERSHIP

Finding New Land

The third and fifth children in the family of John and Charlotte Jenkins were John Jenkins Jnr ("Jack Jenkins") and his younger brother, Francis Jenkins ("Frank Jenkins"). Whilst John Jenkins Snr was clearly not the biological father of the eldest child in the family, Thomas Perrin Surman Jenkins, and may not have been the biological father of the second child, Mary Ann Jenkins, he was almost certainly the father of both Jack and Frank Jenkins and of their sister, Elizabeth Jane Jenkins.[165] Jack was born shortly prior to 6 January 1816 and Frank a little before 14 January 1820. Both were christened in St. James the Great's Church, East Malling.[166]

Like their siblings, Jack's and Frank's early years were marred by poverty and deprivation following the arrest, trial and transportation of their father. Almost certainly, neither received any formal education. In 1826, they left England for good in company with their mother and her other children bound for New South Wales on board the *Grenada*. They arrived in Sydney on 23 January 1827, and joined John Jenkins Snr at *Oldbury*, Sutton Forest soon afterwards. Jack was barely 11 years old on first landing in Australia and Frank barely 7 years old. Neither could have had any real memory of his father.

Following their arrival at *Oldbury*, Jack and Frank Jenkins, together with their older half-brother, Thomas Jenkins, would almost certainly have assisted around the property as best they could, given their varying ages. After the Crown Grant of land at or near to Bong Bong to their mother later in 1827, Jack and Frank probably assisted their father in working that land.[167]

By the early 1830s, John Jenkins Snr was both ready and willing to seek out and secure further pastoral land beyond his wife' Bong Bong property. However, his ability to do so lawfully was constrained. He may well have been financially unable to purchase land, either at auction or by private treaty, within the *Limits of Location*. Moreover, as the holder of a Ticket of Leave, he was legally forbidden to travel beyond those *Limits* in search of land on which to squat. His solution was to send his sons, Jack and Frank, to the Murrumbidgee River Valley as his emissaries.

The two Jenkins boys were dispatched by their father down the Murrumbidgee River Valley in 1832, travelling on horseback. Later in life, Jack Jenkins told his friend James Gormly that on the first occasion he travelled from his parents' Bong Bong home to the Murrumbidgee, "he

---

165 See p. 9 above.
166 See the *Marr, Aitken, Watts Family Tree — Jenkins, John* (http://tinyurl.com/ya5ohz7a) (at 16 November 2019); the *Marr, Aitken, Watts Family Tree — Jenkins, Francis* (http://tinyurl.com/ydhcm5k2) (at 16 November 2019); and McNeill, op. cit., p. 3.
167 See p. 19 above.

managed to procure a horse". On the second occasion, he had to walk the whole distance.[168] Jack would have been about 16 years old at the time of this first venture down the Murrumbidgee. Frank would have been 12 years of age. Given the ages of the boys, they may well have been surreptitiously (and unlawfully) accompanied by their father.

In the event, the Jenkinses in 1832 came to occupy a squatting run in the Murrumbidgee River Valley which they named *Tooyal*. Located on the right bank of the River, the run was situated just to the west of the Malebo Hill and some 15 km west of present-day Wagga Wagga. *Tooyal* initially extended over about 25,600 acres (approximately 10,360 hectares). By 1865, it had grown in size to around 49,920 acres (about 20,202 hectares).[169]

As mentioned above, in the early years of the Jenkins' occupation of *Tooyal*, Jack and Frank Jenkins apparently managed the run on behalf of their father.[170] However, it wasn't long before the two boys were looking westwards down the Murrumbidgee for grazing land of their own. According to Bill Gammage, in 1832, and soon after their arrival at *Tooyal*, they explored as far west as the Yanco Creek, to the south-west of present-day Narrandera, before bringing cattle on to the Colombo Plain to the east of the Creek.[171]

Jack and Frank were undoubtedly very young when they first reached *Tooyal*. However, the rigors of their lives until then would have toughened them, leaving them both resilient and resourceful. They needed to be tough, resilient and resourceful because life on the New South Wales frontier beyond the *Limits of Location* during the 1830s, and for decades afterwards, was not for the soft. As James Ferguson succinctly put it:

"Squatting was not for the faint-hearted. It was a tough life and demanded tough men".[172]

Jack and Frank Jenkins came to know the middle reaches of the Murrumbidgee River and its surrounds well. They moved their cattle widely around the riverine grassy plains. The year 1839 saw them venture on to the *Buckingbong* squatting run along the left bank of the River to the east of current-day Narrandera. The year also saw the two brothers in the thick of what became known as the *Wiradjuri War*.

---

168 See James Gormly, "Pioneers of the Murrumbidgee: Frank and John Jenkins" in the *Gundagai Times and Tumut, Adelong and Murrumbidgee District Advertiser*, Tuesday, 5 December 1916, p. 2. James Gormly lived between 1836 and 1922. Irish by birth, he arrived with his family at Nangus on the Murrumbidgee River in 1844. As a young man, he moved around southern New South Wales and the goldfields of Victoria. He finally settled in Wagga Wagga. Gormly served on the Wagga Wagga City Council from 1883 until 1886 and was Mayor on two occasions. In 1885, he was elected as a Protectionist to the New South Wales Legislative Assembly. From 1904 until his death, he served on the New South Wales Legislative Council. Gormly was an admiring friend of both Jack and Frank Jenkins: see Gordon Buxton, "Gormly, James (1836-1922)" in *Australian Dictionary of Biography* (http://tinyurl.com/uq5k8hc) (at 16 November 2019).

169 See pp. 22-23 above.

170 See p. 23 above.

171 See Gammage, *Narrandera Shire*, op. cit., p. 38.

172 See James Ferguson, *Squatting: Romance & Reality* (2017), p. 92. Later in his book, Ferguson also observed:
"To set out as a squatter was to embrace a life involving long periods of loneliness, rough conditions, and danger from illness, accident or Aboriginal attacks with the chance of destruction always closer than the fortunes dreamed of It was a life lived far from any civilisation."
See Ferguson, op. cit., p 101.

The Wiradjuri War

The traditional country of the Wiradjuri Aboriginal clans covered a large portion of the central south of New South Wales. It extended from Dubbo in the north to Albury in the south, and from Bathurst in the east to Mossgiel in the west.[173] The Wiradjuri population at the time of first contact with Europeans has been estimated at 3,000 persons.[174] The Narrungdera (or Ngarrangdhuray) Clan of the Wiradjuri Nation occupied the land around what is now Narrandera. Late in 1838, they declared war on the invading whites.[175]

It seems that the Narrungdera clansmen initially treated the European explorers and settlers entering their country with courtesy and even a measure of hospitality. Bill Gammage has noted that:

> "In 1829-30, Sturt's men had camped peacefully within their boundaries for a fortnight and apparently the first settlers were hospitably received in 1832."[176]

However, during the second half of the 1830s, hospitality turned to hostility as European invaders claimed ever-expanding swathes of prime land for themselves. In his 1983 PhD Thesis, Peter Read perceptively observed that:

> "The first points of conflict were the areas used regularly by both Aborigines and whites, and of these the permanent waters were the most important. Good Aboriginal campsites

---

173 See Peter John Read, *A History of the Wiradjuri People of New South Wales 1883 — 1969* (PhD Thesis, Australian National University, 1983), pp. 1-2; and Peter Kabaila, *Wiradjuri Places: The Murrumbidgee River Basin* (1995), Vol. 1, p. 4. In 1842, James Dredge, an Assistant Protector of Aborigines in the Port Phillip District of New South Wales, described the Aboriginal peoples' attachment to their lands as historical, material and personal:
"[E]ach tribe had its own territory, well defined by natural boundaries — and amongst themselves well understood and soundly recognised from one generation to another. Within these boundaries of their own country, as they proudly speak, they feel a degree of security and pleasure which they can find nowhere else — here their forefathers lived and roamed and hunted, and here also their ashes rest. And this is the scene of their fondest and earliest recollections....With every nook they are familiar, they know just where their favourite roots are most abundant, the haunts of the Kangaroo, Emu and Opposum — in short, it is their home."
See James Dredge, *Diaries, Notebook and Letterbook, ?1817 to 1845*; diary entry for Monday, 6 June 1842 (State Library of Victoria, MS 11625). See also Jessie Mitchell, *'Country Belonging to Me': Land and Labour on Aboriginal Missions and Protectorate Stations, 1830-1850* (http://tinyurl.com/86mrrvw3) (at 16 November 2019); and the **Wiradjuri Country Map**.

174 See L. R. Smith, *The Aboriginal Population of Australia* (1980), p. 73; and Read, op. cit., p. 3.

175 See Bill Gammage, "The Wiradjuri War 1838-1840" in (1983) 16 *The Push From The Bush: A Bulletin Of Social History* 3, at p. 5. In point of fact, the *Wiradjuri War* of 1838-1840 should properly be called "the second Wiradjuri War". The first Wiradjuri War took place on the Bathurst Plains. A Wiradjuri leader named Windradyne led his men in violent resistance to their dispossession by colonising whites during the early 1820s. After nearly three years of attacks and savage reprisals, Windradyne and his men surrendered to the colonial authorities in Parramatta in 1824. Thereafter, sporadic fighting continued across southern New South Wales over the latter part of the 1830s and into the 1840s: see *Wikipedia — Bathurst War* (http://tinyurl.com/yb9cksd4) (at 16 November 2019); and *The Guardian* (Australian Edition), Sunday, 11 October 2015.

176 See Gammage, "The Wiradjuri War 1838-1840", op. cit., p. 5.

were near water, well drained, elevated above cool air pools, level, sunny, faced to leeward, had a breeze in summer, and had local resources for food and fuel. These same factors generally made good homesites."[177]

Throughout 1837 and 1838, the Riverina was afflicted by a serious drought. The Murrumbidgee and Darling Rivers ceased to flow, and the Murray River was reduced to a trickle. To the Narrungdera, the Europeans were not only occupying their land, they were also competing for depleted resources.[178] Deteriorating relations led to violence. According to evidence given to a New South Wales Legislative Council Committee on 9 July 1839 by Henry Cosby, the Commissioner of Crown Lands for the Lachlan District, white men were habitually carrying guns by early 1838 and searching in their spare time for Aborigines to shoot.[179]

For their part, the Narrungdera men took to attacking the settlers' cattle. By late 1838, cattle were being regularly speared. Many not so speared were being run off the lands they were grazing on. In an earlier report dated 12 May 1839, Commissioner Cosby noted that over the four months since 1 January 1839, and among other squatting runs affected, *Tooyal* had seen 40 cattle speared; with a further 40 speared on *Buckingbong*.[180]

Inter-racial violence on the New South Wales colonial frontier during the 1830s and for years afterwards was by no means restricted to the Murrumbidgee River Valley and surrounds. It was rife wherever new runs were being taken up beyond the *Limits of Location*. On 9 December 1839, Niel Black, a young man who was later to become a prominent squatter in Victoria's Western District, wrote from somewhere near Geelong in his *Journal* that:

> "the best way [for a new white arrival in Australia] is to go outside [the bounds of settlement] and take up a new run, provided the conscience of the party is sufficiently seared to enable him without remorse to slaughter natives right and left. It is universally and distinctly understood that the chances are very small indeed of a person taking up a new run being able to maintain possession of his place and property without having recourse to such means — sometimes by wholesale — but I do not think that this is by any means common, and it is only outside [the bounds of settlement that they are ever called upon to act in so brutal a manner. It, however, seems to be little thought of here as it is only done in defence

---

177 See Read, op. cit., pp. 23-24.
178 See Gammage, "The Wiradjuri War 1838-1840", op. cit., p. 4. In 1914, James Baylis, a friend of Frank Jenkins who had arrived with his parents in Wagga Wagga as an infant, wrote:
"I have heard Frank Jenkins giving evidence before the local Land Board, when he stated that there was a period of 12 years — from 1832 to 1844 — when [the Murrumbidgee River] was not high enough to run into the Yanko and Colombo Creeks, and most of the water in the lagoons dried up. This is borne out by the fact that trees grew up in the beds of the creeks and lagoons, and were killed when the water again filled them. In nearly all the lagoons along the Murrumbidgee River the dead trees can still be seen standing."
James Baylis, *Early History of the Murrumbidgee — Wagga Wagga* (1914), Part 1, p. 6 (http://tinyurl.com/y9pgpbnk) (at 17 November 2019); and James Baylis, "The Murrumbidgee and Wagga Wagga", op. cit., p. 255. See also Ferguson, op. cit., p. 169.
179 See "Evidence of Henry Cosby, 9 July 1839" in *New South Wales Votes and Proceedings* (1839), Vol. 2, p. 68; and Gammage, "The Wiradjuri War 1838-1840", op. cit., p. 5.
180 See the "Cosby Report, 12 May 1839" in *New South Wales State Archives and Records* (AONSW: 4/2438.2); and Gammage, "The Wiradjuri War 1838-1840", op. cit., p. 10.

of self or property. The natives who have not been brought into subjection have a strong propensity to spearing and stealing sheep and cattle, and the settlers agree that lead is the only antidote that effectively cures them of this propensity. When a few are shot the rest become timid and are easily kept at bay....

I am strongly impressed with the opinion that a person bringing a set of decent men with him from home, who would behave as they ought, might here live in perfect safety in the middle of the worst of the natives. They have no desire to take a white man's blood. It is only for the sake of flour or some food of one kind or other that they would take a man's life unless he had injured them, and if he has they are afraid of him."[181]

Bill Gammage described early *Buckingbong* in the following terms:

"In 1839, Buckingbong station stood high on a prior stream dune above the Murrumbidgee, looking south over splendid pioneer country. On most runs forest and want of summer water confined stock to the river, but on Buckingbong swamps and creeks fed vast beds of the nourishing tall spike rush after which the run was named, and plains of saltbush and kangaroo grass extending far to the south and west, kept cattle fed even in drought years."[182]

Gammage went on to recount the origins of European occupation of *Buckingbong*, stating that:

"Michael Byrne took up this country about 1832, but it was Narrungdera heartland, and by 1839 they had forced him to abandon it. Apparently it was reoccupied by Byrne's relative Robert Holt Best (1812-53), son of a wealthy Castle Hill emancipist with Airds Irish connections who had taken up Wagga Wagga run in 1832, but Best too was driven out by Narrungdera spears. As his stockmen were ready to leave, two young men rode up. They bought Buckingbong and about fifteen kilometres of [river] frontage for two cows and two calves, withstood the Narrungdera, and established cattle, so beginning careers which would influence district history for the rest of the century."[183]

---

181   Niel Black, *Journal, 30 September 1839 — 8 May 1840* (State Library of Victoria, Manuscripts, MS 11519, Box 99/1). Around six years after Black's *Journal* entry, an English squatter on the Mornington Peninsula, Henry Meyrick, wrote on 30 April 1846 to his mother:

"The blacks are very quiet here now, poor wretches, no wild beast of the forest was ever hunted down with such unsparing perseverance as they are; men, women and children are shot whenever they can be met with. Some excuse might be found for shooting the men by those who are daily getting their cattle speared, but what they can urge in their excuse who shoot women and children I cannot conceive."

Henry Howard Meyrick, *Letters 1840 — 47* (State Library of Victoria, Manuscripts, MS 7959). A little later in the same letter, Meyrick went on to write:

"For myself, if I caught a black actually killing my sheep, I would shoot him with as little remorse as I would a wild dog. But no consideration on earth would induce me to ride into a camp and fire on them indiscriminatingly as is the custom here whenever the smoke is seen. They will very shortly be extinct."

Ibid.

182   Gammage, *Narrandera Shire*, op. cit., p. 38. According to James Baylis, *Buckingbong* was first named *Boganbong*. The latter name was derived from the Wiradjuri words "bogan", meaning "rushes", and "bong", meaning "dry". Baylis added that there were plenty of rushes "in the big swamp near Buckingbong homestead": see Baylis, "Early History of the Murrumbidgee — Wagga Wagga, op. cit.; and Baylis, "The Murrumbidgee and Wagga Wagga", op. cit., p. 254.

183   Gammage, *Narrandera Shire*, op. cit., p. 38. With regard to the Jenkins brothers' acquisition of Robert Best's interest in *Buckingbong*, James Gormly wrote:

The "two young men" were, of course, Jack and Frank Jenkins.

It is unclear precisely when the Jenkins brothers acquired their interest in *Buckingbong*. However, it appears likely that they acquired that interest when the *Wiradjuri War* was at its height. As Commissioner Cosby noted, the first four months of 1839 saw some 40 head of cattle speared on *Buckingbong*.[184] At least some, and perhaps all, of the 40 cattle were no doubt speared whilst Robert Best and his stockmen occupied the run. However, cattle were still being speared after Jack and Frank Jenkins took over *Buckingbong*. In 1916, James Gormly noted that:

> "For the first year the blacks proved troublesome. Frank Jenkins informed me that on one occasion when riding from Buckingbong to Gillenbah he found several of his cattle had been killed by the blacks. The plan the black men adopted was to hide in the reeds that grew on the water's edge, and watch until the cattle went down the steep bank to drink. Then the blacks would range themselves along the top of the bank and spear the cattle that were below."[185]

Early 1839 saw an escalation of the *Wiradjuri War*, with the Narrungdera men and their allies commencing attacks on the European invaders as well as on their cattle. On 8 January 1839, Denis Denay, an Irish hutkeeper on the *Brewarrina* run near Grong Grong, was speared and tomahawked to death outside his hut. During February, a second transportee, John Williams, was speared to death en route for the *Brillinball* run near present-day Narrandera. In the same month, two transportee servants, John Tomkinson and Joseph Ferguson, were besieged by Narrungdera men in their hut near the *Brillinball* homestead. Tomkinson was struck in the face by a boomerang and wounded in the hand by a spear. In August 1839, two unnamed stockmen were attacked and killed on an outstation of the *Grong Grong* run; the homestead on the *Berembed* run was besieged; and James Byrne, an overlander driving cattle to Adelaide, was attacked to the west of the latter run. Eleven days after the attack on Byrne, four of his stockmen were ambushed, and one had his arm broken by a waddy. Many more whites were killed or wounded in September and October 1839 between Ganmain and the Darling River.[186]

"Frank Jenkins informed me that Best's stockmen had built a hut at Buckingbong when his brother John and himself reached that place. The blacks had speared so many of the cattle that Best's men abandoned the station and on the same day John and Frank Jenkins took up possession of the hut and run."

James Gormly, "Pioneers of the Murrumbidgee: Frank and John Jenkins", op. cit.; and James Gormly, *Exploration and Settlement in Australia* (1921), p. 118.

184   See p. 52 above.

185   James Gormly, "Pioneers of the Murrumbidgee: Frank and John Jenkins", op. cit.; and James Gormly, *Exploration and Settlement in Australia*, op. cit., p. 118. Earlier, in 1906, Gormly wrote:

"The blacks in many instances were a source of annoyance to the early settlers on the Murrumbidgee and Murry. Frank Jenkins informed me that on one occasion he found nine head of his cattle had been killed by the blacks, the stock having been speared as they went to water. At another time Jenkins, when out on his run, discovered that about 200 Aboriginals had surrounded a mob of his cattle and were ringing them around, and within the circle formed the blacks were riddling the cattle with spears all the time."

James Gormly, "Exploration and Settlement on the Murray and Murrumbidgee", op. cit., p. 40. With respect to these cattle losses, Gormly continued in anodyne terms:

"But taking all things into consideration the black man let the intruders on their hunting grounds off very lightly."

Ibid. See also Morris, op. cit., p. 23.

186   See Gammage, "The Wiradjuri War 1830", op. cit., pp. 5-12.

The attacks by the Narrungdera and their allies on the white usurpers left the latter in fear for their lives. In his Report dated 12 May 1839, Commissioner Cosby observed that:

> "The Settlers....are in a Great state of alarm, not daring to go out even the shortest distance from their huts, except in parties of two or three, well armed, and they are obliged to desert their lower Stations altogether, finding it impossible to persuade any men to remain at them, let the wages be ever so high.... The Blacks have gone so far, and struck such terror into the minds of the Settlers, that the White Inhabitants will be compelled to abandon at least 50 miles of the River...."[187]

The affected settlers appealed to the New South Wales Colonial Government for help. However, no assistance was forthcoming. Governor Gipps noted on Commissioner Cosby's Report of 12 May 1839 that:

> "I do not find that anything can be done."[188]

The Europeans were left to their own devices. They did so in a manner familiar to many settlers on the colonial frontier in New South Wales: by hunting down and killing Aboriginal men, women and children.

The *Wiradjuri War* ended in late 1840 or early 1841. It reached an awful climax in a massacre of Aborigines on an island in the Murrumbidgee River, now officially known as Massacre Island, located some 20 km upstream of current-day Narrandera, and about 4 km to the west of the *Buckingbong* homestead.[189] James Baylis wrote that he learned of this massacre from Frank Jenkins, who often conversed with him about "the early days". Frank informed Baylis that in those "early days", the Aborigines had been "very troublesome". According to Baylis. Frank then told him that:

> "at last, all the settlers on both sides of the river determined to give them a lesson; so one day they all went out armed and drove the blacks before them, who took refuge on an island thickly overgrown with reeds in the middle of the river, about seven miles up[by land] from the town of Narrandera, and here they were shot down in numbers. The island is known as the Murdering Island to this day."[190]

There is uncertainty surrounding the number of Aborigines shot on Massacre Island. In an

---

187   *Cosby Report, 12 May 1839*, op. cit.; and Gammage, "The Wiradjuri War", op. cit., p. 10.
188   See the *Cosby Report, 12 May 1839*, op. cit.; and Gammage, "The Wiradjuri War", op. cit., p. 14.
189   See Kabaila, op. cit., p. 92. See also **photos 13 and 14**.
190   Baylis, "The Murrumbidgee and Wagga Wagga", op. cit., p. 256. See also Noel Beddoe, T*he Yalda Crossing* (2012); and "Local massacre retold in novel" in the *Narrandera Argus*, Monday, 7 May 2012. Since 1970, the Island has been officially known as Massacre Island: see *New South Wales Government Gazette* (No. 53), Friday, 17 April 1970, p. 1382.

earlier account of the massacre, Baylis simply noted that "several" were shot.[191] For his part, Bill Gamage has asserted that 60 or 70 men, women and children were trapped on the island and were shot down. According to Gammage, only one man survived — by hiding in the reeds.[192]

What does seem to be almost certainly the case is that Frank Jenkins, and very likely his older brother Jack Jenkins, participated in the Massacre Island massacre. Their participation can readily be inferred from the account of it that Frank gave to James Baylis. That account spoke of the involvement of "all of the settlers on both sides of the river". Given that Massacre Island was situated either on or adjacent to *Buckingbong*, and only a short distance from the run's homestead, it is hard to imagine that the massacre occurred in the absence of the two Jenkins brothers.

Although the *Wiradjuri War* seemingly culminated in the Massacre Island massacre, the Narrungdera men continued to spear settlers' cattle well into the 1840s, and Europeans continued to kill local tribespeople — although not in as ostentatious or public a manner as at Massacre Island.[193] In the words of Bill Gammage:

> "[I]n the mid 1860s Aborigines were to tell Rolf Boldrewood that once they were many around Narrandera, but now they were all gone. 'White fellow shoot 'em like possum', they said."[194]

---

191 See Baylis, "Early History of the Murrumbidgee — Wagga Wagga", op. cit., p. 4.

192 Gammage wrote that the man, given the name "Mungo" by the settlers, received a wound to his eye during the shooting, but nonetheless subsequently worked as a police tracker: see Gammage, *Narrandera Shire*, op. cit., pp. 35 and 131. See also Gammage, "The Wiradjuri War 1838-1840", op. cit., p. 14. It might be noted that Stan Grant, most likely relying on local Wiradjuri oral history, has written that the sole survivor of the massacre was a boy: see Stan Grant, "At Poisoned Waterhole creek I tell my son about the slaughter of our people" in *The Guardian* (Australian Edition), Monday, 12 October 2015. See also Stan Grant, *Talking to my Country* (2016), p. 13; and Morris, op. cit., p. 24.

193 See Gammage, "The Wiradjuri War 1838-1840", op. cit., p. 14. A further possible massacre site is to be found along Poison Waterholes Creek, a non-perennial stream to the south and east of present-day Narrandera. As Peter Kabaila has noted, the written record regarding the naming of Poison Waterholes Creek is largely silent: see Kabaila, op. cit., p. 91. However, local Aboriginal oral history has it that the Narrungdera used to camp beside waterholes in the stream, and that at some now unknown point in time many were killed after Europeans either tipped poison into the waterholes or left poisoned flour nearby for the Aborigines to eat: see Gammage, "The Wiradjuri War 1838-1840", op. cit., p. 14; Kabaila, op. cit., pp. 90-91; Grant, "At Poisoned Waterholes creek I tell my son about the slaughter of our people", op. cit.; and Grant, *Talking to my Country*, op. cit., pp. 12-13. This version of the events leading up to the naming of Poisoned Waterholes Creek was strongly supported by the recollections of the prominent author and social activist, Dame Mary Gilmore, who largely grew up in the Riverina: see Mary Gilmore, "Treatment of Aborigines" in the *Sydney Morning Herald*, Friday, 11 March 1938, p. 8.

As against this, it has long been argued by the descendants of local settlers and others that there was no massacre of Aborigines on Poison Waterholes Creek, and that the latter gained its name after settlers poisoned some of the waterholes in the 1880s to kill some of the numerous dingoes which were then attacking the settlers' sheep, and which were also known to frequent the waterholes: see the *Sydney Morning Herald*, Saturday, 5 March 1938, p. 5; the *Narandera Argus and Riverina Advertiser*, Tuesday, 23 January 1945, p. 2; the *Narandera Argus and Riverina Advertiser*, Monday, 5 February 1951, p. 2; and Gammage, *Narrandera Shire*, op. cit., p. 238. As the poisoned waterholes were said to have been located on the original *Buckingbong* run, it is highly likely that Frank Jenkins at least would have been directly involved in the laying of the poison: see the *Narandera Argus and Riverina Advertiser*, Monday, 5 February 1951, p. 2. See also **photos 15** and **16**.

194 Gammage, "The Wiradjuri War 1830-1840", op. cit., p. 14. See also Henry Campey in *H. and J. Campey Papers* (Mitchell library, Sydney: MS 1380/1).

Photo 1: St. James the Great's Church, East Malling — see footnote 6 on p. 7.

Photo 2: Kemsley Street Road — see footnote 15 on p. 8.

Photo 3: St. Mary the Virgin's Church, West Malling — see footnote 18 on p. 9.

Photo 4: Tooyal, looking west towards the Murrumbidgee River — see footnote 73 on p. 22.

Photo 5: Elizabeth Williams (née Jenkins) — see footnote 85 on p. 25.

Photo 6: Berrima House, Berrima — see footnote 102 on p. 28.

*Photo 7: Jack Jenkins as a young man
— see footnote 108 on p. 30*

*Photo 8: St. Peter's Church, Campbelltown — see footnote 108 on p. 30
(and footnote 206 on p. 59)*

Photo 9: Thomas Perrin Surman Jenkins — see footnote 109 on p. 30.

Photo 10: Frank Jenkins in 1902 — see footnote 117 on p. 31.

Photo 11: John Jenkins' Grave, Berrima — see footnote 129 on p. 32.

Photo 12: Thomas Jenkins' Grave, Buckingbong — see footnote 137 on p. 38.

Photo 13: Massacre Island (1) — see footnote 189 on p. 55.

Photo 14: Massacre Island (2) — see footnote 189 on p. 55.

Photo 15: Poisoned Waterholes Creek (1) — see footnote 193 on p. 56.

Photo 16: Poisoned Waterholes Creek (2) — see footnote 193 on p. 56.

Photo 17: Nangus Homestead in 2015 — see footnote 229 on p. 65.

Photo 18: Location of the North Wagga Flour Mill in 2019 — see footnote 249 on p. 70.

Photo 19: The Star Hotel, South Gundagai in 2019 — see footnote 251 on p. 71.

Photo 20: The Family Hotel (formerly the Gundagai Hotel), Gundagai — see footnote 253 on p. 71.

Expansion and Early Years in the Riverina

Following the *Wiradjuri War*, it would seem that Jack and Frank Jenkins were able to establish a modus vivendi with the remaining local Wiradjuri people. Almost certainly glossing over the complexities of the relationship, James Gormly blandly observed that the:

> "Jenkins brothers soon became on friendly terms with the black tribes, and managed to prevent them from spearing stock."[195]

The relationship was clearly imbued with condescension towards the Aborigines on the part of the brothers. This condescension is evident in the following anecdote recounted by Frank Jenkins to James Baylis:

> "Frank Jenkins has often told me of the early days. His cart was one of the first to go down the river, and the blacks, when they came across the tracks, could not make it out. They followed the tracks for miles, and as the two wheel marks never got any closer they thought it uncanny, and afterwards bolted — 'debbil debbil'."[196]

Bill Gammage has noted that in later years, after the *Wiradjuri War*, the Wiradjuri were driven to dependence on European station holders. Frank Jenkins, for one, let them camp on *Buckingbong* between his vineyard and the Murrumbidgee River. However, they were paid for any work they performed for the squatters only in rations. Many grew addicted to alcohol, and all were readily susceptible to death from pneumonia.[197]

Soon after acquiring *Buckingbong*, Jack and Frank Jenkins formed a further squatting run some 12 km downstream on the left bank of the Murrumbidgee River. They named their new run *Gillenbah*. Lying adjacent to *Buckingbong*, *Gillenbah* was situated directly south of present-day Narrandera. *Buckingbong* covered an area of 57,600 acres [about 23,310 hectares],

---

[195] James Gormly, *Exploration and Settlement in Australia*, op. cit., p. 119. However, it might be noted that on 17 October 1842, the then-Commissioner of Crown Lands for the Murrumbidgee District, Henry Bingham, wrote to the Colonial Secretary in Sydney advising that Aborigines were still spearing Jenkins' cattle, but that he had heard that this was because Jack Jenkins had not treated them well. Bingham further advised that the Jenkins' storekeeper, a Ticket of Leave holder named Thomas Townsend, ought to be required to live in "the settled districts" — ie, within the *Limits of Location* — as the Aborigines had a great dislike of him: see *Letter from Henry Bingham to the Colonial Secretary. 17 October 1842* in *New South Wales State Archives and Records* (AONSW 4/2565.1); and Morris, op. cit., p. 24.

[196] Baylis, "The Murrumbidgee and Wagga Wagga", op. cit., p. 256.

[197] See Gammage, *Narrandera Shire*, op. cit., p. 57.

and *Gillenbah* an area of 25,600 acres [around 10,360 hectares].[198] It would appear that from the outset, the two runs were worked by the brothers as the one enterprise.[199] Whilst Frank made his home on *Buckingbong*, Jack initially made his on *Gillenbah*.[200]

The two Jenkins brothers were evidently indefatigable workers. On a number of occasions, James Gormly wrote of Jack Jenkins' capacity for hard work. In 1916, Gormly observed that:

> "There was no man that I have met that I have obtained so much information from about the early days on the Murrumbidgee as I did from John Jenkins. He had been a traveller on the roads with stock from his boyhood days. He endured hard work and privation from the time he was a child.... He went through the vicissitudes of the pastoralist to the fullest extent."[201]

Mention has earlier been made of Jack and Frank Jenkins making the journey from Berrima to the Murrumbidgee as youngsters in the 1830s on foot.[202] In 1934, Gormly wrote the following account of this epic trip:

> "On one occasion they both walked from their father's residence at Berrima to Buckingbong. John informed me that on that journey Frank and himself stopped a night at Laurence and Peter Cooney's station at Cooney's Creek, near Jugiong. Those men, like most of the old pioneers, were most hospitable. The season was winter and the night cold. There were other travellers at Cooney brothers that night, so the hosts, Cooney brothers, shared their blankets with the travellers and all slept side by side on the earthen floor with their feet to the fire."[203]

Both Jack and Frank necessarily ranged widely over their two runs — and well beyond. James Gormly noted with respect to Jack Jenkins that:
"Before gold was discovered, he had taken mobs of superior fat bullocks from his Gillenbah
> Station and sold them in the Sydney markets at £1/5/- per head."[204]

It was also asserted in Jack's obituary, published in the *Bowral Free Press* on 28 October 1899, that the two brothers were among the first to overland cattle from New South Wales to

---

198 See Vann, op. cit., pp. 99 and 102; and Robert Whitworth, *Bailliere's New South Wales Gazetteer and Road Guide* (1866), pp. 89 and 221.
199 See Campbell, op. cit., p. 54. See also the **Buckingbong** and **Gillenbah Map**.
200 See James Gormly, "Pioneers of the Murrumbidgee: Frank and John Jenkins", op. cit., p. 2; and James Gormly, *Exploration and Settlement in Australia*, op. cit., p. 118.
201 See James Gormly, "Pioneers of the Murrumbidgee: Frank and John Jenkins", op. cit., p. 2; and James Gormly, *Exploration and Settlement in Australia*, op. cit., p. 119.
202 See pp. 49–50 above.
203 James Gormly, "Pioneering Families: The Garners & The Jenkins" in the *Narandera Argus and Riverina Advertiser*, Friday, 3 August 1934, p. 8.
204 James Gormly, "Pioneers of the Murrumbidgee: Frank and John Jenkins", op. cit., p. 2; and James Gormly, *Exploration and Settlement in Australia*, op. cit., p. 119.

Adelaide.[205] However, the newspaper provided no details of this overlanding. Nor would there appear to be any other accessible reference to such an undertaking or undertakings.

On 17 August 1841, Jack Jenkins married Maria Ray in St. Peter's Anglican Church, Campbelltown. The daughter of a farming couple, William and Sarah Ray, from Airds near Campbelltown, Maria was born shortly prior to 18 May 1822.[206] As well as tending to his farming interests, William Ray built and ran *The Plough Inn* near the Bow-Bowing Creek at Campbelltown. It is likely that Jack Jenkins met Maria whilst staying overnight at *The Plough Inn* during trips to and from Sydney to sell stock and to pick up supplies for the *Buckingbong* and *Gillenbah* runs.[207]

Jack Jenkins took his bride to live at *Gillenbah*. Their first dwelling was almost certainly a slab hut roofed with bark. Later in the 1840s, the couple moved to *Buckingbong* after a large, more substantial, residence had been built on the latter to replace the original hut.[208] In all, 10 surviving children were born to Jack and Maria. These were:

- John Francis Jenkins, born shortly before 4 June 1842;
- Charlotte Jenkins, born in Campbelltown a little before 6 June 1844;
- William Henry Jenkins, born at Petersham shortly before 13 February 1846;
- Maria Jenkins, born in Campbelltown shortly prior to 17 December 1847;
- Sarah Anne Jenkins, born in Campbelltown a little before 3 October 1849;
- Frank Thomas Jenkins, born shortly prior to 20 July 1854;
- Eliza Jenkins, born in Gundagai a little before 6 July 1856;
- Elizabeth Jenkins, born shortly prior to 20 August 1858;
- Mary Jane Jenkins, born in Gundagai a little before 4 June 1862; and
- Ridley Walter Jenkins, born in Gundagai shortly prior to 28 January 1867.

Two further children did not survive infancy.[209]

Ian McNeill has described Maria Jenkins as a woman of great strength, both of body and of character. She was said to have been respected for a commanding personality, leavened by religious tolerance and a generous charity.[210] According to an article in the *Sydney Morning Herald* published on 24 December 1920, she was:

> "a noted horsewoman of the fearless and resourceful type in her younger days. In the days when the saddle or the wagon constituted the only means of transport, Mrs. Jenkins travelled, on one occasion, a distance of about 306 miles [roughly 490 km] from Campbelltown in order to reach her destination."[211]

---

205 See the *Bowral Free Press*, Saturday, 28 October 1899, p. 2.
206 See the *Marr, Aitken, Watts Family Tree — Ray, Maria* (http://tinyurl.com/t7svxda) (at 25 November 2019). See also p. 30 above; and **photo 8**.
207 See McNeill, op. cit., p. 9.
208 Ibid.
209 See the *Marr, Aitken, Watts Family Tree — Ray, Maria* (http://tinyurl.com/t7svxda) (at 26 November 2019); and McNeill, op. cit., p. 9.
210 Ibid.
211 See the *Sydney Morning Herald*, Friday, 24 December 1920, p. 8.

According to Dame Mary Gilmore, Maria, like the young Queen Victoria "took snuff".[212]

The 1840s were marked by periods of drought and economic depression in the Riverina and beyond.[213] These were difficult years for Jack and Frank Jenkins. Fear of drought and a search for fresh pastures may well have been reasons which led Frank to take 900 head of cattle down the Murrumbidgee River and, after considerable misadventures which will be detailed below, to ultimately establish a new 30,000 acre [approximately 12,140 hectares] run at Gol Gol on the lower Murray River opposite present-day Mildura.

---

212 See Mary Gilmore, *Old Days, Old Ways: A Book of Recollections* (1934), p. 32.

213 See Claire Fenby and Joëlle Gergis, "Rainfall Variations in South-Eastern Australia Part 1: Consolidating Evidence from Pre-instrumental Documentary Sources, 1788 — 1860" in (2012) 33(14) *International Journal of Climatology 2956*, at pp. 2962 and 2966-2967 (http://tinyurl.com/y4g2to8m) (at 26 November 2019); and p. 52 above. Notwithstanding the drought and economic depression of the 1840s, 1848 saw William Pitt Faithfull acquire *Brewarrena*, the run to the immediate east of *Buckingbong*: see Gammage, *Narrandera Shire*, op. cit., pp. 46 and 49. A decade earlier, eight of Faithfull's men were attacked and killed by Aborigines at the Broken River in Victoria on 11 August 1838 in what popularly became known as the Faithfull Massacre: see Judith Bassett, "The Faithfull Massacre at the Broken River 1838" in (2009) 13(24) *Journal of Australian Studies* 18.

Gold

Things looked up markedly for the Jenkins brothers in the early 1850s with the discovery of gold in Victoria. Ian McNeill has described the impact of gold on squatters in the Riverina thus:

> "within a decade, Australia's white population trebled. Victoria's exploded from 77,345 to 540,342, and Victoria became the wealthiest colony in the world. Gold also made the squatters rich. It created an insatiable market for meat, prices leapt, the Riverina was cleared of stock, prices soared. Cattle which sold for 25/- a head in 1851 realised £26 in 1854, and sheep went from 5/- to 30/- a head. The Riverina became a vast fattening paddock as squatter-dealers drew store cattle and sheep from the north and sold fats to Victoria. Overlanders no longer followed the rivers west to South Australia, but crossed them and went south to Victoria. Wagga, Narrandera and Hay became crossing places: local squatters were literally on the road to a fortune."[214]

Jack and Frank Jenkins took full advantage of the demand in the Victorian goldfields for meat. They fattened their cattle on the reed beds and kangaroo grass of *Buckingbong* and *Gillenbah* before taking them south.[215] In addition to driving their own cattle to Victoria, the brothers purchased cattle from other Murrumbidgee runs to bring them down to the goldfields. Of Jack Jenkins at this time, James Gormly wrote in 1916:

> "Soon after gold was discovered, he was a large purchaser of fat bullocks on the Murrumbidgee stations for Melbourne and the Victorian goldfields markets. He did the purchasing and most of the droving himself. When on the road with mobs of fat cattle that were wild and likely to stampede, he would watch the stock each night for weeks in succession and would only get snatches of sleep while on horseback or lying on the ground holding his horse's bridle. In consequence of the high price of fat cattle on the Victorian goldfields, Jack and Frank Jenkins became rich men."[216]

While Jack Jenkins was purchasing or driving cattle during this period, Frank Jenkins would

---

214 See Gammage, *Narrandera* Shire, op. cit., p. 51: and McNeill, op. cit., p. 11.
215 Ibid.
216 See James Gormly, "Pioneering Families: The Garners & The Jenkins" in the *Narandera Argus and Riverina Advertiser*, Friday, 3 August 1934, p. 8.

sometimes stay behind. On occasions, he would collect stores for the runs by dray from Sydney. In 1852, the one round trip to and from Sydney took him a total of nine months because of floods.[217]

Bushrangers presented a real danger to rural travellers in the 1850s. According to Ian McNeill:

> "This was the period that saw the rise of the bushranger, and one story tells of Maria [Jenkins] sewing sovereigns into her little daughters' petticoats in case of a holdup. As she made regular trips to Campbelltown, it must have been a most necessary precaution."[218]

---

217 See McNeill, op. cit., p. 11.
218 McNeill, op. cit., pp. 9-10.

Acquisition of *Yanco* and *Nangus*

The Jenkins brothers used the monies they made from helping to feed Victorian goldminers by acquiring more grazing lands. In 1854, they purchased the leasehold rights to the *Yanco* run of 57,600 acres [about 23,310 hectares] lying immediately to the west of *Gillenbah* from a George Hill for £6,500. In the same year, Jack and Frank Jenkins also purchased the rights of James and William Macarthur to the *Nangus* run and its stock for £16,000.[219]

Nangus lies on the Murrumbidgee River, some 20 km to the west of Gundagai along the road from Gundagai to Wantabadgery. James and William Macarthur were two of the sons of John Macarthur, the early New South Wales political figure and reputed father of the Australian wool industry. James Macarthur first settled *Nangus* in April 1832.[220] On 23 February 1837, James and William Macarthur jointly paid £10 for an annual licence to "depasture Crown Lands [including *Nangus*] beyond the Limits of Location". They renewed this licence each year until 1847, when they applied for a 14 year lease of *Nangus* — which by then extended over 72,000 acres [around 29,140 hectares]. They were granted this lease in 1848.[221]

In 1848, William Macarthur described *Nangus* as follows:

---

219   See McNeill, op. cit., p. 10; Gammage, *Narrandera Shire*, op. cit., pp. 46 and 52; Vann, op. cit., p. 109; and Whitworth, op. cit., p. 629.

220   See Architectural Conservation Consultants, *Nangus Station Homestead: Report to Accompany Application to Heritage Council of New South Wales for Financial Assistance* (1981) ("*Nangus Station Homestead Report*"), p. 3. The *Nangus Station Homestead Report* is held in the files of the Heritage Council of New South Wales. See further Richard Gormly, *Early History of Nangus Station* (1961), p. 1, also held in the files of the Heritage Council of New South Wales. Richard Gormly was one of the sons of James Gormly: see footnote 168 on p. 50 above, and Campbell, op. cit., p. 50.

221   See Richard Gormly, op. cit., p. 2. The original boundaries of *Nangus* were described in 1848 by metes and bounds as follows: "Bounded on the south by the Murrumbidgee River, (commencing at the south-eastern angle of the run) at the junction with the river of a small creek, called the Oak Tree Creek, (which here is the boundary between Nangus and Kymo run, occupied by Mr. Andrews), and extending thence down the course of the river nearly west about 720 chains [approximately 14½ km] in a direct line to the junction with the river of a small creek at the south-west extremity of Tenandra Flat; thence by that creek to a point about 60 chains [about 1.2 km] west of its mouth at the extremity of a spur from Mount Tenandra, this point forming the south-west angle of the run; on the west by a line extending from the south-west angle above-mentioned in a north north-west direction along the summit of the above spur until its junction with Mount Tenandra range, and thence along the summit of Mount Tenandra range to a high point distant about 320 chains [around 6½ km] in a north north-west direction from the above-mentioned south-west angle of the run, from this point by a marked tree line extending due north over a tract of low country without landmarks about 600 chains [approximately 12 km] to a tree marked as the north-west angle of the run, this western boundary line separating it from the run occupied by Mr. James Thorn; on the north by a marked tree line extending due east from the north-west angle above-mentioned about 400 chains [about 8 km] to the summit of Mount Kooba range, at a spot about 50 chains [approximately 1 km] distant from its north-west extremity, thence by the summit of that range extending first south-east, then north-east to its junction with the main range, thence by a line extending along the summit of the main range in a direction generally about south-east to its junction with Mount Kymo range, which point may be termed the north-eastern angle of the run, and is distant about 750 chains [around 15 km] in a direct line south-east from the above mentioned intersection of Mount Kooba range by the due east and west marked tree line above-mentioned, the whole of this northern line being bounded by Mr. Taaffe's run; on the east by a line extending along the summit of Mount Kymo range in a south south-west direction to its termination at the Oak Tree Creek, about 40 chains [approximately 800 m] above its mouth, thence by that creek to its junction with the Murrumbidgee River at the starting point first mentioned, this eastern line being bounded by the run of Mr. Andrews."
See *Supplement to the New South Wales Government Gazette* (No. 109), Tuesday, 27 September 1848, p. 1315.

> "This run called 'Nangus' contains about 70,000 acres [about 28,328 hectares], all very open forest....There are about nine miles [around 14½ km] of river frontage in a direct line with about 3 — 4,000 acres [1,200 -1,600 hectares] of rich alluvial flats — watered by lagoons as well as the river — the remainder consists of sound dry forest land, not rich but good sheep land."[222]

The Macarthurs built an imposing brick homestead on *Nangus*. They originally called this homestead *Clarendon House*.[223] The main building faces north and is situated just above the rather steep local valley walls of the Murrumbidgee River, the flood plain of which comes quite close to the rear of the house.

Doubts persist as to precisely when and how the *Nangus* homestead was constructed. As late as 1848, Edward Beckham, who was then the Commissioner of Crown Lands for the Lachlan District, described *Nangus* as supporting slab huts and a mere four residents who lived in them.[224] However, it could be that the main homestead was then extant but only lived in when either or both of the Macarthurs visited *Nangus*. In any event, it would seem that the most authoritative view is that at least the ground floor of the homestead was built in the 1830s — a decade more consistent with the building's Georgian style of construction.[225]

It has also been asserted that whilst the ground floor of the *Nangus* homestead was constructed by the Macarthurs in the 1830s, the upper storey was added by Jack Jenkins in the 1850s.[226] The authors of the *Nangus Station Homestead Report* take issue with this assertion, arguing that:

---

222   See Maurice Cantlon, *Homesteads of Southern New South Wales: 1830-1900* (1981), p. 120. Some 11 years earlier, on 7 May 1837, Thomas Walker provided the following description of *Nangus*:

"[T]oday, we passed through Mr. Jenkins's and Messrs. J. S. and W. McArthur's cattle stations. The latter, called Nangus, is a beautiful run, and has a more fine back run than most on the river; to the northward, it extends as far as the low flat country through which the Lachlan flows; it is watered not only by the river, but by lagoons and creeks in the heart of it. The cattle on it looked better than any we had lately seen; indeed most of the cattle on the various runs have lately been sent away owing to the deficiency of pasturage, but from it, no such migration has been found necessary."

See Thomas Walker, *A Month in the Bush in Australia* (1838), p. 18. The "Mr. Jenkins" referred to here was almost certainly a Robert Pitt Jenkins, who squatted on the *Bangus* run to the south-east of *Nangus* at Tumblong in about 1831. He was no relation of Jack and Frank Jenkins: see *Wikipedia — Tumblong, NSW* (http://tinyurl.com/y6n2x6n5) (at 13 December 2019); and Parliament of New South Wales, *Mr. Robert Pitt Jenkins (1814-1859)* (http://tinyurl.com/y32cpgat) (at 13 December 2019). It is of interest to note that a small island in the Murrumbidgee River forming part of *Nangus* was apparently one of the early goldfields in the Gundagai area. Now known as Nangus Island, it was originally named McArthur Island: see *Wikipedia — Gundagai* (http://tinyurl.com/mybx35s) (at 13 December 2019); and *Wikipedia — William Macarthur* (http://tinyurl.com/y9ka9vjv) (at 13 December 2019).

223   See "National Trust of Australia (NSW) Listing Proposal" in *Nangus Station Homestead Report*, p. 1.

224   Edward Beckham, "Crown Land Commissioners' Correspondence: Itinerary for 1848" in *New South Wales State Archives and Records* (AONSW 4/2393.2-2843); and Cantlon, op. cit., p. 120. Earlier, on 27 October 1836, Major Thomas Mitchell, the New South Wales Surveyor General, spent the night at *Nangus* without making mention of a substantial homestead. He wrote:

"We have arrived on the Murrumbidgee, seventy-five miles below the point where that river quitted the settled districts, and ceased to form a county boundary. I found the upper portion of this fine stream fully occupied as cattle stations, which indeed extended also, as I was informed, much lower down the river; and such was the thoroughfare in that direction that I found a tolerable cart road from one station to another. I passed the night at the house of a stockman in charge of the cattle of Mr. James MacArthur, and I was very comfortably lodged."

Sir Thomas Mitchell, *Three Expeditions into the Interior of Eastern Australia* (1838), Vol. 2, p. 314.

225   See Australian Heritage Commission, *The Heritage of Australia: The Illustrated Register of the National Estate* (1981), p. 186; and Cantlon, op. cit., p. 120.

226   See Australian Heritage Commission, *The Heritage of Australia: The Illustrated Register of the National Estate* (1981), p.186; and Cantlon, op. cit., p. 120.

> "There is no good evidence that the lower and upper floors were built separately. Indeed, the ground floor plan with its ample original provision for a staircase would indicate that the upper floor is contemporary with the lower."[227]

Notwithstanding continuing controversy surrounding its date and manner of construction, the homestead on the *Nangus* property is probably the most southerly Colonial Georgian homestead building in New South Wales, and a well-preserved example of a Nineteenth Century eastern Murrumbidgee River homestead.[228] In the words of the *Nangus* registration entry in the *Register of the National Estate*:

"As a distinctive piece of architecture with historical connections, it is of outstanding value."[229]

Soon after *Nangus* was acquired by the Jenkins brothers in 1854, Jack Jenkins moved with his wife and children to live in the run's homestead, whilst Frank Jenkins and his immediate family remained at *Buckingbong*. It would seem that the last five of Jack and Maria Jenkins' surviving children were born at *Nangus*, and that Jack and Maria continued to live on that property until at least 1889.[230]

---

227   See *Nangus Station Homestead Report*, p. 5.
228   Ibid. See also a letter dated 16 June 1981 from Mrs Jill Morrow, the Honorary Secretary of the Riverina Regional Committee of the National Trust of Australia (NSW), to Mr P C James, the Deputy Director of the National Trust of Australia (NSW), held in the files of the Heritage Council of New South Wales.
229   See Australian Heritage Commission, *The Heritage of Australia: The Illustrated Register of the National Estate* (1981), p. 186. See also **photo 17**.
230   See James Gormly, *Exploration and Settlement in Australia*, op. cit., p. 119; and Richard Gormly, op. cit., p. 3.

Partnership Dissolution

For some time after 1854, Jack and Frank Jenkins continued to hold and work their runs in partnership with one another. They worked the runs industriously and with great overall success. James Gormly noted that:

> "By hard work and perseverance, the men progressed in the face of all difficulties until at one time they had twenty thousand head of cattle on their Buckingbong and Gillenbah properties."[231]

In addition to raising and selling cattle, the brothers built up flocks of sheep on their properties for the wool market.

However, while the close personal bond between Jack and Frank Jenkins remained unwavering over the balance of their joint lives, their business interests came to diverge with time. Whilst both brothers continued to improve their jointly-held squatting properties, with Jack developing *Nangus* and Frank building up *Buckingbong* and *Gillenbah*, Frank moved in the late 1850s and early 1860s to acquire leasehold interests in his own right in a number of other large runs in the central south of New South Wales. These acquisitions will be dealt with in some detail below. For his part, Jack Jenkins launched himself into a range of often unsuccessful non-pastoral enterprises.

By the end of the 1860s, the business partnership between Jack and Frank Jenkins was at an end. Their geographic separation and diverging business interests were almost certainly responsible for what amounted to a "velvet divorce". In 1868, Jack transferred his leasehold interests in *Buckingbong*, *Gillenbah* and *Yanco* to Frank, and the latter transferred his interest in *Nangus* to Jack.[232]

---

231 See James Gormly, *Exploration and Settlement in Australia*, op. cit., p. 119.
232 See *Supplement to the New South Wales Government Gazette* (No. 96), Friday, 16 April 1869, pp. 1047 and 1049.

JACK JENKINS ALONE
(1816 — 1899)

Early Speculative Ventures

Jack Jenkins was evidently an ebullient man. Bill Gammage noted that he came to be referred to locally as "Roaring Jack". Gammage went on to say that:

"In the great days of the 50s, he was to shoe his horses with gold. His short stocky figure was ever restless along the Murrumbidgee, buying and selling land, building flour mills and smithies and hotels and stores, constructing a paddle steamer at Nangus near Gundagai, taking on anything with an adventure or a quid in it."[233]

For his part, James Gormly described Jack as a "sanguine speculator".[234] Gormly further observed that:

"He was a man that went into many enterprises that did not prove as successful as his pastoral pursuits."[235]

Many of Jack Jenkins' speculative ventures were centred on the growing township of Gundagai to the east of *Nangus*. According to James Gormly, Jack:
"purchased a large number of houses in South Gundagai, which gave him a poor return."[236]

It is not presently known whether he put all or any of these houses out to rent, or whether he simply sought to resell them at a profit. In any event, it would seem that his residential property speculation did not reward him to much, if any, extent.

As may be seen above, Bill Gammage wrote of Jack building smithies and stores.[237] Little has been unearthed in relation to these ventures.[238] However, it seems unlikely that they earned Jack much money which he was able to retain or profitably invest in the long term.

Jack Jenkins was responsible for the construction of two flour mills. The first was located at Spring Flat near North Gundagai and was steam powered. Jack apparently left the operation of this mill to William Hamilton Hayes. The latter came to be Jack and Maria Jenkins'

---

233 See Gammage, *Narrandera Shire*, op. cit., p. 38.
234 See "Pioneering Families: The Garners & The Jenkins" in the *Narandera Argus and Riverina Advertiser,* Friday, 3 August 1934, p. 8.
235 See James Gormley, *Exploration and Settlement in Australia*, op. cit., p. 119.
236 See "Pioneering Families: The Garners & The Jenkins" in the *Narandera Argus and Riverina Advertiser,* Friday, 3 August 1934, p. 8.
237 See Gammage, *Narrandera Shire*, op. cit., p.38; and see also above.
238 Among the stores erected by Jack Jenkins were those occupying a row of buildings on the south side of Sheridan Street, Gundagai. These buildings were located between what was originally Bibo's Bakery and is now the Gundagai Bakery in the east and what was originally the Assembly Hall and is now Gundagai Appliances and Plumbing in the west: see the *Gundagai Times and Tumut, Adelong and Murrumbidgee District Advertiser*, Friday, 20 October 1899, p. 2.

son-in-law; marrying their second child and eldest daughter, Charlotte Jenkins, at Gundagai on 13 October 1869.[239] According to James Gormly, this mill did not prove to be "a profitable speculation".[240]

Jack's second flour mill was somewhat larger than his Spring Flat mill. This second mill was erected at the intersection of what were then known as the Junee and Clarendon Roads (now Hampden Avenue and Mill Street) in North Wagga, and came to be called the *Britannia Steam Flour Mills*.[241] The mill was initially run by a J. Chapman and then by William Hayes' brother, Henry Smithers Hayes.[242] Steam powered, with brick walls, a shingle roof and rising to three storeys, it was a substantial structure. It produced flour with the use of a 16 horsepower [about 12 kilowatts] engine and a boiler which was 20 feet [6 metres] long and 4 feet 6 inches [approximately 1.4 metres] in diameter.[243] In 1866, Jack advertised "the best fine flour available" at £26 a ton, second grade flour at £20 a ton and wheat at between 9/6d and 10/- a bushel. The flour was marketed under the brand name of "Snowdrift".[244]

Two flour mills had earlier been constructed in Wagga Wagga to the south of the Murrumbidgee River. However, grain growers on the northern side of the River were required to pay tolls to carry their wheat to these mills across the only bridge. This was known as "*the Company Bridge*" and was owned by local businessmen and property owners.[245] In building his mill at North Wagga, Jack Jenkins clearly sought to win the custom of the "north bank" growers.[246]

The *Britannia Steam Flour Mills* was substantially damaged by a fire in 1867. It was then rebuilt by Jack.[247] It is not known how profitable it proved to be while in Jack's hands. In the early 1880s, he sold it to Henry Hayes who installed new and more sophisticated machinery in the mill.[248] However, on 16 January 1885, the mill burned to the ground and was not replaced.[249]

---

239   See the *William Duncombe/Mary Haughton Family Website — William Hamilton Hayes [2229]* (http://tinyurl.com/se7bz3t) (at 10 February 2020); and the *Mary Wade Family Website — Charlotte Jenkins* (http://tinyurl.com/y2hmhxpe) (at 10 February 2020).

240   See "Pioneering Families: The Garners & The Jenkins" in the *Narandera Argus and Riverina Advertiser*, Friday, 3 August 1899, p. 8.

241   See the *Illustrated Sydney News*, Saturday, 17 March 1883, p. 14; and the **North Wagga Flour Mill Drawing**.

242   See the *William Duncombe/Mary Haughton Family Website — Henry Smithers Hayes [2227]* (http://tinyurl.com/rgbuhnz) (at 10 February 2020).

243   Ibid.

244   Ibid. See also William Ellis, "Mill Street" in *The Street Names of Wagga Wagga* (http://tinyurl.com/yxe63kuo) (at 10 February 2020).

245   See *City of Wagga Wagga — Wagga Bridge* (http://tinyurl.com/yxopezzu) (at 10 February 2020).

246   See Morris, op. cit., p. 66.

247   See the *Wagga Wagga Advertiser*, Saturday, 17 January 1885, p. 2.

248   See Morris, op. cit., p. 66; and the *William Duncombe/Mary Haughton Family Website — Henry Smithers Hayes [2227]* (http://tinyurl.com/rgbuhnz) (at 10 February 2020)

249   See the *Wagga Wagga Advertiser*, Saturday, 17 January 1885, p. 2; Morris, op. cit., p. 66; and James Gormly, *Exploration and Settlement in Australia*, op. cit., p. 368. See also the **North Wagga Flour Mill Site Plan** and **photo 18**.

Hotels

Jack Jenkins apparently acquired interests in no less than four hotels in South Gundagai: *Gasse's Hotel*, the *Rose Hotel*, the *Eagle Hotel* and the *Star Hotel*.²⁵⁰ The first three of these hotels, and Jack's interest in them, were seemingly ephemeral. All three have now disappeared without leaving any physical traces.

However, one of the four South Gundagai hotels was a substantial structure and, although heavily modified, is still extant. The *Star Hotel* was built by a Thomas Lindley in Mount Street, South Gundagai in 1856.²⁵¹ It was purchased by Jack Jenkins soon afterwards. Jack subsequently transferred the hotel to Henry Jenkins, the ninth child and sixth son of Jack's half-brother, Thomas Perrin Surman Jenkins. In turn, Henry Jenkins sold the *Star Hotel* to a James Hawthorne for £475 in 1895.²⁵²

Jack Jenkins owned but one hotel in Gundagai proper, and he held it for many years. In 1858, and at about the same time as he acquired the *Star Hotel* from Thomas Lindley, Jack also purchased Lots 4 and 5 in Sheridan Street, Gundagai from Lindley. On this site, he constructed a two-storey brick hotel. Jack called it the *Gundagai Hotel*.²⁵³ Jack was likely the absentee licensee of this hotel himself until 1872, when a John Fry probably took over the licence from him.²⁵⁴ In 1883, Jack sold the hotel to a William Deighton. The latter changed its name to *The Family Hotel*. It is still known by that name today.²⁵⁵

The *Gundagai Hotel* played a significant role in the history of Gundagai. In its earliest days, whiskey apparently sold for 2/9d a bottle from the premises, with gold nuggets being accepted as tender alongside the coin of the realm.²⁵⁶ The first offices of the Commercial Banking Company of Sydney were located in the premises, as were the local offices and stables of Cobb and Co. Petrich's Billiard Room was to be found in the hotel, and the Gundagai Masonic Lodge used the premises for its meetings.²⁵⁷

The *Gundagai Hotel* presumably constituted an asset of considerable and continuing value

---

250   See the *Gundagai Times and Tumut, Adelong and Murrumbidgee District Advertiser*, Friday, 17 February 1893, p. 4.

251   See **photo 19**.

252   See McNeill, op. cit., p. 10. See also the *Ancestry: Stokes Family Tree — Thomas Perrin Surman Jenkins* (http://tinyurl.com/yyz89ncq) (at 11 February 2020)

253   See *The Family Hotel* (http://tinyurl.com/yxnggxqg) (at 11 February 2020); and **photo 20**.

254   John Fry also managed the *Nangus* run for Jack Jenkins until about 1876: see McNeill, op. cit., p. 10. For almost a decade, the hotel was informally known as "*Fry's Hotel*": see the History Notice Board affixed to the front street wall of the hotel ("the *Notice Board*"). At all times during Jack's ownership of it, the hotel was probably operated on a day-to-day basis by managers appointed by him.

255   See McNeill, op. cit., p. 10.

256   See the *Notice Board*.

257   Ibid.

to Jack Jenkins. However, when he finally sold it to William Deighton in 1883, Jack's fortunes were already in decline. The sale was probably one of necessity rather than choice, procuring cash to pay off debt.

At some time between 1846 and 1869, Jack Jenkins purchased *The Plough Inn* at Airds near Campbelltown, together with its adjacent two-storey residence, from his mother-in-law, Sarah Ray, who had managed it since her husband's death. He also purchased the 50 acre [around 20 hectares] *Mt Pleasant Estate* on the Camden Road. In 1855, he sold this land to his brother-in-law, William Ray Jnr. The latter was insolvent by 1869, and the Australian Joint Stock Bank seized and sold the *Mt Pleasant Estate* at a mortgagee's auction for less than half its true worth. Jack subsequently conveyed *The Plough Inn* to John Francis Jenkins, his oldest child, in 1875. By 1877, William Ray Jnr's fortunes had improved, and in that year John Francis Jenkins sold *The Plough Inn* to his Uncle William.[258]

---

258 See McNeill, op. cit., p. 10.

Paddle Steamer

Perhaps Jack Jenkins' most audacious commercial venture was his paddle steamer, the *Nangus*.[259] Assembled on the banks of the Murrumbidgee River on Jack's *Nangus* run, the paddle steamer made its maiden voyage in 1865. On 22 September 1865, the *Sydney Morning Herald*, quoting from the *Wagga Wagga Express*, described the vessel's arrival at Wagga Wagga on Friday, 15 September 1865, and the events leading up to it, thus:

> "As the presence of a steamer at Wagga Wagga is an event of some importance...we may mention that the *NANGUS* reached her moorings near the southern bank of the Murrumbidgee near Church Hill on Friday evening at 7,00 pm. She is an iron vessel, 70 ft in length, drawing a little over 18″ of water, and is propelled by an engine of 12 hp driving a pair of side wheels 8′ x 2′. She is owned by John Jenkins of Nangus Station, near Gundagai where she was built by Mr Chapman, engineer of Sydney (constructed by Geo. Chapman & Co, Sydney, transported by dray to Gundagai and re-erected there), who, in company with her proprietor, accompanied her down the river on her maiden trip. She has two barges in tow, also of iron, and is intended for the upper Murrumbidgee trade (Gundagai to Hay). The steamer and barges are calculated to carry 60 tons of cargo, but on this occasion has a little over 20 tons. The vessels remained until Thursday when they proceeded downstream, the river being just as required for the voyage.... It is 7 years since the first steamer ploughed the Murrumbidgee near Wagga and 5 years since they advanced this far.... It is to be hoped that [the resumption of river trade on the upper Murrumbidgee] at the present moment by Mr Jenkins will pave the way for a much greater effort at no distant period."[260]

As generally informative as it may have been, it would appear that this *Sydney Morning Herald* article was probably wrong in referring to the voyage which brought the *Nangus* to Wagga Wagga on 15 September 1865 as being the vessel's maiden voyage. Some support for it having been the maiden voyage was provided by Richard Gormly in 1961, who observed:

---

[259] It is perhaps of interest to note that in a newspaper letter published in 1926, one Patrick Hogan, whose late father, James Hogan, apparently worked on the *Nangus* run and helped launch the paddle steamer, observed that the vessel had been named the *Myria Nangus*. Jack Jenkins' wife's Christian name was, of course, "Maria", and it is possible that Patrick Hogan, long after the event, confused "Myria" for "Maria". Be this as it may, he appears to be the only person on record to refer to the paddle steamer by any other name than simply the *Nangus*: see the *Tumut and Adelong Times*, Tuesday, 9 March 1926, p. 1.

[260] See the *Sydney Morning Herald*, Friday, 22 September 1865, p. 5. See also the *Sydney Mail*, Saturday, 23 September 1865, p. 4; and Ronald Parsons, *Ships of the Inland Rivers* (3rd revised ed., 1996), p. 112; and Morris, op. cit., p. 77.

> "The Goulburn 'Herald' of 6/9/1865 reported that on the last day of August, John Jenkins of Nangus had started his steamer 'Nangus' with two barges in tow on the Murrumbidgee River near his station. The barges and steamer, capable of carrying 30 to 40 tons, were loaded with flour and potatoes for the towns of Hay and Deniliquin."[261]

It could well have taken some two weeks for the *Nangus* to have picked its way downstream from Jack Jenkins' run to Wagga Wagga.

However, a report in the *Tumut and Adelong Times* on 31 July 1865 is suggestive of at least one earlier voyage. The report stated that:

> "We regret to learn that one of Mr Jenkins' barges, tender to the Nangus, has been snagged near Mundarlo, and her crop of potatoes lost."[262]

Moreover, in the first edition of his book, *Ships of the Inland Rivers*, Ronald Parsons noted that the *Nangus* was reported to have arrived at Lang's Crossing [Hay] in June 1865 with a cargo from the *Nangus* run.[263]

It seems unlikely that the *Nangus* paddle steamer was ever a profitable enterprise for Jack Jenkins. Most of the produce carried by it, and by its barges, was probably produced on Jack's *Nangus* run. The paddle steamer would only have been able to operate when water levels on the upper Murrumbidgee River were high. River snags would have inhibited it from travelling at speed. In any event, the *Nangus* had a short life, sinking either in 1867 or 1868.[264] How and precisely where it met its end remains unclear. One story has it that after being moored out of service and used as part of an informal bridge across the River at Wagga Wagga, it was pulled over by its securing ropes and flooded.[265] According to another account, the *Nangus* sank after hitting a snag near Wagga Wagga.[266] It likely foundered in the Murrumbidgee River close to the eastern end of Kincaid Street.[267] Its remains were said to be still visible as late as 1913.[268]

---

261 See Richard Gormly, op. cit., p. 3.
262 See the *Tumut and Adelong Times*, Monday, 31 July 1865, p. 2.
263 See Ronald Parsons, *Ships of the Inland Rivers* (1987), p. 100.
264 See *Wikipedia — Gundagai: Riverboat Trade* (http://tinyurl.com/y6ond7hn) (at 11 February 2020); and Alex McConachie, "Search is on for paddle-steamer's watery grave" in *The Daily Advertiser*, Thursday, 21 March 2013.
265 Ibid.
266 See *Wikipedia — Gundagai: Riverboat Trade* (http://tinyurl.com/y6ond7hn) (at 11 February 2020).
267 See the *Tumut and Adelong Times*, Tuesday, 9 March 1926, p. 1.
268 See the *Australasian Underwater Cultural Heritage Database — Nangus [1314]* (http://tinyurl.com/yyqvntq9) (at 11 February 2020).

Middle Years

It seems clear that Jack Jenkins derived the better part of his income during his middle and later years from his *Nangus* run. He used the property principally for raising cattle and sheep. He was apparently able to increase the value of his stock by agisting his herds and flocks over hot summers on the 58,000 acre [around 23,470 hectares] *Nottingham Forest* run adjacent to the Goobarragandra River in the foothills of the Australian Alps to the southeast of Tumut. Jack's brother, Frank Jenkins, also used this run for agistment purposes, and it would appear that by 1886, the property was held in Frank's name.[269] It is probable that while moving his stock backwards and forwards between his properties in the central south of New South Wales and the *Nottingham Forest* run, Frank would have spent time with his brother Jack at *Nangus*.

By the 1860s, Jack Jenkins was clearly farming parts of his *Nangus* run. It is highly likely that he was growing potatoes on a section or sections of the property's rich river flats.[270] Given his flour mills in both North Gundagai and North Wagga, he probably also cropped wheat. It further appears that Jack also established a vineyard from which he made his own wine.[271] Interestingly, it seems that in the mid 1880s, Jack sub-leased around 300 acres [121 hectares] of alluvial land at *Nangus* to a Chinese entrepreneur, Dang Ah Chee, for growing tobacco.[272]

Maria Jenkins was no doubt kept very busy raising her 10 surviving children, several of whom apparently had significant musical abilities. Tutors and governesses were engaged by her to supervise their education. In an era when most clothes were hand-sewn, Maria was reputed to have been the owner of the first mechanical sewing machine in the Murrumbidgee River valley. In addition to managing her children and household, Maria saw to the cultivation of a fine garden at *Nangus*.[273]

---

269   See William Hanson, *The Pastoral Possessions of New South* Wales (1889), pp. 114-114; the *Micalong Swamp Flora Reserve No. 70 Working Plan*, p. 9 (http://tinyurl.com/y3z9zxp8) (at 11 February 2020); Anon., *Richard Morris Rivers — West Blowering Station* (http://tinyurl.com/y6nx7o3z) (at 11 February 2020); and Whitworth, op. cit., p.428. See also the *Australian Town and Country Journal*, Saturday, 24 June 1876, p. 16; and Gammage, *Narrandera Shire*, op. cit., p. 96.

270   See p. 74 above.

271   See McNeill, op. cit., p. 10.

272   See the *Gundagai Times*, Tuesday, 5 October 1886; and Barry McGowan, Tracking *the Dragon* (2015), p. 37.

273   See McNeill, op. cit., p. 10.

St Paul's Anglican Church, Nangus

Jack and Maria Jenkins were committed Anglicans. Prior to 1878, services for local Anglicans were held in a room located in the *Nangus* homestead.[274] Jack and Maria worked with others to secure the construction of a church on the north-western margin of the *Nangus* run. On 3 April 1877, Maria was called upon to lay the foundation stone of that church.[275] The first service in St. Paul's Church, Nangus was conducted on 21 May 1878.[276] Over time, a small village, also known as "Nangus" grew up in the immediate vicinity of the Church.

Jack and Maria, together with the immediate members of their family, would have been regular parishioners at St. Paul's Church. On 30 July 1887, Jack and Maria's youngest child, Ridley Walter Jenkins, died of heart failure at the age of 20 years and 6 months. He was buried by his parents in the Nangus village graveyard.[277] In the 1920s, two further Jenkins sons were interred in Ridley Jenkins' grave.[278]

Following the deaths of both Jack and Maria, their second youngest child, Mary Jane Beveridge (née Jenkins), arranged for two stained glass windows to be installed in the chancel wall of St. Paul's Church immediately above the alter in honour of her parents.[279]

---

[274] See the *Gundagai Times and Tumut, Adelong and Murrumbidgee District Advertiser*, Friday, 31 May 1878, p. 2; and Anon., *St. Paul's, Nangus: Centenary 1878 — 1978* (1978), p. 5.

[275] In its edition of 6 April 1877, the *Gundagai Times and Tumut, Adelong and Murrumbidgee District Advertiser* wrote:
"The building committee, as a slight token of their great regard for her, and in recognition of the earnest way in which she works for the church, had requested Mrs. Jenkins, of Clarendon House, Nangus, to lay the foundation-stone. In their name and his own the vicar then called upon her to perform that ceremony. After wielding the trowel and mallet, Mrs. Jenkins declared the foundation-stone of St. Paul's Church to be well and truly laid."
See the *Gundagai Times and Tumut, Adelong and Murrumbidgee District Advertiser*, Friday, 6 April 1877, p. 2. See also Anon., *St.Paul's, Nangus: Centenary 1878 — 1978* (1978), pp. 2-3.

[276] See the *Gundagai Times and Tumut, Adelong and Murrumbidgee District Advertiser*, Friday, 31 May 1878, p. 2; and Anon., *St. Paul's, Nangus: Centenary 1878 — 1978* (1978), pp. 3-4. See also **photo 21**.

[277] See the *Cootamundra Herald*, Saturday, 6 August 1887, p. 4. See also **photo 22**.

[278] The two other Jenkins brothers buried in Ridley Jenkins' grave in the Nangus village graveyard are William Henry Jenkins, who died on or about 23 October 1923, and Frank Thomas Jenkins, who died on or about 8 May 1925. Neither is referred to on their brother Ridley's headstone: see "Re Gundagai" post by Ros Phillips dated 3 June 2004 in *RootsWeb* (http://tinyurl.com/y27s5dk6) (at 16 February 2020).

[279] See **photos 23**, **24** and **25**.

Legal Troubles

In an obituary for him published in the *Bowral Free Press and Berrima District Intelligencer* on 28 April 1899, Jack Jenkins was described as:

"a man of extraordinary vitality and vigour, widely known, and much beloved, industrious and benevolent, and possessed of the most guileless of dispositions."[280]

However, there was clearly a dark side to Jack's character. His ebullience was probably accompanied by a readily-aroused temper, together with a willingness to resort to force in serious confrontations. This willingness to resort to force ultimately resulted in his exposure to very serious legal jeopardy.

It would seem that Jack was summoned to appear before the Wagga Wagga Magistrates on several occasions in 1849 and 1850 for non-payment of wages owed to his employees. In 1853, he was fined £3 by the same Bench of Magistrates for using abusive language.[281]

Reference has been made above to Jack Jenkins' likely involvement in the Massacre Island massacre of Aborigines in late 1840 or early 1841 during the Wiradjuri War.[282] No white was ever brought to account for this slaughter. However, an act of threatened violence did bring Jack to court in 1873. In early May of that year, he was involved in a heated argument with a "Mr Moore", of the firm of Moore and Dunlop, Commission Agents. In the course of that argument, Jack threatened to strike Moore with "a loaded whip" — that is, a whip with a weighted handle. Charged with using threatening language, he was bound over to keep the peace in the Wagga Wagga Police Court on 6 May 1873.[283]

In 1877, an act of actual violence led to a great deal more legal trouble for Jack Jenkins. On 18 June 1877, and at Goobarragandra on or near to the Jenkins brothers' *Nottingham Forest* run to the south-east of Tumut, Jack confronted James Brogan, a shepherd then in his employ. He accused Brogan of stealing his dog. According to a witness, Duncan McCallum, Brogan, in an "impertinent manner", denied taking the dog; asserting that it had simply followed him and telling Jack to "tie your dog up". Apparently enraged, Jack then hit Brogan on his head with the handle of Jack's sheep whip. This apparently opened an artery on the left side of Brogan's

---

280   See the *Bowral Free Press and Berrima District Intelligencer*, Saturday, 24 June 1899, p. 2.
281   See Sherry Morris, *Biographical Notes — John Jenkins ("Johnny")* (Manuscript held by the Wagga Wagga City Library).
282   See pp. 55-56 above.
283   See the *Wagga Wagga Express and Murrumbidgee District Advertiser*, Wednesday, 7 May 1873, p. 2.

head, leading to significant bleeding. Thereafter, Brogan sought medical assistance from a Dr Gilbert Selfe in Tumut, who was able to staunch the bleeding.

Jack was subsequently charged with unlawfully and maliciously wounding Brogan. This charge was heard by Judge David Forbes and a Jury in a Wagga Wagga Quarter Sessions Court hearing conducted on 29 July 1877. After being instructed by Judge Forbes that they could do so, and after considerable deliberation, the Jury found Jack guilty not of malicious wounding, but of an assault occasioning actual bodily harm. Judge Forbes then sentenced Jack to be imprisoned for three months in Goulburn Gaol with hard labour, and further to be fined £100.[284] However, rather than commencing his term of imprisonment at Goulburn Gaol, the New South Wales Government arranged for Jack to be immediately removed from Wagga Wagga to serve his sentence instead in Gundagai Gaol.[285]

Jack appealed his conviction to the New South Wales Supreme Court. His appeal was heard by a Full Court consisting of Chief Justice Martin and Justices Faucett and Manning on 31 August 1877. The only point at issue in the appeal was whether Judge Forbes had been correct in instructing the Jury during the trial that they could find Jack guilty of assault occasioning actual bodily harm when the only charge preferred against him was one of unlawful and malicious wounding. In the event, the Full Court concluded (with Justice Manning nonetheless expressing serious doubts with respect to the question) that the Trial Judge's instruction to the Jury had indeed been incorrect.[286] The conviction was accordingly set aside and an order made that Jack be discharged from custody.

In Wagga Wagga at least, the order of the Full Court setting aside Jack Jenkins' conviction was seemingly welcomed. On 1 September 1877, the editor of the *Wagga Wagga Advertiser* wrote:

> "Considerable satisfaction was expressed in town last night when it became known that the conviction of Mr John Jenkins of Nangus had been quashed. Deep sympathy has all along been felt for this much persecuted gentleman, and the opinion universally shared throughout the district is that he should never have been committed upon such a charge, much less convicted."[287]

---

284 See the *Wagga Wagga Advertiser*, Saturday, 30 June 1877, p. 4; and the *Freeman's Journal*, Saturday, 7 July 1877, p. 16. For his part, the editor of the *Wagga Wagga Advertiser* was highly critical of the Jury's verdict, observing:
"The verdict arrived at against Mr John Jenkins of Nangus is viewed with much dissatisfaction by everyone who can appreciate sterling worth when they find it in anyone, be he old or young."
See the *Wagga Wagga Advertiser*, Saturday, 30 June 1877, p. 2.

285 See the *Wagga Wagga Advertiser*, Wednesday, 1 August 1877, p. 2.

286 In his judgment, Chief Justice Martin held that:
"I think that the circumstance of aggravation that this assault occasioned actual bodily harm ought to have been set forth in the Information in this case. I do not think a Judge ought to have the discretionary power of sentencing a Prisoner for something with which he is not charged. I therefore think that the Jury were not at liberty to find the verdict which they did, because there was no count in the Information charging an assault occasioning actual bodily harm, and on that ground the conviction ought to be set aside."
See *The Queen v Jenkins* [1877] Knox's Reports 295, at 298.

287 See the *Wagga Wagga Advertiser*, Saturday, 1 September 1877, p. 2. The editor continued:
"Mr. Jenkins has not only been wrongfully imprisoned for two months, but contrary to the sentence, the payment of the fine was sometime since insisted upon, and a levy of distress made upon his property. The amount of £100 was of course paid, with about £6 expenses, and this sum has now to be refunded to him."
Ibid.

Unfortunately for Jack, the legal consequences of his whip handle blow to James Brogan's head did not end with the Full Court's decision of 32 August 1877. On 26 March 1878, James Brogan died at his home at Spring Valley near Goulburn. On instructions from the New South Wales Attorney General, Jack was charged with Brogan's manslaughter.[288]

On 9 August 1878, Jack Jenkins faced a committal hearing in the Tumut Police Court before a Police Magistrate, Arthur Vyner. During the committal, evidence was of course adduced of the altercation between Jack and Brogan which led to the former inflicting the blow to the latter's head. However, the balance of the hearing was directed to the question of what caused Brogan's death.

The Court heard from Peter Brogan Jnr, James Brogan's brother. Peter Brogan testified that he had seen his brother frequently at Spring Valley during the six weeks prior to his death. Over this period, Peter Brogan stated that he had observed James Brogan bleeding on a number of occasions from his left nostril. On one such occasion, the bleeding lasted for about three hours.

The Court then heard from a Dr Lewis Davidson. Dr Davidson gave evidence that he had attended James Brogan on the day before the latter's death and found him to be suffering from loss of blood. Brogan told Dr Davidson that he had been bleeding severely off and on since he had been struck on the head. Dr Davidson opined that Brogan had died from the effects of blood loss. A post-mortem examination revealed that Brogan's brain was healthy but drained of blood. He concluded:

> "I am of opinion that the blow may have been an indirect cause of the bleeding; I discovered no disease in any of the organs sufficient to cause death..."[289]

However, Dr Davidson conceded under cross-examination that:

> "I have never had any experience of a case of death from secondary haemorrhage caused by a blow to the head, but it is feasible nevertheless; any severe loss of blood might occasion a state of system prone to bleeding."[290]

Two medical practitioners gave evidence on behalf of Jack Jenkins. The first, Dr Robert McKillop, deposed that:

> "I have never known of secondary haemorrhage produced by a blow such as that described today; I have never read of it in any medical work; I have searched medical

---

288   See the *Sydney Morning Herald*, Tuesday, 13 August 1878, p. 6.
289   Ibid.
290   Ibid.

works for such cases; if there had been profuse bleeding before the blow, I should hardly think the blow had anything to do with the subsequent bleeding."[291]

The second of the two doctors called for the Defence was a Dr Patrick Kennedy. In the course of his evidence, the latter stated:

"I cannot conceive how secondary haemorrhage could follow from a blow on the head; haemorrhagic diathesis is a constitutional disease, and could not be produced by great loss of blood; if I knew that James Brogan had been subject to profuse bleeding before he received the blow spoken of, I should think he died of a constitutional tendency to haemorrhage."[292]

Two lay witnesses were called on Jack Jenkins' behalf. The first, Maurice Kiley, deposed that he was a grazier. He had employed James Brogan for some two or three months after Jack and had known him for two years prior to that. Kiley stated with regard to Brogan:

"I once heard him say that he would have been a smart man, but that he was subject to bleeding at the nose and fits."

However, Kiley also stated that he had never seen Brogan bleed at the nose, nor saw him suffer a fit.[293]

The last lay witness was a labourer, Alfred Harris. In his evidence, Harris stated:

"I knew James Brogan previous to him being struck by John Jenkins, at least I had seen him three or four times. I saw him bleeding at the nose last March twelve months [i.e. before being struck by Jack]. He was holding a handkerchief to his nose, and as he walked away I saw blood on the handkerchief."[294]

At the conclusion of the committal hearing, Police Magistrate Vyner held that Jack had a case to answer on the manslaughter charge. To that charge, Jack pleaded not guilty. The Police Magistrate then ordered that "he take his trial" at the Wagga Wagga Circuit Court in the sittings commencing on 1 October 1878.[295]

As matters turned out, Jack Jenkins did not face trial for the manslaughter of James Brogan. In early September 1878, the New South Wales Attorney General abandoned the prosecution

---

291 Ibid.
292 Ibid. In haematology, haemorrhagic diathesis is an unusual susceptibility to bleed: see *Wikipedia — Bleeding Diathesis* (http://tinyurl.com/y47qfwaj) (at 16 February 2020).
293 See the *Sydney Morning Herald*, Tuesday, 13 August 1878, p. 6.
294 Ibid.
295 Ibid.

by filing a *nolle prosequi* declaration with the Supreme Court.[296] Undoubtedly, the Attorney General concluded that given the medical and other evidence adduced during the committal hearing with respect to the cause of Brogan's death, the Crown stood virtually no chance of proving beyond reasonable doubt at trial that Jack's blow had caused that death.[297] Jack's relief at this outcome can only be imagined.

---

[296] See the *Sydney Morning Herald*, Friday, 6 September 1878, p. 6.

[297] This seemingly obvious explanation for the Crown's abandonment of Jack Jenkins' trial did not occur to, or alternatively satisfy, the *Sydney Morning Herald*'s editorial writer, who railed:

"Why the Crown ordered the prosecution and now refuses to proceed with the same is inexplicable, and it does seem that Mr. Jenkins and the witnesses have been cruelly put to a deal of needless trouble and expense, else that justice has miscarried."

Ibid.

Financial Strains

In his book *Exploration and Settlement in Australia*, James Gormly observed of Jack Jenkins:

> "Jenkins had a weakness that caused him to go into speculations outside his pastoral business, and these speculations brought him in his old age into financial straits. While Jenkins stuck to the business he best understood he prospered, but when he went into building, and constructing a steamer (to ply the river), most of such ventures proved to be losing concerns. I have known few men, if any, who worked as long and as hard as did John Jenkins; yet when he died at eighty-six he was not a rich man."[298]

There was a clear connection between Jack's financial woes in later life and his stewardship of the *Nangus* run. Over time, Jack witnessed his original holding reduced greatly in size and become burdened with debt. The reduction in the run's size was intimately connected with changes in New South Wales land laws.

---

[298] See James Gormly, *Exploration and Settlement in Australia* (1921), p. 368.

Evolving Land Laws

It might be recalled that when Jack and Frank Jenkins, and probably their father, first occupied the *Tooyal* run in 1832, they did so strictly as trespassers in the eyes of the law. However, following the introduction in 1837 of depasturing licences with respect to squatters' runs beyond the *Limits of Location*, such a licence was first issued to John Jenkins Snr in that year.[299] A depasturing licence was similarly granted in 1837 to James and William Macarthur with respect to their *Nangus* run.[300] Jack and Frank Jenkins would almost certainly have acquired a licence covering their *Buckingbong* and *Gillenbah* runs soon afterwards.

The introduction of depasturing licences satisfied very few squatters. The causes for their dissatisfaction were summarised by Cecil King as follows:

> "[T]he charging of a licence fee still left the basic problem of land tenure unresolved, because the licence had to be renewed annually, the licensee made any improvements at his own risk, and he was left to bargain with his neighbours about the boundaries of his runs, since there were no Crown surveys — pastoralists hesitated to develop their holdings. Runs were unfenced, buildings were of bark, ...drains for stock watering avoided.... Yet the wool industry was booming, and its very importance impelled some early determination of the squatters' legal position..."[301]

In essence, the squatters wanted greater security of tenure for their runs. They agitated for that greater security in Britain. The Conservative Government of Sir Robert Peel, which was elected to office in 1841, proved to be more receptive to the squatters' agitation than had its predecessor, the Whig Government of Lord Melbourne.[302]

In 1846, the Peel Government enacted the *Sale of Waste Lands Act 1846* (Imp).[303] This statute was closely followed by the consequential promulgation of an *Order of the Queen in Council* dated

---

299   See pp. 25 and 31 above.
300   See Campbell, op. cit., p. 22.
301   See Cecil King, *An Outline of Closer Settlement in New South Wales, Part 1: The Sequence of the Land Laws, 1788 — 1956* (1957), p. 48.
302   In a dispatch dated 30 January 1845, Peel's Secretary of State for War and the Colonies, Lord Stanley, stated:
    "I know that the great source of the wealth of New South Wales, the production of wool, has been mainly the work of those who are termed squatters....[T]hey include many of the most educated, the most intelligent, and the wealthiest of the inhabitants of the colony. I believe, moreover, that they constitute a body whose influence in the colony, out of the Legislature, is very great..."
    See Campbell, op. cit., p. 7.
303   More formally, the *Act to Amend an Act for Regulating the Sale of Waste Land Belonging to the Crown in the Australian Colonies* (9 and 10 Vic. c. 104).

9 March 1847 ("the *Order in Council of 1847*").[304] Taken together, these measures authorised the New South Wales Government to grant leases of runs of land beyond the *Limits of Location* to such persons as the Colonial Governments in Australia thought fit for terms of up to 14 years.[305]

By 1848, Jack and Frank Jenkins had been granted a 14 year lease of *Buckingbong* by the New South Wales Government; with that lease covering both *Buckingbong* proper and the adjacent *Gillenbah* run.[306] James and William Macarthur had likewise acquired a 14 year lease over their *Nangus* run.[307]

The *Order in Council of 1847* contained a further provision of immediate importance. Clause 6 provided that:

> "[I]t shall be lawful for the [New South Wales Government] to sell such lessee any of the lands comprised in the lease granted to such lessee, provided that the quantity of lands sold to such lessee shall not be less than one hundred and sixty acres, and that the price to be paid for the same shall not be below the general minimum price of one pound for each acre; provided also, that if the portion or lot of any such run sold to such lessee be less in extent than three hundred and twenty acres, the expenses of the survey of the portion so sold shall be paid by the purchaser."[308]

At some point in time between 1848 and 1850, it would seem that James and William Macarthur took advantage of clause 6 of the *Order in Council of 1847* to purchase 320 acres [around 129 hectares] of their *Nangus* run by then under lease.[309] It might readily be assumed that the 320 acres so purchased contained the property's homestead.

When Jack and Frank Jenkins acquired the Macarthurs' interest in *Nangus* in 1854, they clearly would have secured a conveyance of the 320 acres of freehold land forming part of the run as well as an assignment of what remained of the Macarthurs' leasehold interest in the property.[310] There is nothing to suggest that the Jenkins brothers purchased any further portion or portions of *Nangus* prior to the passage of the Robertson Land Acts in 1861.

---

304 See the *Port Phillip Gazette and Settlers' Journal*, Saturday, 14 August 1847, p. 1.

305 Clause 2 of the *Order in Council of 1847* provided that:
"The rent to be paid for each several run of land shall be proportioned in the number of sheep or equivalent number of cattle which the run shall be estimated as capable of carrying, according to a scale to be established for the purpose, by authority of the Governor. Each run shall be capable of carrying, at least 4,000 sheep, or an equivalent number of cattle, according to the scale aforesaid, and not in any case be let at a lower rent than ten pounds per annum, to which two pounds ten shillings per annum shall be added for every additional thousand sheep, or equivalent number of cattle which the run shall be estimated as capable of carrying."
Ibid.

306 See Campbell, op. cit., p. 54; and Whitworth, op. cit., p. 89. It would seem that Jack and Frank Jenkins' father, John Jenkins Snr, also obtained a 14 year lease of his *Tooyal* run in or about 1848: see Campbell, op. cit., p. 50. However, it appears that by 1865, *Tooyal* had passed into the hands of mortgagees, Mort, Cameron & Buchanan: see Vann, op. cit., p. 69. See also Alan Barnard, "Mort, Thomas Sutcliffe (1816-1876)" in *Australian Dictionary of Biography* (http://tinyurl.com/y3poz9bn) (at 16 February 2020).

307 See p. 63 above.

308 See the *Port Phillip Gazette and Settlers' Journal*, Saturday, 14 August 1847, p. 1.

309 Between 1848 and 1850, the area of the *Nangus* run under lease dropped from 72,000 acres [a little over 29,137 hectares] to 71,680 acres [about 29,007 hectares]: see Campbell, op. cit., p. 50; and Richard Gormley, op. cit., p. 3.

310 See p. 63 above.

In the years following the promulgation of the *Order in Council of 1847*, and particularly after the gold rushes of the early 1850s, the political tide turned against the squatters. Agitation to "unlock the land" grew in New South Wales, as in Victoria. Pressure mounted to allow the landless access to the vast holdings of the squatters, and to curb the political influence of the squatter class. In the words of Bill Gammage, progressives in New South Wales reasoned:

> "To destroy the squatters, to advance democracy, and to ensure progress, the runs must be cut up."[311]

Leadership of those seeking to unlock the squatters' hold on pastoral land outside the *Limits of Location* fell to John Robertson. In January 1861, Robertson assumed the position of Secretary for Lands and Works in the Cowper Government of New South Wales. After a monumental struggle, he succeeded in securing the passage of his two Land Acts.[312] In October 1861, the New South Wales Parliament enacted the *Crown Lands Alienation Act 1861*[313], the object of which was to provide for the conversion of non-freehold land under squatter control into small freeholdings, and the *Crown Lands Occupation Act 1861*, which was designed to regulate the leasing of Crown Lands.[314]

Put simply, the combined effect of the two Robertson Land Acts was as follows:
- The Order in Council of 1847 was repealed, and Crown lands beyond the Limits of Location which enclosed "the settled districts" were opened up for selection and sale.
- Subject to limitations referred to below, any person could select and ultimately obtain freehold title to between 40 and 320 acres of Crown land, other than town land, reserves or goldfields, for £1 an acre; with a deposit of 5/- per acre and the balance either to be paid at the end of three years or deferred indefinitely upon payment of 5% interest per annum.
- Selectors were required to live on their selections for at least three years, and during that period spend at least £1 an acre in improving those selections.
- Land held by squatters under Crown leases granted prior to 22 February 1858 was exempt from sale during the currency of those leases; with each squatter being given a pre-emptive right to purchase one twenty-fifth of his leased lands in addition to improved areas.
- Upon the expiration of existing pastoral leases, new leases of previously leased lands outside the settled districts which had not been selected by selectors in accordance with the Robertson Land Acts could be issued for terms of no more than five years.

Some of the selectors seeking to take advantage of the Robertson Land Acts were genuine, would-be settlers. Others were simply land speculators, selecting land with a view to its ultimate re-sale at a profit after three years. Attempts by selectors, whether bona fide settlers or speculators, led them into open, and often bitter, conflict with squatters. The latter were

---
311   See Gammage, *Narrandera Shire*, op. cit., p. 62.
312   See Bede Nairn, "Robertson, Sir John (1816-1891)" in *Australian Dictionary of Biography* (http://tinyurl.com/y42edrrq) (at 17 February 2020).
313   See 25 Vic. No. 1 (NSW).
314   See 25 Vic. No. 2 (NSW).

generally outraged by what was occurring. Some sold out. Many others sought to exploit exemptions and loopholes in the Acts to deny their lands to selectors, and instead to secure freehold title to as much of their runs as they could. In some cases, the squatters were able to secure all or most of their runs by arranging for family members, friends or paid agents to select portions of the runs — portions which were ultimately conveyed back to the squatters concerned. This subterfuge was known as "dummying". Squatters also attempted to acquire in their own names portions of their runs in strategic locations so as to effectively deny would-be selectors access to water. This stratagem was known as "peacocking".[315]

It is presently unclear whether the Jenkins brothers took any, and if so what, steps in the years immediately following the enactment of the Robertson Land Acts to prevent would-be selectors from laying claim to portions of *Nangus* after the expiration of the 14 year lease of the run granted in 1848.[316] Nor is it clear what portion or portions of the property selectors were successful in claiming. Again, it is presently uncertain whether the Jenkins brothers together, or Jack independently, used the Acts to acquire freehold title to a further portion or portions of *Nangus*. However, what is clear is that over the period between 1850 and 1865, the area of *Nangus* under Crown lease dropped from 71,680 acres [around 29,007 hectares] to 57,000 acres [about 23,000 hectares].[317]

---

315 See generally here Gammage, *Narrandera Shire*, op. cit., pp. 62-64.
316 See p. 63 above.
317 See footnote 309 on p. 84 above; Vann, op. cit., p. 66; and Whitworth, op. cit., p. 396.

Financial Decline

As previously mentioned, Frank Jenkins transferred his interest in *Nangus* to his brother Jack in 1868.[318] Almost immediately afterwards, Jack Jenkins mortgaged the run to the Australian Joint Stock Bank.[319] No doubt Jack used the money advanced by the Bank under the mortgage to effect improvements on *Nangus* and/or to further pursue his multifarious other business ventures and investments. The Australian Joint Stock Bank's loan was refinanced by Jack on at least one and possibly more occasions as, by the late 1880s, his interest in *Nangus* was subject to a different mortgage — one in favour of the Bank of New South Wales.[320]

Continuing pressure in New South Wales to open up leased pastoral land to closer settlement following the widespread "gaming" of the Robertson Land Acts by squatters and speculators led to the enactment of the *Crown Lands Act of 1884* (NSW).[321] Among other important measures in that Act, pastoral leaseholders were each required to surrender half of their leased run to the New South Wales Government in return for enhanced security of tenure on what remained. At the Government's discretion, the resumed areas were to be open to survey and sale to selectors in lots of up to 640 acres [about 258 hectares]. The original leaseholders were offered lesser leases of the resumed land pending such sale to selectors.

It is unclear precisely what impact the new Act had on Jack Jenkins' *Nangus* leased land. It seems that the Act, like the earlier Robertson Land Acts, was widely circumvented by affected pastoralists by means of the use of family and other "dummy" selectors. Whether Jack resorted to such tactics is not presently known. However, it seems likely that the new Act would have resulted in at least some reduction in the size of his leasehold lands.

Be that as it may, it would appear the by 1891, Jack Jenkins had lost *Nangus*, with the Bank of New South Wales foreclosing on its mortgage.[322] New South Wales Stock Returns for 1892 reveal that the Bank was then in possession of *Nangus*; and that the property then extended over some 25,000 acres [about 10,117 hectares] and carried 33,974 sheep, 1,643 head of cattle and 44 horses.[323]

Whilst Jack had been unsuccessful in at least some of his business ventures, and had also

---

318   See p. 66 above.
319   See *Supplement to the New South Wales Government Gazette* (No 96), Friday, 16 April 1869, p. 1047.
320   See Richard Gormly, op. cit., p. 3.
321   See 48 Vic. No. 18 (NSW).
322   See Richard Gormly, op. cit., p. 3.
323   Ibid.

probably been somewhat improvident, the primary reason for his loss of *Nangus* would appear to have been the economic upheavals of the late 1880s and the early 1890s.[324]

The 1880s had commenced as boom years for Australian primary producers. Commodity prices had been high and bank loans abundant. However, exuberant lending by banks and other financial institutions led to over-investment in properties and the emergence of an asset "bubble".

By the late 1880s, the boom had run its course. Commodity prices had fallen by up to 50%. This led to depreciations in land values. The results were loan and overdraft defaults and mortgage foreclosures. These developments undermined the stability of Australian lending institutions. British investors, conscious of declining Australian returns, began to withdraw from funding the Australian capital market. Loan defaults multiplied and land became difficult to sell. The "bubble" had burst. The near collapse of Barings Bank in Britain in 1890 due to risky investments in Argentina triggered the collapse and ultimate restructuring of no less than 14 Australian lending banks between 1891 and 1893. All of this financial turmoil was associated with the commencement of the 1890s depression in the eastern Australian colonies — a perfect storm.[325]

Jack Jenkins clearly found himself unable to weather the storm. There are some indications that he tried to shore up his declining financial position by selling some of his freehold land. Thus, towards the middle of 1889, he was able to sell the small island in the Murrumbidgee River forming part of *Nangus* to a neighbour, William Bootes of *Mundarlo*, for £4 an acre.[326] Prior to leaving *Nangus*, Jack was also able to sell some of his sheep for the very low prices of 6d and 9d a head. The sheep so sold were taken to Wagga Wagga and boiled down.[327] However, these endeavours were ultimately to no avail, and Jack was forced to hand *Nangus* over to its mortgagee, the Bank of New South Wales.

According to Bill Gammage, Frank Jenkins went so far at about this time as to borrow the enormous sum of £80,000 to clear his older brother's remaining debts; thus saving Jack from the ignominy of bankruptcy.[328]

It would appear that on first vacating *Nangus*, Jack and Maria Jenkins may have moved north to live with their third son, Frank Thomas Jenkins, and the latter's family on Frank's pastoral property near Eugowra on the Lachlan River to the west of Orange.[329]

In 1893, Jack Jenkins was sued for £7,000 by the Union Bank of Australia upon a written

---

324 See p. 69 above.

325 See David Merrett, "The Australian Bank Crashes of the 1890s Revisited" in (2013) 87 *Business History Review* 407, at pp. 409-417.

326 See the *Gundagai Times and Tumut, Adelong and Murrumbidgee District Advertiser*, Tuesday, 27 August 1889, p. 2. See also footnote 222 on p. 64 above. Interestingly, when the Bank of New South Wales sought to sell *Nangus* at auction in 1898, the only bid received was at a price of £2 an acre; at which figure the Bank refused to sell; see Richard Gormly, op. cit., p. 4

327 See George Seymour, "Days of Cheap Sheep" in *MyHeritage — George Seymour*, p. 12 (http://tinyurl.com/yxdpz6kv) (at 18 February 2020).

328 See Gammage, *Narrandera Shire*, op. cit., p. 96. See also McNeill, op. cit., pp. 12-13.

329 Frank Thomas Jenkins was seemingly the first selector to purchase land in the Eugowra District: see Parliamentary Standing Committee on Public Works, "Minutes of Evidence — Railway from Molong to Parkes and Forbes", February 1890, Vol. 6 *New South Wales Votes and Proceedings*, p. 145.

guarantee for that amount which Jack was said to have provided to the Bank for monetary advances loaned by the Bank to Frank Thomas Jenkins. Jack disputed the claim.

The trial of the Bank's action against Jack was heard in the New South Wales Supreme Court in Sydney on 19 and 20 June 1893 before Justice Windeyer and a jury of four. Jack gave evidence in his own defence. Describing himself as a grazier from Eugowra, he deposed that he had verbally agreed to guarantee certain promissory notes for a lesser total amount given by his son to the Bank. However, he had been presented by the Bank with a written guarantee for the larger sum. Stating that he was illiterate, he said that he executed the written guarantee upon the Bank representing to him that the document referred only to the promissory notes. Jack's defence was unsuccessful, and the Jury quickly found in favour of the Bank.[330]

There are a number of uncertainties surrounding the Union Bank of Australia's action against Jack Jenkins. Was Jack really illiterate or even functionally illiterate? Presumably, he could at least sign his own name. Did the property at Eugowra in fact belong in equity, as well as legally, to Frank Thomas Jenkins? Or was Frank simply his father's legal nominee? Was Jack really living at Eugowra at the time of the trial or was he simply using the property as a convenient address? Was the Eugowra property itself ultimately lost by foreclosure to the Union Bank of Australia? And was part of the £80,000 advanced by Jack's younger brother, Frank Jenkins, in 1893 on Jack's behalf used to pay Jack's Judgment debt to the Union Bank of Australia? These questions presently stand unanswered.

---

[330] See the *Sydney Morning Herald*, Tuesday, 20 June 1893, p. 3; the *Sydney Morning Herald*, Wednesday, 21 June 1893, p. 7; and the *Wagga Wagga Express*, Saturday, 24 June 1893, p. 4.

Final Days

Whatever his true address was in 1893, Jack Jenkins spent his last years with his wife, Maria, on his brother Frank's *Buckingbong* property. According to his friend James Gormly, who visited him shortly prior to his death, Jack's memory was:

> "as acute as it had always been. He was able to give me a fund of information about the pioneering days on the Murrumbidgee, the Lower Lachlan and the Lower Murray that no other man in the State could impart."[331]

Jack Jenkins died on *Buckingbong* at the age of 83 years on 16 October 1899. His Death Certificate gave his cause of death as "Bronchitis" of four days' duration.[332] In part echoing James Gormly, the *Bowral Free Press and Berrima District Intelligencer* wrote of his death:

> "He was hale and hearty and retained his faculties up to the last, and only succumbed to an attack of paralysis following upon a severe chill through getting wet while watering his garden and neglecting to change his clothes."[333]

Jack was buried by the Reverend G Nobbs on 18 October 1899 in Plot H30 of the Old Church of England Division in the Narrandera Cemetery.[334]

In an obituary published on 20 October 1899, the *Gundagai Times and Tumut, Adelong and Murrumbidgee District Advertiser* wrote of Jack Jenkins:

> "There died at Buckingbong, Narrandera, this week, at the residence of his brother, Mr. Fred.[sic] Jenkins, a figure as well known to Gundagai as the Prince Albert bridge, in the person of Mr. J. Jenkins. Death occurred at the age of 86 [sic] years. Deceased was one of the very earliest settlers about this district. He acquired that famous property, the Nangus Estate — one of the best estates in this part of the colony. He was a very wealthy man in the early days of Gundagai. He settled here over half a century ago. To his enterprise Gundagai owes much, as he was seized with the spirit of speculation when others were idle…. He was even reckless in some of his speculations, and should

---

[331] See James Gormly, "Pioneering Families: The Garners & The Jenkins" in the *Narandera Argus and Riverina Advertiser*, Friday, 3 August 1934, p. 8.

[332] See *New South Wales Register of Births, Deaths and Marriages — Deaths: John Jenkins* (1899/14209).

[333] See the *Bowral Free Press and Berrima District Intelligencer*, Saturday, 28 October 1899, p. 2.

[334] See *New South Wales Register of Births, Deaths and Marriages — Deaths: John Jenkins* (1899/14209). See also **photos 26** and **27**.

have been an immensely wealthy man. A few years ago, he became somewhat enfeebled, and left the Nangus station, which has since been controlled by the Bank of New South Wales, and went to live with his brother at Buckingbong, where he died as stated. After his departure for Narrandera, all his Gundagai property was sold."[335]

Maria Jenkins, Jack's widow, lived on for almost 25 years following the death of her husband. She moved from *Buckingbong* to live with her youngest living child, Mary Jane Beveridge (née Jenkins), at the latter's home in Epping, New South Wales. Maria died at her daughter's home on Tuesday, 22 April 1924 at the great age of 101 years and 11 months. Of her demise, the *Gundagai Times* wrote on 29 April 1924:

"Deceased was a most interesting woman, and an encyclopaedia of early days events, and her chats about blacks and bushrangers were most interesting, and her lively recollections of the stirring old days and of the exploits of bushrangers that made life far from quiet in country districts were realistic. Ben Hall and the Moonlight gang entered into deceased's existence, and her memory was keen when she spoke of them; in fact, one of Moonlight's gang (Bennett) worked at Nangus.

The clouds rolled back when deceased thought of her husband and the blacks. How the natives speared cattle, and how her husband cured them of the habit, and how mobs of cattle were taken to Adelaide.

Our grand old woman has gone to meet her Maker, and she leaves behind her a host of friends, grand-children and great grand-children to mourn the loss of one of the most interesting personalities that ever lived in our grand district, and whose memory will be ever cherished."[336]

Jack Jenkins was a complex man who led a tumultuous life. Although portrayed as a man much beloved, benevolent and possessed of the most guileless of dispositions, Jack clearly had a darker side; manifested by his likely treatment of Aboriginal men, women and children during the *Wiradjuri War*, and by an evident propensity to resort at times to violent behaviour which brought him into contact with the law.[337] He was possessed of enormous vigour, and by an entrepreneurial spirit which was sometimes ill-advisedly expressed. A man who was probably functionally illiterate, and who spent his formative years in a Kent workhouse, he amassed great wealth in a new land only to see his fortune dissipate with the great financial crash of the early 1890s. Jack Jenkins was not simply a squatter; he was a true pioneer who, with his brother Frank, made a major contribution to opening up the Riverina to European settlement.

---

335 See the *Gundagai Times and Tumut, Adelong and Murrumbidgee District Advertiser*, Friday, 20 October 1899, p. 2.
336 See the *Gundagai Times*, Tuesday, 29 April 1924, p. 2. In an earlier incarnation of the same newspaper, it had described Maria, at the time of Jack Jenkins' death, as being:
"dearly loved by all the old hands about Gundagai for her gentle and kind qualities..."
See the *Gundagai Times and Tumut, Adelong and Murrumbidbee District Advertiser*, Friday, 20 October 1899, p. 2.
337 See pp. 55-66 above and p. 77-81 above.

FRANK JENKINS ALONE
(1820 — 1902)

Early Years on the Murrumbidgee River

The youngest of John and Charlotte Jenkins' children, Frank Jenkins, was born a little prior to 14 January 1820. He was baptised as Francis Jenkins on that date in St. James the Great's Church, East Malling in Kent.[338]

Much of Frank's early life up until his settlement on the middle reaches of the Murrumbidgee River has been traced in detail above. His formative years were intimately entwined with those of his older brother, Jack Jenkins. Yet the characters of the two brothers were quite different. "Roaring Jack" was flamboyant, somewhat reckless in his commercial dealings and probably quick-tempered. On the other hand, as Bill Gammage has written:

> "Frank lacked his brother's flashiness but matched his courage and energy, and he too lived a full and adventurous life. He raced fast thoroughbreds, was a generous host to every man, married three times and in later life, some said, was known in every bedroom in Narrandera. Yet his great loves were *Buckingbong* and cattle, and he devoted his long life to them. John was the adventurer, Frank the anchor.[339]

Frank Jenkins' early days on the *Buckingbong* run were marked by danger, isolation and unremitting endeavour. First arriving at the property with his brother Jack in 1839 at the height of the *Wiradjuri War*, he was faced with the very real threat of being speared by one of the Aboriginal war parties. Along with Jack, he was almost certainly among the whites who massacred some of the 60 to 70 Aboriginal men, women and children who were ambushed on Massacre Island near *Buckingbong* in late 1840 or early 1841. Frank no doubt saw that massacre as a wartime necessity rather than the genocidal crime that it surely was.[340]

As mentioned above, soon after taking up the *Buckingbong* run in 1839, the two Jenkins brothers also acquired the neighbouring *Gillenbah* run to the immediate west of *Buckingbong*.[341] Although they would almost certainly have employed stockmen to assist in running the two properties and the cattle on them, the brothers clearly worked hard and long hours themselves.

Marketing their produce prior to the commencement of steam navigation on the Murrumbidgee River, followed by the coming of rail transportation, was both difficult and

---

338 See the *Marr, Aitken, Watts Family Tree — Surman, Charlotte Elizabeth* (http://tinyurl.com/y8zfn83x) (at 20 February 2020); and McNeill, op. cit., p. 3.

339 See Gammage, *Narrandera Shire*, op. cit., p.38.

340 See pp. 56-56 above. In later years, Frank Jenkins adopted a somewhat more benevolent attitude towards local Aborigines; employing some of them (if only for rations) and allowing others to camp at times on *Buckingbong* between his vineyard and the Murrumbidgee River: see p. 57 above.

341 See pp. 57-58 above.

time-consuming for both brothers. In 1917, the pastoralist Cuthbert Featherstonhaugh recounted that:

> "Frank Jenkins used to take cheeses and hams and bacon from Buckingbong to Sydney in the old days in a bullock dray. Just imagine starting in those early days over what was scarcely a bush track some 400 miles [a little over 643 km] with a load of farm produce for Sydney. Plenty of grit that."[342]

Periodic flooding around *Buckingbong* hampered and delayed both marketing produce and procuring supplies for that run and for *Gillenbah*. James Baylis observed that the Murrumbidgee River would yearly flood into the Sandy and Old Man Creeks to the south of *Buckingbong*. He recalled how Frank Jenkins once set out for Sydney with two drays, he driving one, taking wool bales for sale. By virtue of being blocked by floods, it took him some nine months to return with provisions for *Buckingbong*.[343]

---

[342] See Cuthbert Featherstonhaugh, *After Many Days* (1917), p. 95. Featherstonhaugh implies that the Jenkins brothers were raising pigs as well as grazing cattle in their early days on *Buckingbong*.

[343] See James Baylis, "Notes on Buckingbong Station" in *Recollections of the Murrumbidgee District* ("*Recollections*") (manuscript held in the Mitchell Library, Sydney: 1832-1888, Ab 139/1); Peter Freeman, *The Homestead: A Riverina Anthology* (1982), pp. 196-197; and Gammage, *Narrandera Shire*, op. cit., p. 52.

First Marriage and Family

On 23 August 1842, Frank Jenkins married Rebecca Charlotte Higgins in St. John the Evangelist's Catholic Church in Campbellfield. Born shortly prior to 4 July 1826, Rebecca was the second child of John Higgins, a Campbellfield farmer, and his wife, Hannah ("Anna") Higgins (née Winfield).[344] It seems likely that Frank first met Rebecca during one of his trips between *Buckingbong* and Sydney.

It would appear that Frank and Rebecca Jenkins lived initially on *Gillenbah* but later moved to *Buckingbong*.[345] They went on to have six surviving children together. These were:

- Lydia Ann Jenkins, born a little before 20 March 1844;
- Francis Jenkins, born shortly prior to 5 July 1845;
- John Jenkins, born shortly before 16 August 1847;
- Ridley William Jenkins, born in 1850;
- Robert James Jenkins, born in 1852; and
- Charlotte Elizabeth Jenkins, born in 1854.[346]

---

[344] See the *Marr, Aitken, Watts Family Tree — Higgins, Rebecca Charlotte* (http://tinyurl.com/r4tmd9e) (at 24 February 2020); *Australian Royalty — Rebecca Higgins (1826-1856)* (http://tinyurl.com/y6ak9wbh) (at 24 February 2020); and McNeill, op. cit., p. 9.

[345] Ibid.

[346] See the *Marr, Aitken, Watts Family Tree — Higgins, Rebecca Charlotte* (http://tinyurl.com/r4tmd9e) (at 24 February 2020).

Statesman and *Gol Gol*

In late 1846 or early 1847, and at the ripe young age of about 27 years, Frank Jenkins embarked on an ambitious venture. Leaving his wife and young children behind at *Buckingbong*, he set off down the Murrumbidgee River with some 900 head of cattle, 10 horses, a bullock-drawn wagon containing supplies and six men.[347] On reaching the junction of the Murrumbidgee with the Murray River, the party continued along the right bank of the latter river. In taking the route that he did, Frank was following that taken in 1830 by the explorer Charles Sturt, and subsequently by overlanders en route to the newly-founded Adelaide.

On about 1 March 1847, and on reaching a point some 60 miles [around 97 km] downstream of the confluence of the Murrumbidgee and Murray Rivers, Frank Jenkins took his party across to the left bank of the latter with the intention of establishing a new run fronting the Murray River. The land he chose for the run encompassed the site where the City of Mildura and its surrounds now lie. Frank gave the name *Statesman* to the property. Although he subsequently sought to acquire a depasturing licence for the run in his own name, there can be little doubt that he would have regarded his brother, Jack Jenkins, as an equal, if silent, partner in the venture.

In a letter he sent from *Statesman* on 1 July 1847 to a Melbourne agent, John Clark, Frank described the proposed dimensions of the run as follows:

> "Extent of new run 25 miles [along] the Murray River, commencing at Mr Hawdon's top boundary line and about 1½ miles back [inland], being the whole of the grazing land. It is hemmed in by Malley [Mallee] scrub."[348]

Once across the Murray River, Frank and his men set about constructing a hut as the nucleus for a planned homestead. Then, leaving his cattle and some of his horses on the property under the charge of his overseer, William Rae, Frank set off down the River with his bullock wagon and its driver. He appears to have had two objects in mind. Firstly, he needed to secure further supplies from Adelaide for the new run and the men he had left on it. Secondly, he intended to

---

[347] Frank Jenkins subsequently named his six accompanying men as:
  William Rae — Overseer;
  Jesse Dear — Stock Keeper;
  James Slye — Hut Keeper;
  John Renolds — Labourer;
  William Holdin — Labourer; and
  James Williams — Bullock Driver.
  See letter from Frank Jenkins to John Clark dated 1 July 1847: *Public Records Office Victoria* ("*PROV*"), VPRS 5359 and VPRS 5920, Pastoral Run Files, 1840-1878, No. 798, Mildura.

[348] Ibid. The area claimed for *Statesman* would have been about 24,000 acres or around 9,710 hectares.

register his claim to the property in Adelaide. He formed that intention in the mistaken belief that the run lay in the Province of South Australia rather than in the Colony of New South Wales. Disabused of that belief in Adelaide, Frank was advised that he would have to apply for a depasturing licence for the property in Melbourne. He then made his way back up the Murray River to *Statesman* with the supplies he had purchased in Adelaide.[349]

While Frank Jenkins was journeying to and from Adelaide, the brothers Hugh and (Thomas) Bushby Jamieson were on the hunt for their own squatting run on the lower Murray River. Hugh Jamieson had been managing the *Murray Downs* run opposite Swan Hill. A year earlier, in 1846, the Jamiesons' friend, John Hawdon Jnr, together with the latter's business partner, Armourer Foster, had taken up the *Kulnine* (or *Culnine*) run to the immediate west of *Statesman*.

On 25 May, and apparently at Hawdon's suggestion, the Jamieson brothers made application for a depasturing licence for a run to the east and south of *Statesman* which they sought to call *Cantells*. However, their application was rejected on 31 May 1847 by the Commissioner of Crown Lands for the Wimmera District, William Wright, on the ground that part of the land for which the licence was sought had already been licensed to John Kidd and James Brown as the *Carwarp* run. Wright went on to verbally advise the Jamiesons that it was nevertheless open to them to make application for a depasturing licence for any currently unlicensed land, with a frontage of up to 25 miles to the Murray River, lying between the Hawdon and Foster run to the west and the Kidd and Brown run to the east.[350] This was precisely the land which Frank Jenkins was seeking for his *Statesman* run.

The Jamieson brothers quickly chose to follow Wright's advice. Although they almost certainly would have been aware of the presence of Frank Jenkins' hut, men and cattle on the proposed *Statesman* run, they would equally have been aware from Wright that no New South Wales licence had as yet been granted with respect to the property. Accordingly, they took immediate steps to secure such a licence. However, rather than applying for one in their own names, they seemingly reached an agreement with a prominent Melbourne identity, William Foster Stawell. In consequence, Stawell applied for a licence to the run in his own name in 1847.[351] Instead of *Statesman*, Stawell, and presumably the Jamiesons, chose to call the run *Yerre Yerre*.[352]

---

349   In his letter to John Clark dated 1 July 1847, Frank wrote, inter alia, that:
"I have formed a station here on the first of March last — expecting I was in the Adelaide District, but having made an application there found that I was not in that District...."
Ibid. It might be noted that the northern section of the boundary between South Australia and what was then the Port Phillip District of New South Wales was not finally surveyed and demarked through to the Murray River by Edward Riggs White until 17 December 1850: see letter from Edward White to Robert Hoddle dated 18 December 1850 in *State Records of New South Wales*, Lands Department, Ministerial Branch, Correspondence, 1911.

350   See Application for a Depasturing Licence for *Cantells* dated 25 May 1847, together with Memorandum dated 31 May 1847 recording Commissioner Wright's advice that day to Hugh Jamieson: *PROV*, VPRS 5359 and VPRS 5920, Pastoral Run Files 1840-1878, No. 798, Mildura.

351   In 1847, William Foster Stawell was a leading Melbourne barrister. On Victoria's separation from New South Wales in 1851, Lieutenant Governor La Trobe appointed him to be the new Colony's first Attorney General. In February 1857, he was appointed Chief Justice of the Supreme Court of Victoria. Stawell was knighted in July of that year: see Charles Francis, "Stawell, Sir William Foster (1815-1889)" in *Australian Dictionary of Biography* (http://tinyurl.com/yyxf5695) (at 24 February 2020).

352   *Yerre Yerre* was apparently named after a local tribe of Aborigines, better known today as the Jarijari: see *Wikipedia — Jarijari* (http://tinyurl.com/y4zx5bhz) (at 24 February 2020).

The precise terms of the agreement apparently reached between the Jamieson brothers and Stawell are presently unknown. Presumably, the latter applied for the licence to *Yerre Yerre* as a nominee for the Jamiesons. The agreement may have obliged him to assist in stocking the run with sheep in return for a share in the resulting profits.

On or shortly after 1 July 1847, Frank Jenkins lodged his own application for a depasturing licence for his proposed *Statesman* run. Using the services of an agent, John Clark, the application and an accompanying letter were filed in Melbourne with Commissioner Wright.[353] A month later, Frank filed a Stock Return for *Statesman* dated 1 August 1847 with Wright.[354] There is nothing to suggest that Frank was aware of Stawell's licence application for the proposed *Yerre Yerre* run when he lodged his *Statesman* licence application and letter or his Stock Return.

Towards the beginning of September 1847, Stawell was advised by Wright that his application for a licence to depasture *Yerre Yerre* had been approved. On 9 September 1847, Wright saw fit to personally advise Frank Jenkins that because of the grant of the licence to Stawell, Frank's own application had been refused.[355]

Having been legally "claim jumped" by Stawell and the Jamieson brothers, Frank had no option but to take his men and cattle back across the Murray River. Once across, he established a new run of some 30,000 acres [about 12,140 hectares] on the right bank of the River. He initially called this run *Gall Gall*.[356] However, the property was later re-named *Gol Gol*. For their part, it would appear that the Jamiesons immediately occupied *Yerre Yerre* on Frank's departure from the property, stocking it with sheep.[357]

One can only speculate as to why Frank Jenkins went to the lengths which he did to establish a run on the lower Murray River. As suggested above, it might have been due to a perceived need to find fresh pastures in a period of recurrent drought in the Riverina.[358] An intriguing possible alternative reason is that the proposed new run was seen by the Jenkins brothers as an agistment resting point for their cattle being taken overland from the Riverina to market

---

353 See p. 98 above.

354 See Stock Return dated 1 August 1847: *PROV*, VPRS 5359 and VPRS 5920, Pastoral Run Files 1840 — 1878, No. 798, Mildura.

355 See annotation to the *Statesman* Depasturing Licence Application dated 1 July 1847: *PROV*, VPRS 5359 and VPRS 5920, Pastoral Run Files 1840-1878, No. 798, Mildura. See also Mildura & District Genealogical Society Inc., "The Naming of Mildura" in (2008) 8(2) *The Grapeline*, pp. 6 and 7; and Thomas Bridge (ed.), *Letters from Victorian Pioneers* (1983), p. 377.

356 See Vann, op. cit., p. 42; and Whitworth, op. cit., p. 213.

357 On 23 June 1848, William Stawell applied to the Superintendent of the Port Phillip District, Charles La Trobe, to convert his depasturing licence for *Yerre Yerre* into a lease: see Application for a Lease of *Yerre Yerre* by William Stawell dated 23 June 1848: *PROV*, VPRS 5359 and VPRS 5920, Pastoral Run Files 1840-1878, No. 798, Mildura. The power to grant such leases had been vested in the New South Wales Government by the *Order in Council of 1847*: see pp. 83-84 above. In essence, the Order was designed to provide a mechanism by which squatters could convert their licensed runs via leases into freehold holdings. In the Port Phillip District, La Trobe refused to grant any such lease applications, including that made by Stawell. La Trobe was opposed in principle to what he saw as an avenue for squatters to "lock up" large areas of land under his jurisdiction. He took the view that although licence holders could apply to him for leases of their runs, he was not obliged by the Order to grant any such applications: see Richard Brown, "Unlocking the Land" in *Looking at History*, 6 April 2013 (http://tinyurl.com/lqrhu7v) (at 25 February 2020); A. G. L. Shaw, "Victoria's First Governor" in (2003) 71 *The Latrobe Journal* 85 at p. 95 (http://tinyurl.com/k4pcovb) (at 25 February 2020); and *The Argus*, Saturday, 21 August 1852, p. 2.

For some presently unknown reason, William Stawell transferred his licence to *Yerre Yerre* to an Edward James Hogg of Prahran on 8 August 1853. Presumably, Hogg continued to hold the licence as some form of nominee or silent partner of the Jamieson brothers. Finally, Hogg transferred the licence on 2 January 1858 to Hugh and Bushby Jamieson: see Ralph Billis and Alfred Kenyon, *Pastoral Pioneers of Port Phillip* (2nd ed., 1974), p. 243; and Robert Spreadborough and Hugh Anderson, *Victorian Squatters* (1983), p. 255. By virtue of a letter dated 20 March 1858 from the Jamieson brothers to Commissioner Wright, the name of the run was changed from *Yerre Yerre* to *Mildura*: Ibid.

358 See p. 60 above.

in Adelaide. It might be noted that Jack Jenkins' obituary published in the *Bowral Free Press and Berrima District Intelligencer* on 28 October 1899 asserted that the two brothers had been among the first to overland cattle to Adelaide.[359] In like fashion, the obituary for Jack's widow, Maria Jenkins, published in the *Gundagai Times* on 29 April 1924 made mention of Frank Jenkins having taken "mobs of cattle" overland to Adelaide.[360] However, these two obituaries apart, there would appear to be no record or mention of any such venture currently extant.

Having claimed the *Gol Gol* run in or shortly after September 1847, it seems likely that Frank Jenkins' stay on the property was brief, and that he made a fairly quick return to his family on *Buckingbong*. He probably left William Rae, his overseer, in initial charge of the new run. However, by early 1850 at the latest, *Gol Gol* was effectively in the hands of Frank's sister, Elizabeth Williams (née Jenkins), and her husband, Henry Williams.[361] Although Frank remained registered as the lessee of *Gol Gol* until the 1860s, it would appear that he never resumed the management or any active control of the run.[362]

---

[359] See the *Bowral Free Press and Berrima District Intelligencer*, Saturday, 28 October 1899, p. 2.
[360] See the *Gundagai Times*, Tuesday, 29 April 1924, p. 2. See also p. 91 above.
[361] Elizabeth and Henry Williams' tenth child, Ridley Williams, was born on *Gol Gol* shortly prior to 3 June 1850: see *Ancestry — Elizabeth Jane Jenkins* (http://tinyurl.com/y6raf4tm) (at 25 February 2020).
[362] See Vann, op. cit., p. 99; and Whitworth, op. cit., p. 213.

Wealth and Sorrow

As mentioned above, Frank and Jack Jenkins were able to earn their fortunes during the Victorian gold rushes by supplying an exploding population of miners with beef on the hoof.[363] As James Gormly observed:

> "In consequence of the high price of fat cattle on the Victorian goldfields, John and Frank became rich men."[364]

Although Jack Jenkins was responsible for driving most of the Jenkins brothers' cattle from the Riverina to Victoria, Frank also led cattle drives from time to time to the southern goldfields. In his *Recollections of the Murrumbidgee District*, James Baylis wrote of one such drive. In that drive, Frank was overlanding cattle from *Buckingbong* to the Bendigo diggings. Because *Buckingbong*, like all Riverina runs, was essentially unfenced at the time, stock would occasionally walk off the property and wander through surrounding areas. On the cattle drive in question, Frank camped for the night at Conargo near Deniliquin. During the night, a number of cattle walked in to drink at the adjacent creek. Among them were some with the Jenkins' brand on them. These wanderers were immediately secured and taken on with the rest of the cattle from *Buckingbong* to the diggings.[365]

The 1850s brought Frank Jenkins great wealth. However, it also brought him great grief. On 23 November 1853, his second child and eldest son, Francis Jenkins Jnr, drowned in the Murrumbidgee River at *Buckingbong* at the age of 8 years. The boy's body was taken to Bong Bong and interred there in the Christ Church Anglican graveyard.[366] Frank was struck by tragedy again in 1856. On 20 June in that year, his wife Rebecca died at *Nangus* in childbirth. She was buried in her son Francis' grave in the Christ Church graveyard at Bong Bong.[367] Rebecca was only 30 years of age when she died. Her death left Frank with the care of five young children.

Frank Jenkins used portions of his new wealth to acquire further pastoral runs. As mentioned

---

363   See p. 61 above.
364   See James Gormly, "Pioneering Families: The Garners & The Jenkins" in the *Narandera Argus and Riverina Advertiser*, Friday, 3 August 1934. p. 8.
365   See James Baylis, "Notes on Buckingbong Station" in *Recollections*, op. cit.; and Freeman, op cit., pp. 197-199.
366   See the *Marr, Aitken, Watts Family Tree — Jenkins, Francis* (http://tinyurl.com/ybnw7zam) (at 25 February 2020); McNeill, op. cit., p. 11; and *Bell's Life in Sydney and Sporting Reviewer*, Saturday, 17 December 1853, p. 3.
367   See the *Marr, Aitken, Watts Family Tree — Higgins, Rebecca Charlotte* (http://tinyurl.com/r4tmd9e) (at 25 February 2020); and Mc Neill, op. cit., p. 11. On 23 August 1869, Frank's mother, Charlotte Jenkins, was buried in the same plot as her daughter-in-law and grandson in the Christ Church graveyard at Bong Bong: see the *Marr, Aitken, Watts Family Tree — Surman, Charlotte Elizabeth* (http://tinyurl.com/y8zfn83x) (at 25 February 2020). See also pp. 31–32 above.

above, he purchased the leasehold rights to the *Yanco* and *Nangus* runs with his brother Jack in 1854.[368] In 1857, Frank acquired the *Morundah* run in his own right. This run, to the south-west of *Gillenbah*, extended over 82,000 acres [about 33,184 hectares][369] In January 1859, he purchased the rights to the *South Thononga, South Thonoga Block A* and *South Thononga Bock B* runs from James Maiden and D. Denny. These runs, together totalling 120,000 acres [around 48, 562 hectares] in area, were located on the left bank of the Lachlan River to the north-west of *Buckingbong*.[370]

---

368   See p. 63 above.
369   See Whitworth, op. cit., p. 370; Gammage, *Narrandera Shire*, op. cit., p. 52; and McNeill, op. cit., p. 11.
370   See the *Goulburn Herald and County of Argyle Advertiser*, Wednesday, 19 January 1859, p. 4; Vann, op. cit., p. 68; and Whitworth, op. cit., p. 506

Second Marriage and Family

On 14 February 1859, and shortly after his acquisition of the *South Thonoga* runs, Frank Jenkins married for the second time. He was 39 years old at the time of this marriage, which was solemnised in St. James' Anglican Church, Sydney.[371] His bride, Mary Anne Higgins, was aged 16 years.

It would appear that Mary Anne was no relation of Frank's first wife, Rebecca Charlotte Jenkins (née Higgins). Mary Anne was born in Berrima shortly prior to 14 July 1842.[372] She was the third daughter of James Jerome Higgins and his wife, Mary Anne Higgins (née Winton). James and Mary Higgins arrived in Sydney from Dublin in November 1833 as free immigrants. Soon after their arrival, they settled in Berrima, where James Higgins became a storekeeper, postmaster and ultimately coroner.[373] No doubt Frank Jenkins met and wooed Mary Anne during visits he made from time to time to his parents' Berrima home in Jellore Street, which was located a short distance from Mary Anne's home in Market Street.

Mary Anne bore Frank a total of seven children, being:

- Walter Augustus Jenkins, born shortly before 22 October 1859;
- Emily Grace Jenkins, born shortly prior to 12 December 1860;
- Marcus Henry Jenkins, born shortly before 28 December, 1861;
- Albert Winton Jenkins, born in 1864;
- Clara Florence Jenkins, born in 1865;
- Edward Ridley Jenkins, born in 1871; and
- Ada Mary Jenkins, also born in 1871.[374]

---

371 See the *Sydney Morning Herald*, Thursday, 17 February 1859, p. 1.
372 See the *Marr, Aitken, Watts Family Tree — Higgins, Mary Anne* (http://tinyurl.com/yaefjg2f) (at 26 February 2020).
373 See Chris Thompson, "No. 18 of Berrima 1841 — James Jerome Higgins, Market Place" in *The 36 Households: Harper's Mansion, Berrima* (http://tinyurl.com/y3azfpw2) (at 26 February 2020).
374 See the *Marr, Aitken, Watts Family Tree — Higgins, Mary Anne* (http://tinyurl.com/yaefjg2f) (at 26 February 2020).

Further Property Acquisitions

Following his marriage to Mary Anne, Frank Jenkins' wealth and property entitlements continued to grow; with the growth fuelled by the exploding demand for meat in the Victorian goldfields. In an informative article republished in the *Narandera Argus and Riverina Advertiser* in 1934, James Gormley wrote of a chance meeting he had with Frank in Sydney during these boom years. Gormly recalled that:

> "In those booming days, I chanced to be staying at the same hotel as Frank Jenkins. He then informed me that he had just arrived by steamer from Melbourne, where he had sold a mob of fat cattle. He asked me to accompany him in a cab to a stock and station office, as he was then taking seven thousand sovereigns which he had brought from Melbourne in a box to pay for a station he had purchased on the Murrumbidgee. What a haul for robbers had there been any about! Of course we would have put up a fight if attacked. I had the six-chamber revolver that I used to carry when on the goldfields."[375]

In 1859, the same year as he acquired the *Thononga* runs and married Mary Anne Higgins, Frank also acquired the *Little Swamp* run of 18,000 acres [approximately 7,284 hectares] to the immediate south of *Buckingbong*.[376] The following year, 1860, he purchased the lease of the *Colombo Creek* run adjacent to his *Morundah* run and to the west of *Buckingbong*.[377] In 1861, Frank purchased the lease of the *Lake Walgiers* run.[378] This run, later known as the *Lake Waljeers* run, was located on the right bank of the Lachlan River to the west of Frank's *Thononga* runs. It had an area of some 46,080 acres [around 18,647 hectares]. However, it seems that Frank did not hold the lease of *Lake Walgiers* for long. By 1866, it was held by a John Peter.[379] As mentioned above, Frank also acquired a lease of the *Nottingham Forest* run at some point prior to 1886. This latter run was situated in the foothills of the Australian Alps to the south-east of Tumut. It would appear that both Frank and his brother, Jack Jenkins, agisted stock from time to time on this property, which extended over about 58,000 acres [about 23,472 hectares].[380]

---

375 See James Gormly, "Pioneering Families: The Garners and the Jenkins" in the *Narandera Argus and Riverina Advertiser*, Friday, 3 August 1934, p. 8. It might be noted that 7,000 sovereigns in, say, 1860 would be worth around $600,000 in 2020: see Anon., *MeasuringWorth* (http://tinyurl.com/y5kpae96) (at 26 February 2020).

376 See Gammage, *Narrandera Shire*, op. cit., p. 52; McNeill, op. cit., p. 11; and Whitworth, op. cit., p.318.

377 See Gammage, *Narrandera Shire*, op. cit., p. 52; and McNeill, op. cit., p. 11. The *Colombo Creek* run was subsequently renamed the *Colombo Plains* run, perhaps due to the ephemeral nature of the water flow in the Creek.

378 See Gammage, *Narrandera Shire*, op. cit., p. 52; and McNeill, op. cit., p. 11.

379 See Whitworth, op. cit., pp. 309-310. As to John Peter, see Gammage, *Narrandera Shire*, op. cit., p. 51-52.

380 See p. 75 above. See also the *Sydney Mail and New South Wales Advertiser*, Saturday, 23 January 1892, p. 176.

As well as his extensive land holdings in southern New South Wales, Frank Jenkins also held lands in both Queensland and Victoria.[381] The nature and precise locations of his holdings in Queensland are presently unclear. However, he apparently held a Queensland run as early as 1876.[382] In or about May 1887, Frank acquired three separate properties in the Warrego District to the south-south-east of Barcaldine: *Wellwater*, *Mangalore* and *Nive Junction*.[383]

In Victoria, Frank apparently owned a pastoral property at Derrinal to the south-east of Bendigo.[384] He may well have used this property as a "stop-over" point for cattle he was sending to the Victorian goldfields and to Melbourne from his New South Wales runs. It is unclear how large the property was other than to say that the *McIvor Times and Rodney Advertiser* referred to it on 21 August 1902 as being "considerable".[385] Frank may have owned another pastoral property at Glenaire near to Cape Otway[386] He certainly owned land on the outskirts of Melbourne.[387]

---

381 See McNeill, op. cit., p. 12. See also p. 132 below.
382 See the *Corowa Free Press*, Tuesday, 14 November 1876, p. 3. The name given to this run is currently unknown.
383 See *The Argus*, Saturday, 7 May 1887, p. 8; *The Capricornian*, Saturday, 21 May 1887, p. 8; the *Maitland Mercury and Hunter River General Advertiser*, Saturday, 28 May 1887, p. 13; and the *Queensland Figaro and Punch*, Saturday, 4 June 1887, p. 11. See also p. 132 below.
384 See the *McIvor Times and Rodney Advertiser*, Thursday, 14 August 1902, p. 2.
385 Ibid. See also p. 132 below.
386 See p. 132 below.
387 See p. 117 below.

The *Buckingbong* Homestead

The original *Buckingbong* homestead was probably a slab hut roofed with bark and situated on a high bank overlooking the Murrumbidgee River.[388] Over time, the building was enlarged and then replaced by connected brick and timber structures. In turn, these structures were progressively altered over the course of Frank Jenkins' occupancy of the property. In 1978, an assessment of the *Buckingbong* homestead provided to the National Trust of Australia (NSW) in response to a listing proposal described it, and ancillary buildings, thus:

> "The Buckingbong Homestead is two brick buildings, in Flemish bond style, joined by a later brick extension. The left hand building with its high pitched roof contains the bedrooms, all opening out onto the verandah. The Homestead has been simply built and furnished, and has been subject to a number of alterations and additions. The right hand building was originally the living and dining area. It has been converted into a kitchen. There appear to be later extensions to the rear.... All verandah windows are six pane sash windows. At the rear is a large original kitchen with a food passageway extending through to the dining room. This kitchen has been unused for a long time.... There is a small courtyard but the back verandah has been completely enclosed with weatherboard to make a hallway. The large cellar lies in the hallway. All mantle pieces are timber. In separate buildings facing this courtyard are the old laundry and adjoining empty rooms. These buildings were cement rendered.... Some of the rear chimneys have pebble dash on them....
>
> Originally the carriage-way extended up to the front door. Opposite the front entrance is a small brick building with weatherboard extensions to the north and western sides. The front steps also lead down to a large cellar underneath....
>
> There are two stables. One is of timber with undressed uprights, and adzed and semi-dressed beams. It is in a fair condition. The other building is of brick, in colonial bond style, on stone foundations. The loft walls and gables are of weatherboard.... Internal posts are undressed and the floor is of brick. There is a harness room.... Both buildings are roofed in corrugated iron.
>
> Beyond the stables is a milkshed. It is an iron building with undressed and semi-dressed uprights and beams. The floor and yard area are covered in brick to prevent them becoming boggy."[389]

---

388 See p. 54 above. See also the *Narandera Argus and Riverina Advertiser*, Friday, 3 August 1902, p. 8.
389 See the *Jenkins Family File*, pp. 45-46. See also Freeman, op. cit., p. 200; and the *Marr, Aitken, Watts Family Tree — Stories, Buckingbong Station* (http://tinyurl.com/y23c4p65) (at 26 February 2020).

The listing proposal was approved by the Council of the National Trust of Australia (NSW) on 30 October 1978.[390] Over the years since 1978, the *Buckingbong* homestead has been extensively renovated and modernised.[391]

In addition to enlarging, renovating and embellishing the *Buckingbong* homestead, Frank Jenkins also developed its immediate surrounds. He put lawns, gardens, orchards and tennis courts around the homestead — and, indeed, around each of his outstations.[392] Frank further planted a vineyard with some 300 grape vines adjacent to the homestead.[393] It would appear that fine wine was made from his grapes, and that this wine was stored in one of his cellars on site. In March 1871, Frank was granted a licence to distil brandy from the wine produced from his vineyard.[394] It would further seem that he went to the extent of bringing out an expert from France to make both his wine and his brandy.[395] According to James Gormly, who knew the property well, the *Buckingbong* homestead was:

"the best appointed home on the lower [Murrumbidgee] River."[396]

---

[390] See the *Jenkins Family File*, p. 44.

[391] See **photos 28**, **29** and **30**.

[392] The *Buckingbong* garden was said to have been planted with ornamental and European trees and an orchard which contained apple, pear, fig, peach, nectarine, plum, orange, locquat, walnut and almond trees; together with around 200 lemon trees: see the *Narrandera Argus*, Wednesday, 29 January 2014, p. 5.

[393] Ibid.

[394] See the *Sydney Morning Herald*, Wednesday, 15 March 1871, p. 5.

[395] See Gammage, *Narrandera Shire*, op. cit., p. 79; and the *Narrandera Argus*, Wednesday, 29 January 2014, p. 5.

[396] See James Gormly, "Pioneering Families: The Garners & The Jenkins" in the *Narandera Argus and Riverina Advertiser*, Friday, 3 August 1934, p. 8.

Religion

Religion clearly had its place in the lives of Frank Jenkins and his family. Although both Frank and Mary Anne were Anglicans, they were seemingly not adverse to the ministries of nonconformists.[397] In 1864, they were visited at *Buckingbong* by an itinerant Quaker evangelist, Joseph Westwood. At the time, Westwood was preaching throughout the Riverina. He approached *Buckingbong* from the opposite side of the Murrumbidgee River. As to his movements immediately thereafter, he noted in his Journal:

> "**Saturday, January 2nd, 1864** — Leaving my horse and gig, 'cooed' to the opposite bank where a man came to my relief and rowed [me] across to Buckingbong. Hospitably received by Mrs. Jenkins and her sister, Miss Higgins. Obtained permission to spend the night and hold divine service on the Sabbeth. In the evening in company with Mrs Jenkins and her sister, angled in the river and caught a beautiful perch. Baited with raw beef.
>
> **Lord's Day, 3rd.** — Preached morning and evening, and had a good attendance of family and servants.
>
> **Monday, 4th.** — Before leaving, Mr. Jenkins presented me with a three pound cheque; also received one pound for books which I had sold."[398]

---

[397] Interestingly, Frank married his first wife, Rebecca Higgins, on 23 August 1842 in St. John the Evangelist's Catholic Church, Campbellfield: see p. 76 above. Rebecca was likely a baptised Catholic from a family of Catholics. However, following her death, she was buried by Frank in the graveyard of an Anglican church, Christ Church, Bong Bong: see p. 81 above. Frank himself was buried in the Anglican section of the Narrandera Cemetery following an Anglican funeral: see pp. 103-104 below. It is accordingly unlikely that Frank was ever a serious convert to Catholicism — if, indeed, he converted at all.

[398] See Joseph Westwood, *The Journal of Joseph Westwood* (1865), pp. 388-389.

A Further Tragic Loss

Although surrounded in his middle and later years by the fruits of wealth, Frank Jenkins was never far from tragedy. His eldest son, Francis Jenkins Jnr, had drowned in the Murrumbidgee River in 1853. His first wife, Rebecca Jenkins, died in childbirth in 1856. These were nowhere near the last of the bereavements suffered by Frank.

On 12 December 1866, Frank's third son, Ridley William Jenkins, died at the *Duke of Rothsay* hotel in Elizabeth Street, Melbourne following what was reported as being "a long and painful illness".[399] He was 16 years of age when he died. Presumably, Ridley had been staying at the hotel with family members whilst receiving specialist medical care in Melbourne for his illness. The precise nature of that illness is presently unknown. Ridley was buried in the grave of his father's first cousin, John Clark Jnr, in the Melbourne General Cemetery on 14 December 1866.[400]

---

399 See *The Argus*, Saturday, 15 December 1866, p. 4.
400 See *The Argus*, Friday, 14 December 1866, p. 8; and *Victoria Deaths Register — Ridley William Jenkins* (1866/11390).

Building in Narrandera and Wagga Wagga

Simultaneously with both extending and consolidating his Riverina pastoral empire, Frank Jenkins put a great deal of effort over many years into developing a township on the Murrumbidgee River downstream of *Buckingbong*. As early as 1846, Frank, together with his brother, Jack Jenkins, had constructed an inn on their *Gillenbah* run. This inn, which was probably a rude, slab and bark shanty, was subsequently known as the *Bush Inn* and managed by a John Dill. The inn was located on a stock route running south from central New South Wales via the Mirrool Creek to the Murrumbidgee River opposite the inn, and then across the River by ford and down the Yanco Creek and lower creeks to the Murray River and Victoria.[401]

By 1848, Frank and Jack Jenkins had built a store and a smithy near to their *Bush Inn*. In 1856, they purchased a 65 hectare block of freehold land which surrounded these buildings; the first blocks of freehold land sold by the New South Wales Government in the district.[402]

In 1852, John Dill built a punt to ferry passengers and stock across the Murrumbidgee River adjacent to the nascent Gillenbah settlement. He replaced that punt in 1858 with a larger one capable of transporting bigger stock numbers. It seems highly likely that the Jenkins brothers had some form of financial interest in these punts. In 1858, Dill applied to the New South Wales Government for a licence to operate a post office at the Gillenbah settlement. Unfortunately, he later died in the same year. Later still in 1858, Thomas Fennell moved up from the Bendigo diggings to take over the operation of both the punt and the *Bush Inn*.[403]

In early 1859, the New South Wales Government approved the erection of a post office at the Gillenbah settlement. Shortly afterwards, one Knox Ellis was appointed as postmaster. Ellis built a new store closer to the southern terminus of the punt. By 1859, the little Gillenbah settlement apparently consisted of the Jenkins brothers' inn, store, smithy and huts associated with the *Gillenbah* run; together with the punt, forcing yards (pens used to force cattle into races for movement to other locations), a breaking yard, a vegetable garden and the makings of a racetrack.[404] According to Bill Gammage, two days of racing were held on the racetrack in February 1859.[405]

The growth of a village by the Murrumbidgee River on the *Gillenbah* run was not welcome

---

401 See Gammage, *Narrandera Shire*, op. cit., pp. 122 and 124.
402 See Gammage, *Narrandera Shire*, op. cit., p. 122.
403 Ibid. Thomas Fennell could well have been related to Frank's third wife, Brigid Maria Jenkins (née Fennell). However, a family connection has yet to be established.
404 Ibid.
405 Ibid.

news to Edward Flood. Flood occupied the *Narrandera* run on the opposite bank of the River to *Gillenbah*. It would seem that he was also anxious to control punting across the Murrumbidgee, and to see to the establishment and government recognition of a town on his side of the River. In Flood, the Jenkins brothers were faced with an eminent, but also ruthless, adversary.[406] The opening salvos in the battle between the Frank and Jack Jenkins and Edward Flood were described by Bill Gammage in his *Narrandera Shire* as follows:

> "On 30 March 1858, John Dill complained to the Secretary for Lands that Narrandera station workers were obstructing his punt and molesting his passengers, and the following month surveyor Edward Fisher reported many complaints of interference with the punt, culminating in severing its warp, which prevented it from operating. Flood and the Jenkins' had begun a duel to control the coming village."[407]

In the event, Flood won the day so far as the location of a new town was concerned. In 1859, the New South Wales Government instructed a government surveyor, Edward Twynam, to survey a site for the town on the *Narrandera* run. In June 1860, Twynam submitted his plan for a town covering an area of 327 acres [around 132 hectares]. The town was officially gazetted as "Narrandera" on 28 April 1863.[408] Although Flood may well have used his political influence with respect to the selection of the site, there can be little doubt that the right bank of the Murrumbidgee River was a preferable location for settlement to the left bank. The site chosen by Twynam was generally higher and less likely to flood than the flat land surrounding the Gillenbah hamlet across the River.

By about 1860, Jack Jenkins had moved with his immediate family from *Buckingbong* to *Nangus*, leaving Frank on the former run to do battle with Edward Flood.[409] Frank initially fought this battle on two fronts. In the first place, he sought to promote alternative villages to the surveyed Narrandera town. He saw to the establishment of both a wheelwright's shop and a butchery in his Gillenbah hamlet. By 1866, this small settlement boasted a population of some 25 people. A short way further down the Murrumbidgee River, and near to its

---

406   Edward Flood was born in Sydney in 1805, the illegitimate son of an Irish convict father. Trained as a carpenter, he quickly built a business and pastoral empire. Flood acquired the *Narrandera* run of 76,000 acres [about 30,756 hectares] in 1841. Within a decade, he apparently acquired further runs in the Clarence River District, over 650,000 acres [some 263,046 hectares] of pastoral land on the lower Darling River in addition to *Narrandera* and further runs on the Lachlan River. In 1842, Flood was elected an alderman on the first Sydney Council. In 1849, he was Mayor of Sydney. In 1851, he was elected to the New South Wales Legislative Council. In 1859, he was briefly Secretary for Public Works in the Cowper Ministry. He resigned from Parliament in 1860 to devote himself to his pastoral business enterprises. Flood died in 1888: see R. W. Rathbone, "Flood, Edward (1805-1888)" in *Australian Dictionary of Biography* (http://tinyurl.com/yxwf462u) (at 27 February 2020).

407   See Gammage, *Narrandera Shire*, op. cit., p. 123. There was clearly no love lost between the Frank Jenkins and the Flood family. In the late 1840s, Edward Flood's brother, James Flood, deftly exploited the provisions of the *Order in Council of 1847* to secure the eviction of Frank's brother-in-law, James Garner, from the latter's *Ulong* run: see p. 43 above. Further, in October 1849, Frank's half-brother, Thomas Jenkins, who was then managing John and Frank Jenkins' *Gillenbah* run, secured the prosecution of Edward Flood's son, George Flood (who was managing the *Narrandera* run on his father's behalf), for horse stealing: see Gammage, *Narrandera Shire*, op. cit., p. 45.

408   See *Supplement to the New South Wales Government Gazette* (No. 73), Tuesday, 28 April 1863, p. 986.

409   See Gammage, *Narrandera Shire*, op. cit., p. 124. See also p. 65 above. In 1868, Jack transferred his interests in *Buckingbong*, *Gillenbah* and *Yanco* to Frank, and Frank his interest in *Nangus* to Jack, as parts of an amicable dissolution of their partnership: see p. 66 above.

junction with the Yanco Creek, he built both an inn and a store, and secured the declaration of a government stock pound beside these structures. Further south, and on his *Yanco* run, he constructed two more inns and established a second vineyard on Cuddell Creek. Unfortunately for Frank, none of these ventures were to prosper.[410]

On 10 June 1861, the post office at Gillenbah closed, and a replacement post office was opened in Narrandera.[411] Between April and November 1870, nine separate floods washed away most of the structures in the Gillenbah settlement, together with the punt; thus proving the wisdom of constructing the new town on the right, and not the left, bank of the Murrumbidgee River.[412] All that now remains of village development at Gillenbah, and on the Yanco and Cuddell Creeks, are a service station, a motel and a caravan park at Gillenbah.

Frank Jenkins' second front in his battle with Edward Flood lay within the surveyed site for the town of Narrandera itself. The first sale of allotments in the new town took place in Wagga Wagga on 22 October 1860. Of the 56 lots offered for sale, Frank's associates purchased 21 and Flood's associates 32, with the remaining three lots being purchased by parties unrelated to either Frank or Flood. At the second sale of Narrandera allotments conducted on 22 February 1861 in Wagga Wagga, all of the lots on offer were sold to associates of either Frank or Flood.[413]

In 1862, Frank saw to the construction of the *Royal Hotel* on the south-western corner of Larmer and Cadell Streets in Narrandera. Bill Gammage has written of this hotel:

> "It had 36 rooms, and quickly became Narrandera's social and administrative centre, housing the post office between 1870 and 1876, court sittings in its 'Hall of Justice' until 1879, Anglican church services until 1880, council meetings in 1885-6, and Pastures and Stock Board meetings in 1886."[414]

Three years after constructing the *Royal Hotel*, Frank in 1865 erected a further inn in Narrandera known as the *Farrier's Arms*. The latter was constructed of canvas and appears to have been ephemeral.[415]

The battle between Frank Jenkins and Edward Flood for property and commercial control of Narrandera continued virtually until Flood's death in 1888. In 1874, a further 36 allotments in the town were offered for sale. Of these, associates of Frank purchased 9 lots and those of Flood 13 lots. Both men concentrated on extending their respective holdings along the Larmer Street towards the south, the early heart of Narrandera.[416]

---

410   See Gammage, *Narrandera Shire*, op. cit., p. 124.
411   See Gammage, *Narrandera Shire*, op. cit., p. 125.
412   See Gammage, *Narrandera Shire*, op. cit., pp. 126-127. However, it might be noted that Frank Jenkins launched a new punt connecting Gillenbah with Narrandera on 1 May 1872: see Gammage, *Narrandera Shire*, op. cit., p. 127. The punt was acquired by the Narrandera Council in October 1885 and finally replaced by a bridge over the Murrumbidgee River in July 1891: see Gammage, *Narrandera Shire*, op. cit., p. 146.
413   See Gammage, *Narrandera Shire*, op. cit., pp. 124-125.
414   See Gammage, *Narrandera Shire*, op. cit., p. 126. See also **photos 31** and **32**. Much of the *Royal Hotel* still stands, although now as a private residence and not as a hotel.
415   See Gammage, *Narrandera Shire*, op. cit., p. 126.
416   See Gammage, *Narrandera Shire*, op. cit., pp. 127 and 133.

Things changed for Narrandera in many ways with the arrival of the railway in 1881. Not least of these ways was in the pattern of the town's growth. Narrandera's station on the new line was located about 1.6 km to the north of Larmer Street. As the population of the town increased, the focus for settlement moved northwards of Larmer Street. Gradually, East Street supplanted the latter as the commercial hub of Narrandera. This significantly disadvantaged both Frank and Flood, who found themselves unable to extend their holdings in pace with the changing pattern of town development.[417] Both men were also challenged by land selectors laying claim to parts of their respective runs, thereby requiring each of them to turn his attention and finances toward the preservation of his pastoral holdings. And so, in the words of Bill Gammage:

> "The railway and the landseekers rescued the town from the squatters who wanted to be squires."[418]

Frank Jenkins also turned his hand (and considerable energies) to property development in Wagga Wagga. In 1866, he built two substantial buildings on Fitzmaurice Street in that town. He rented one to Messrs Battersby and Pendleton, builders and cabinet makers.[419] The other was rented to a W C Hunter, who established a book and gift sales store in it.[420] Frank also constructed four further, adjacent commercial buildings in Fitzmaurice Street, which he leased to a variety of businesses. However, by 1882, he had sold them all. This was fortunate for him as on the night of 4 January 1882, all four of the adjacent structures were consumed by fire.[421]

---

417 See Gammage, *Narrandera Shire*, op. cit., pp. 131 and 133.
418 See Gammage, *Narrandera Shire*, op. cit., p. 138. See also the *Narrandera Argus*, Wednesday, 29 January 2014, p. 14.
419 See the *Wagga Wagga Express and Murrumbidgee District Advertiser*, Saturday, 24 March 1866, p. 2.
420 See Morris, op. cit., p. 60. This building was located at what is now 110 Fitzmaurice Street, Wagga Wagga: Ibid. The Hunter business continued trading from the site until well into the 1960s.
421 See the *Wagga Wagga Advertiser*, Thursday, 5 January 1882, p. 2. One poor soul was not as lucky as Frank. A child in one of the burning buildings could not be rescued and died in the conflagration: Ibid.

The Fruits of Success Coupled with More Tragic Losses

Notwithstanding his ventures with respect to urban property development in Narrandera and Wagga Wagga, Frank Jenkins' first and abiding love apart from his family was his life on the land as a grazier. Although *Buckingbong* and his other runs were initially stocked predominantly with cattle, Frank ultimately found that his lands were better suited to raising sheep. By 1876, and with an estimated 47,700 head of sheep, he was said to have been one of the largest flock owners in southern New South Wales.[422]

The year 1872 started badly for Frank. It proved to be disastrous for one of his employees. On 22 January of that year, a fierce bush fire was found to be raging along the boundary between Frank's *Yanco* and *Gillenbah* runs. Every

> available station hand was sent to fight the flames. One of Frank's overseers, a Bartholomew Burke, apparently raced on horseback to get ahead of the fire. Burke was thrown when his horse stumbled. Stunned, he was tragically burned to death. He was subsequently buried in the *Buckingbong* cemetery.[423]

In June 1872, an anonymous writer, referred to only as "Our Special Correspondent", who authored a series of articles in the *Australian Town and Country Journal* over the course of 1871 and 1872 whilst travelling through southern New South Wales, visited *Buckingbong* and described it as:

> "one of the largest stations in the Riverina. Its area is 350 square miles [about 907 square kilometres]; this includes five stations altogether. It has a frontage of twenty-four miles [around 40 km] to the Murrumbidgee...."[424]

The anonymous writer was shown around parts of *Buckingbong* by Frank Jenkins. Frank first took his guest some 8 km downstream of the *Buckingbong* homestead to the run's woolshed.

---

422 See the *Mining Record and Grenfell General Advertiser*, Saturday, 11 March 1876, p. 2. See also the *Wagga Wagga Advertiser*, Tuesday, 4 August 1902, p. 2. Although Frank's runs proved to be well-suited to the raising of sheep, the husbandry of the animals presented him with major difficulties from time to time. Chief of these difficulties was probably scab disease. In 1857 alone, Frank lost some 6,180 sheep to scab: see Gammage, *Narrandera Shire*, op. cit., p. 229.

423 See *The Empire*, Tuesday, 30 January 1872, p. 2.

424 See the *Australian Town and Country Journal*, Saturday, 29 June 1872, p. 18.

This was located on the bank of the Murrumbidgee River in close proximity to Massacre Island. The anonymous author described the woolshed as "a very substantial building", built of stone and with a galvanised iron roof. Wool was baled within it using a screw wool press.[425]

Frank next took the writer to inspect a quarry on *Buckingbong*. This quarry was apparently worked by a R. McDougall and produced what was said by the writer to be "beautiful stone". The writer went on to observe of the stone:

> "It comes off in layers, and is excellent for tablets, monuments, etc. Many of the blocks are used for door and window sills about Wagga Wagga, and some of the thicker layers are now being used in the construction of the Hay bridge."[426]

The writer was finally taken by Frank to inspect some of the latter's prize animals; including a stud bull known as *Fairy Prince*, which had been imported from England and which Frank had purchased for 390 guineas. The writer was also shown a number of the Jenkins family's horses. He observed:

> "One horse in particular, General, the property of Mr Jenkins, Junr., distinguished himself considerably at the last Hay races, where he carried off most of the principal prizes."[427]

If 1872 started badly for Frank Jenkins, its ending was even worse. On 22 November 1872, Frank's eldest surviving son, John Jenkins, died at the residence of his father-in-law, Dr William Large, in Wagga Wagga after what was described as "a short illness".[428] John was 25 years old at the time of his death.

---

[425] Ibid. See also Eric Irvin (ed.), *Letters from the River* (1959), p. 17. Bill Gammage has noted that Frank Jenkins gave a riverboat operator, James Roach, "sawmill rights" on *Buckingbong* in return for cheap steamer shipping rights. It would appear that most of Frank's baled wool clip was sent to Sydney for sale. However, some was shipped by steamer down the rivers to Adelaide: see Gammage, *Narrandera Shire*, op. cit., p. 218. See further George Main, *The Regeneration of Rural Place* (2005), p. 61. No trace of the *Buckingbong* woolshed remains extant today.

[426] See the *Australian Town and Country Journal*, Saturday, 29 June 1872, p. 18. A slab of stone from the *Buckingbong* quarry was an official New South Wales exhibit at the Melbourne International Exhibition, which opened in the Exhibition Buildings on 1 October 1880: see the *Clarence and Richmond Examiner and New England Advertiser*, Tuesday, 12 October 1880, p. 4.

[427] Ibid. It seems that Frank Jenkins had long been interested in horse racing. In December 1853, he officiated as a steward at a North Wagga race meeting: see the *Supplement to the Goulburn Herald*, Saturday, 24 December 1853, p. 1. See also p. 111 above. He probably also had an interest in sports shooting. In 1889, he was appointed the patron of the Narrandera Sporting Gun Club: see Gammage, *Narrandera Shire*, op. cit., p. 148.

[428] See the *Sydney Morning Herald*, Tuesday, 3 December 1872, p. 1.

Auburn-villa and Still More Tragedy

In late 1873 or early 1874, Frank Jenkins purchased a substantial house on a large block of land near Melbourne. The property, then known as *Auburn-villa*, originally faced onto Auburn Road in a locality originally called Upper Hawthorn and currently known as Auburn. The house was constructed for a John Tankard in 1867. At the time Frank purchased the property, it was largely surrounded by market gardens, orchards and at least one vineyard.

A likely reason for Frank's purchase of *Auburn-villa* may have been to enable one or more of his younger children to attend school in Melbourne. It seems that at least one of Frank's daughters, Emily Jenkins, lived in the house for a time whilst attending the Presbyterian Ladies' College, which was then located in East Melbourne.[429] Although *Auburn-villa* was located in what was at the time a semi-rural area, it was not far by train to Melbourne travelling from the nearby Hawthorn railway station.

Auburn-villa could not have generated too many happy memories for Frank Jenkins. On 16 January 1877, his second wife, Mary Anne Jenkins, succumbed to liver cancer at the house. She may well have been living there for some time whilst receiving specialist medical care in Melbourne prior to her death. Mary Anne was buried in the Boroondara Cemetery on 18 January 1877. She was 36 years old when she died.[430]

Frank was struck by tragedy yet again less than a month after Mary Anne's death. On 13 February 1877, his 17 years old son, Walter Augustus Jenkins, was fatally wounded in his bedroom at *Auburn-villa* after being shot in the head at close range by a friend, William Love. At the time that he shot Walter, Love was playing with a revolver which he erroneously thought was both unloaded and defective. Walter died the following day, 14 February 1877. On 15 February 1877, he was interred, like his mother, in the Boroondara Cemetery.[431] Shortly afterwards, Frank Jenkins understandably sold *Auburn-villa*.[432] By then, the property must have become the focus of terrible memories for him.

---

429 See contents of a letter written by Emily Jenkins' grandson, Ray Pugh, dated 4 August 2008 in the *Marr, Aitken, Watts Family Tree — Parker, Walter Robert* (http://tinyurl.com/uaj4bg4) (at 29 February 2020). According to Pugh, Emily as a teenager was also "a communicant member" of the congregation at St Paul's Anglican Cathedral in Melbourne: Ibid. See also McNeill, op. cit., p. 12.

430 See the *Marr, Aitken, Watts Family Tree — Higgins, Mary Anne* (http://tinyurl.com/yaefjg2f) (at 29 February 2020).

431 See *The Argus*, Thursday, 15 February 1877, pp. 1, 6 and 8; *The Australasian*, Saturday, 17 February 1877, p. 21; and the *Wagga Wagga Advertiser*, Saturday, 17 February 1877, p. 2.

432 See Gwen, McWilliam, *Hawthorn Street Index: A Brief History of the Streets of Hawthorn* (2004), p. 26. After Frank parted with the ownership of *Auburn-villa*, its name was changed to *Aidaville*. Still later, it was given the name *Fairmount*. In 1925, the grounds of *Fairmont* facing Auburn Road were subdivided into lots and sold by the property's then owner, Albert Williams. The original house still stands, with substantial extensions and modifications, at 6 Fairmount Road, Auburn: see *Open Houses 2019: St Joseph's School Hawthorn: Fairmount Road, East Hawthorn* (http://tinyurl.com/y3zvhe7b) (at 29 February 2020); Context, *City of Boroondara Municipal-Wide Heritage Gap Study* (2019), Vol. 6. pp. 146-149; McWilliams, op. cit., p. 25; and *Answers: What is Extra History of Hawthorn?* (http://tinyurl.com/y58hpz5n) (at 29 February 2020). See also **Drawing of Auburn-villa** and **photo 33**.

Third Marriage

Mary Anne Jenkins' death again left her widower with the sole parental care of a number of young children. Frank Jenkins' load in this regard was perhaps lightened when, on 27 February 1878, he married for the third time. His bride on this occasion was Bridget Mary Fennell. Bridget was some 26 years younger than Frank, having been born in Appin, New South Wales in 1846.[433] Her father, Patrick Fennell, was an Irish convict who arrived in Sydney on board the *Mangles* on 8 November 1822.[434] Patrick Fennell married Bridget's mother, Eleanor ("Ellen") Fennell (née Dillon), in Sydney in about 1827.[435] Ellen Fennell was the daughter of another Irish convict, Thomas Dillon, who reached Sydney on 11 January 1800 on board the *Minerva*.[436]

The Jenkins and Fennell families had already been joined by marriage prior to Frank's union with Bridget. In 1867, John Francis Jenkins, the eldest son of Frank's brother, Jack Jenkins, had married Bridget's sister, Catherine Mary Fennell. Moreover, Bridget's brother, Daniel Joseph Fennell, had married Jack Jenkins' daughter, Sarah Anne Jenkins, in 1874.[437] It is perhaps worth noting that Frank and Bridget were married in the home of John Francis Jenkins and his wife, Catherine Jenkins, at Tumbleton near Young. The celebrant was a Catholic priest, Father Edmond McCarthy.[438]

---

433 See the *Marr, Aitken, Watts Family Tree — Fennell, Brigid Maria* (http://tinyurl.com/y9d94rsy) (at 29 February 2020); and *New South Wales Register of Births, Deaths and Marriages — Marriages: Frank Jenkins and Bridget Fennell* (No. 5305/1878).

434 Patrick Fennell was born in or near to Limerick in about 1799. A "ploughman" by original occupation, he apparently became involved with the so-called *Rockite* movement at an early age. The *Rockites* waged a sporadic agrarian rebellion in southern Ireland in the second and third decades of the Nineteenth Century. In essence, the movement was a reaction to local high rents, rural evictions, debt and Protestant oppression of Catholics. In September 1821, Patrick Fennell and his older brother John were captured by local authorities after participating in a violent raid on the village of Shanagolden. The edition of the *Limerick Times* published on 26 September 1821 recounted this raid in the following terms:

"Sunday night, at Shanagolden, an armed party of 200, many wearing white bands on their hats, attacked the village in search of firearms. They first went to the post office and on being told the family had no muskets, they broke the furniture and threatened to murder the inhabitants. They next proceeded to the Bridewell and broke it open, thence to other houses and after demolishing the doors and windows of each they attacked, entered and took what arms they could get. A reward was offered by the Post Master for their capture."

Following their arrest, the two Fennell brothers were sentenced to death at the Limerick Spring Assizes in May 1822. However, their death sentences were subsequently commuted to transportation to New South Wales for seven years apiece. After his emancipation in 1837, Patrick Fennell came to hold the licence for the *Victoria Hotel* in Appin, acquired a number of depasturing licences as a squatter in south-western New South Wales and became a partner in a coaching business: see Valerie Thompson, "Men of the Mangles, 1822" in (Winter, 2002) *The Old Limerick Journal* pp. 36-37; Frank Murray, *Mangles Indent* (http://tinyurl.com/y494jtaq) (at 29 February 2020); and Kate Press and Valerie Thompson, *West Limerick Families Abroad* (2001), pp. 72-73.

435 Ibid.

436 Thomas Dillon was sentenced at the Limerick Autumn Assizes in October 1798 to transportation for seven years to New South Wales for "cow stealing": see *Wikitree — Thomas Dillon* (http://tinyurl.com/y6sqytoj) (at 29 February 2020); and *Convict Records of Australia — Thomas Dillon* (http://tinyurl.com/y5du7qe6) (at 29 February 2020).

437 See the *Marr, Aitken, Watts Family Tree — Jenkins, John Francis* (http://tinyurl.com/y38fe4h8) (at 29 February 2020); the *Marr, Aitken, Watt Family Tree — Fennell, Daniel* (http://tinyurl.com/y6s2zeej) (at 29 February 2020); *and* McNeill, op. cit., pp. 11 and 12.

438 See *New South Wales Register of Births, Deaths and Marriages — Marriages: Francis Jenkins and Bridget Fennell* (No.

Frank and Bridget Jenkins had no children together. Nonetheless, their marriage seems to have been a happy one. Bridget apparently loved *Buckingbong*, and much of the credit for its fine gardens belongs to her.[439] However, notwithstanding his marriage to Bridget, Frank's life was soon again marked by deep sorrow.

5305/1878). John Francis Jenkins had conditionally purchased some 60 acres [around 24 hectares] of land as a selector at Tumbleton in February 1877: see the *Goulburn Herald and Chronicle*, Saturday, 24 February 1877, p. 3. Although Frank and Bridget Jenkins were married in a Catholic ceremony, Frank was both baptised and buried as an Anglican: see p. 9 above and p. 131 below. See also p. 109 above.

439   See McNeill, op. cit., p. 12.

Yet More Tragedies

On 23 October 1879, Frank's eldest surviving son, Robert James Jenkins, was found dead in his bedroom at *Buckingbong*. He was 27 years old at the time of his death. According to his Death Certificate, his cause of death was either an epileptic attack or a stroke. Robert was duly buried in the family cemetery at *Buckingbong*.[440]

Some four months after Robert Jenkins' death, Frank Jenkins' second daughter, Charlotte Elizabeth Berthon (née Jenkins), died on 2 March 1880 at *Buckingbong* of "phthisis" [pulmonary tuberculosis]. Like her brother, Robert Jenkins, Charlotte was interred in the family cemetery on *Buckingbong*.[441]

Frank Jenkins' woes continued into 1881. In July of that year, he was thrown from his buggy after it hit a log on *Buckingbong*. Frank was caught between the Buggy's wheels and severely bruised. His injuries were such that he was required to travel to Melbourne for medical treatment.[442]

---

[440] See *New South Wales Register of Births, Deaths and Marriages — Deaths: Robert James Jenkins* (No. 9311/1879); the *Wagga Wagga Advertiser*, Saturday, 25 October 1879, p. 2; the *Gundagai Times and Tumut, Adelong and Murrumbidgee District Advertiser*, Tuesday, 28 October 1879, p. 2; and the *Marr, Aitken, Watts Family Tree — Jenkins, Robert James* (http://tinyurl.com/y4v4l78q) (at 29 February 2020).

[441] See *New South Wales Register of Births, Deaths and Marriages — Deaths: Charlotte Elizabeth Berthon* (No. 10597/1880); the *Sydney Morning Herald*, Saturday, 15 May 1880, p. 1; and the *Marr, Aitken, Watts Family Tree — Jenkins, Charlotte Elizabeth* (http://tinyurl.com/utgxldy) (at 29 February 2020). Charlotte was married to Charles Berthon, a district engineer with the Harbours and Rivers Branch of the New South Wales Public Works Department. For several years, he was the officer-in-charge of a party detailed to perform de-snagging work on the Murrumbidgee River. Greatly depressed by the death of Charlotte, he committed suicide by hanging himself at Narrandera on 11 May 1880 in a fit of what was said to be "temporary insanity". He, too, was buried in the cemetery on *Buckingbong*: see the *Evening News*, Thursday, 13 May 1880, p. 2; the *Maitland Mercury and Hunter River General Advertiser*, Thursday, 20 May 1880, p. 3; the *Riverine Herald*, Saturday, 22 May 1880, p. 2; and Freeman, op. cit., p. 200.

[442] See the *Albury Banner and Wodonga Express*, Friday, 29 July 1881, p. 16.

Photo 21: St. Paul's Church, Nangus — see footnote 276 on p. 76.

Photo 22: Ridley Jenkin's Grave, Nangus — see footnote 279 on p. 76.

Photo 23: St. Paul's Church Windows, Nangus (1) — see footnote 279 on p. 76.

Photo 24: St. Paul's Church Windows, Nangus (2) — see footnote 279 on p. 76.

Photo 25: St. Paul's Church Windows, Nangus (3) — see footnote 279 on p. 76.

Photo 26: Jack Jenkins' Grave, Narrandera (1) — see footnote 334 on p. 90.

Photo 27: Jack Jenkins' Grave, Narrandera (2) — see footnote 334 on p. 90.

Photo 28: Buckingbong Homestead in 1902 (1) — see footnote 391 on p. 108.

Photo 29: Buckingbong Homestead in 1902 (2) — see footnote 391 on p. 108.

Photo 30: Buckingbong Homestead in 2015 (3) — see footnote 391 on p. 108.

Photo 31: The Royal Hotel, Narrandera in 1924 — see footnote 414 on p. 113.

Photo 32: The former Royal Hotel, Narrandera in 2019 — see footnote 414 on p. 113.

Photo 33: Fairmount (formerly Auburn-villa) in 2019 — see footnote 432 on p. 117.

Photo 34: Frank and Bridget Jenkins in 1902 (1) — see footnote 481 on p. 131.

Photo 35: Frank and Bridget Jenkins in 1902 (2) — see footnote 481 on p. 131.

Photo 36: Frank Jenkins' Grave, Narrandera — see footnote 486 on p. 131.

Photo 37: The Williams' Cannon, (courtesy of The Royal Geographical Society of South Australia Inc.) — see footnote 525 on p. 145.

Photo 38: Ridley Williams as a young man — see footnote 548 on p. 153.

Photo 39: Wigley Gorge in 2019 — see footnote 640 on p. 176.

Photo 40: Wigley Waterhole (c. 1915) — see footnote 640 on p. 176.

Photo 41: Central Australian Pioneers' Memorial, Alice Springs in 2019 (1)
— see footnote 642 on p. 176.

Photo 42: Central Australian Pioneers' Memorial, Alice Springs in 2019 (2)
— see footnote 642 on p. 176.

Photo 43: St. Saviour's Church, Glen Osmond — see footnote 663 on p. 180.

Photo 44: Ridley Williams' Grave, Morphett Vale — see footnote 670 on p. 181.

Confronting Selectors

As mentioned earlier, Frank Jenkins' greatest love apart from his family was for the lands on which he had squatted. The Robertson Land Acts of 1861, which were unambiguously aimed at opening up squatting runs beyond the *Limits of Location* enclosing "the settled lands" for selection and sale, put those lands at dire risk of alienation.[443] Following the passage of these Acts, Frank was to spend a great deal of his time, energies and monies defending his holdings. He concentrated his efforts on his five adjoining runs of *Buckingbong*, *Gillenbah*, *Little Swamp*, *Morundah* and *Yanco*.

Most squatters in the Riverina, and elsewhere in New South Wales, were outraged by the 1861 Land Acts. To quote Bill Gammage, the squatters believed that:

> "they had pioneered the bush, enduring blacks, droughts, floods and depressions, and now they were to have the eyes picked from their runs by newcomers whose only purpose might be to hold them to ransom. In any case, they said, much of the land not [already] freehold was fit only for grazing."[444]

In endeavouring to fight off selectors, squatters employed a suite of stratagems; principally exploiting perceived loopholes in the Lands Acts, often with the connivance of Lands Department officers. These stratagems were outlined in graphic detail by an anonymous "Special Correspondent" in a lengthy article entitled "Land Selection in Riverina" published in *The Age* on 16 May 1873.[445]

In the first place, squatters who had not already purchased the lands on which their homesteads stood used the entitlements granted by the *Crown Lands Alienation Act 1861* to select those lands and purchase them on a deposit of 5/- per acre, rather than paying the sum of £1 per acre as previously required by the *Order in Council of 1847*.[446]

Secondly, squatters were entitled under the *Crown Lands Alienation Act* to claim grants of land around improvements, such as huts, dams and sheep yards, which they had constructed on their runs, at the rate of one acre of land for every £1 expended on the improvements. In many cases, the "improvements" relied on by squatters to found claims to freehold land grants were nothing more than shams, such as the construction of rude, easily demountable huts.

---

443   See pp. 85 above.
444   See Gammage, *Narrandera Shire*, op. cit., p. 62.
445   See *The Age*, Monday, 11 May 1874, p. 3. See also *The Leader*, Saturday, 16 May 1874, p. 8.
446   See p. 85 above. See also Gammage, *Narrandera Shire*, op. cit., p. 62.

Further, and often with the aid of corrupt or simply compliant local officials, these "improvements" were frequently valued at exorbitant figures; thereby giving the squatters access to greater freehold acreages.[447]

Thirdly, the Land Acts provided for the creation of reserves for timber, minerals, travelling stock, water and the like. As these reserves remained within the squatters' runs on which they lay, the squatters concerned applied for the declaration of as many reserves as they could as a bar to selectors and selection. Of these declared reserves, those protecting sources of water were far and away the most important to the squatters. In the words of Bill Gammage:

> "Water was the key to holding land — even a small farmer had to water his horses. The squatters were allowed to reserve one mile of [water] frontage in four, and to extend any water reserve to their back boundaries so that stock anywhere on the run could get to water. So they drew water reserves to protect their boundaries, linked them when necessary with [their own] freehold or selections, and prosecuted for trespass any would-be selector daring to cross. When they had secured the rest of the run, they had the reserves progressively revoked and selected the land."[448]

Fourthly, and perhaps most significantly, many squatters "picked the eyes out" of their own runs by not only using the Land Acts to select 320 acres [around 130 hectares] each for themselves, but also by procuring spouses, children, relatives and trusted others to select, or "dummy", other lots in strategic locations on their runs for them. The lands so selected would often be positioned on the runs in such fashion as to deny selectors meaningfully sized and shaped allotments. Lands thereby left unselected would then be surveyed and purchased by the squatters in question at upset prices. Further, squatters were almost always able to make arrangements to subsequently purchase the lands selected by their "dummies".[449]

Challenges were made in New South Wales to the legality of squatters using their underage children to "dummy" for them. However, the Privy Council ruled in *O'Shannassy v Joachim and Others* that land grants made prior to the enactment of the *Lands Acts Amendment Act 1875* (NSW) to those under the age of 21 years were indeed legal.[450] The Act confirmed the validity of all land grants to those under 21 years old made before its passage, and of all subsequent grants to those of and above the age of 16 years only. The Act also increased the maximum size for selections from 320 acres [about 130 hectares] to 640 acres [around 260 hectares], and gave squatters a pre-emptive right to buy 640 acres for every 3,200 acres [approximately 1,295 hectares] they undertook to improve.[451]

---

447   See *The Age*, Monday, 11 May 1874, p. 3; and Gammage; *Narrandera Shire*, op. cit., p. 62.
448   See Gammage, *Narrandera Shire*, op. cit., p.63; and *The Age*, Monday, 11 May 1874, p. 3.
449   See Gammage, *Narrandera Shire*, op. cit., p. 64; and *The Age*, Monday, 11 May 1874, p. 3. The "upset price" was the price fixed by the New South Wales Government as the minimum price for which the land in question could be sold.
450   See *O'Shanassy v Joachim and Others* [1876] UKPC 7.
451   See 39 Vic. No. 13 (NSW). See also Gammage, *Narrandera Shire*, op. cit., p. 66.

The stratagems thus employed by the squatters were roundly condemned by selectors and those seeking to unlock the land for closer settlement. However, they were instrumental in enabling many squatters to secure freehold title to all or the greater parts of their runs.[452]

It would appear that Frank Jenkins used all of the squatters' stratagems to defend his Riverina runs. These runs extended over some 224,046 acres, or around 907 square kilometres.[453] Bill Gammage has noted that:

> "Such a huge area could not be locked up by reserves, but Frank did his best, and reserves for water, timber, travelling stock roads, minerals and a botanic garden soon dotted the leases. They locked up over 28,500 hectares [some 285 square miles], and made access to other land very difficult. Frank also took care to reserve or freehold the swamps on which both he and the Narrungdera [Aborigines] had built their fortunes, but essentially the old pioneer defended his runs by dummying."[454]

Frank apparently used the services of many "dummies". Bill Gammage has graphically described the variety of persons so relied on by Frank as follows:

> "Frank Jenkins was a popular man. His haystacks were burnt now and then, but his generosity and hospitality were bywords, and he seems to have had little trouble finding dummies. Some were men sheltered in old age in return for bequeathing their selections: in June 1890, John Bailly, aged 77, fell into a fire on his Buckingbong selection, and died soon after, leaving his block to Jenkins. Some were professionals, men who selected on several district runs and forfeited soon after, allowing the squatter to buy the blocks at auction: on 3 January 1877, for example, Frank bought 2,570 hectares in this way. Some were relatives, from as far as Adelaide and possibly England. Some were Narrandera townsmen, or bank managers, or squatters and financiers like Samuel McCaughey and Henry Miller of Melbourne. Some were members of large families, like Hugh Moffat and his many children, who dummied for Jenkins before being helped to select their own blocks on his lease. 'Mr. Moffat [has] sold to me through Mr Blair [of Richard Goldsbrough and Company] for 30/- per acre', Jenkins wrote in January 1886, 'William Dunn has transferred his land to

---

452   The bitterness engendered by the squatters' tactics in resisting the incursions of selectors can be seen reflected in the "Special Reporter's" concluding remarks in his article "Land Selection in Riverina":

        "Hitherto there has been an unequal fight between a few strangers in a strange country and an organised unscrupulous class, who appear to have the Lands department in their pay, from the surveyors on the ground to the Ministers in Sydney. The selectors are, however, gaining fast in strength, and by organisation are turning upon the squatters their own tactics. In a short time the number of votes will admit of a selector's man being returned to Parliament. When this is accomplished one effective step will have been taken towards the exposure of a system of rottenness and corruption on the part of the Lands department that is only equalled by the utter meanness and purse-proud arrogance of the Riverina squatters, who have had their riches thrust upon them by a long and uninterrupted enjoyment of these fertile lands at a nominal fee."

    See *The Age*, Monday, 11 May 1874, p. 3.

453   See p. 115 above.

454   See Gammage, *Narrandera Shire*, op. cit., p. 85. See also pp. 51-52 above.

me. So far I have not lost a selection, but only for his honesty I might have lost it for there is not a scrap of writing to show how he got the money to take it up or any security for it.' In 1887 Jenkins was hoping to buy out the last of his dummies.

Jenkins also employed tenants. They had their own selections, but were secured to Jenkins possibly by private contract, and certainly by debt, for he staked their selections, improvements and supplies. They worked as required and defended him against hostile selectors, but they also farmed and grazed on their own account, sometimes paying Jenkins a share of the profits. In time some passed their blocks to their children, others sold out to Jenkins.... [I]n 1893 Jenkins was able to tell a visitor that there were only one or two hostile selectors on [his runs]."[455]

By about 1884, Frank Jenkins had in large measure protected his Riverina runs from incursions by selectors — particularly by hostile selectors. The latter probably included members of the Macpherson family.[456] Frank had even managed to extend his boundaries a little to the east and to the south-west.[457] However, the passage of the *Crown Lands Act 1884* (NSW) caused him to radically restructure those parts of his lands still held by him under Crown leases.[458]

Under the terms of the 1884 Act, each squatter in the defined "Central Division" of New South Wales was required to divide his non-freehold land into two equal areas: a "leasehold" area and a "resumed" area. The leasehold area was available for re-leasing to the squatter for 10 years and was exempted from sale to selectors during this period. The resumed area was held open to selection. However, the squatter was entitled to continue to occupy unselected portions of this area from year to year under Crown licence. The squatter was also entitled to select land himself within the resumed area.

In response to the *Crown Lands Act*, Frank Jenkins consolidated his five adjoining Riverina runs into one. He then divided the consolidated property in two; taking up a 10 year lease on the "leasehold" half (which of course contained his homestead, already held by him as freehold property, and to which he gave the *Buckingbong* name, and an annual Crown licence on the remaining "resumed" portion.[459]

---

455 See Gammage, *Narrandera Shire*, op. cit., pp. 84-85. Frank Jenkins' Adelaide relations were probably children of his late sister, Elizabeth Williams (née Jenkins). However, Gammage's reference to a relative or relatives from England possibly acting as a dummy or dummies for Frank presents a bigger mystery. There doesn't appear to have been any relative of Frank who would fit this description. Samuel McCaughey, who lived from 1835 until 1919, was another large Riverina squatter. He became Frank's close friend and, as will be seen below, was of great assistance to Frank in the latter's last years. A Member of the New South Wales Legislative Council and a great philanthropist, McCaughey was knighted in 1905: see Peter Hohnen, "McCaughey, Sir Samuel (1835-1919)" in *Australian Dictionary of Biography* (http://tinyurl.com/yxdtw4bc) (at 2 March 2020).

456 The latter were likely related to Ewen Macpherson of Peechelba station in Victoria. One of the daughters of the latter had played the piano under duress for the bushranger, "Mad" Dan Morgan in the Peechelba homestead on the night before Morgan was shot dead on 9 April 1865. A younger daughter, Christina Macpherson, played the tune to which Banjo Paterson wrote "Waltzing Matilda" at *Dagworth* station in Queensland in 1895: see the *Ovens and Murray Advertiser*, Tuesday, 11 April 1865, p. 2; Gammage, *Narrandera Shire*, op. cit., p. 85; and W. Benjamin Lindner, *Waltzing Matilda: Australia's Accidental Anthem: A Forensic History* (2019), passim.

457 See Gammage, *Narrandera Shire*, op. cit., p. 85.

458 See 48 Vic. No. 18 (NSW).

459 See Gammage, *Narrandera Shire*, op. cit., p. 85. See also **Plan of *Buckingbong* in 1885**.

Financial Woes

Frank Jenkins' battle to protect his runs from selectors was both long and costly for Frank. He was forced to borrow heavily and frequently to finance the costs associated with his defensive measures and with the construction of necessary improvements on his properties. Frank's lender of choice was Richard Goldsbrough and Company ("Goldsbrough"), which secured its loans to Frank by taking mortgages of his property.[460] As his debt to Goldsbrough grew, Frank's ability to service it decreased. By the late 1870s, the boom years of earlier decades for Riverina meat and wool were ending.[461] As commodity prices flattened, Frank found it more and more difficult to cope.[462]

By 1879, Frank owed Goldsbrough £60,000. Under pressure from the latter, he offered *Buckingbong, Gillenbah, Yanco, Little Swamp* and *Morundah* for sale in the early 1880s, with a reserve price fixed at £150,000. On offer were 19,480 acres [around 7,883 hectares] of freehold land, 11,000 acres [about 4,452 hectares] of land under selection by Frank and his "dummies", 164,000 acres [approximately 66, 368 hectares] of land under Crown leases, 75,000 sheep and 3,000 head of cattle.[463]

By late January 1880, it appeared that Frank had succeeded in selling his runs to the brothers William and Joseph McGaw for £170,000.[464] The McGaw brothers were the lessees of *Kooba*, a large run located to the north of the Murrumbidgee River between Narrandera and Griffith.

In the expectation that Frank Jenkins would leave the district after the completion of the sale of his runs to the McGaws, Frank's friends and neighbours in and around Narrandera organised a valedictory banquet for him.[465] The banquet was held on 1 June 1880 at McMahon's Hall, Narrandera, and was attended by around 40 men. After speeches, Frank was presented with an illuminated testimonial address, which in substance read:

> "We, the residents of Narrandera, and the surrounding district, cannot allow you to depart from amongst us without an expression of sincere regret that the friendly

---

460   See p. 123 above.

461   See Merrett, op. cit., p. 410.

462   See Gammage, *Narrandera Shire*, op. cit., p. 96; the *Narrandera Argus*, Wednesday, 29 January 2014, p. 5; and McNeill, op. cit., p. 12. Gone were the days when his abundant riches allowed Frank to affect an indifference to money. Bill Gammage has recounted an anecdote which no doubt exemplified Frank's apparent lack of regard for cash in his halcyon days:
"Once, when told he could clear £100,000 by selling Buckingbong, he replied: 'What is £100,000? I've handled a power of money in my time.'"
See Gammage, *Narrandera Shire*, op. cit., p. 150.

463   See Gammage, *Narrandera Shire*, op. cit., p. 96.

464   See the *Wagga Wagga Advertiser*, Thursday, 29 January 1880, p. 2; and Irvin, op. cit., p. 49, n. 15.

465   See the *Wagga Wagga Advertiser*, Tuesday, 6 May 1880, p. 2.

relations which have subsisted for almost half a century between you and all classes of our community are now on the eve of being severed. If it is a merit to have won the cordial esteem of all with whom you have come into contact, you may justly claim the proud distinction that now, at the close of your long sojourn in this neighbourhood, you bear away with you the good wishes of all for the future welfare of yourself and family. With the assurance of our conviction that the void created by your departure will be long felt by all who have been honoured by your acquaintance, and trusting you will bear in mind the many devoted friends you leave behind, we beg to subscribe ourselves, dear sir, yours sincerely (for the committee), Jas. Bowes, hon. Treasurer; John L. King, hon. Secretary."[466]

For some presently unascertained reason, Frank Jenkins' sale of his runs to the McGaw brothers foundered before completion. It may be that the McGaws were unable to raise the necessary finance. Frank tried to sell the runs again in 1881. Again, he was unsuccessful. Goldsbrough was apparently left with little option but to continue supporting him.[467]

Between 1881 and 1884, Frank's overall indebtedness rose from £78,000 to £160,000. In 1884, his nephew, John Francis Jenkins, was bankrupted and lost his Tumbleton selection. Frank must have stood as guarantor for at least some of his nephew's debts, as John's bankruptcy left Frank liable for a further sum of around £39,000.[468] Goldsbrough's response to this extra debt burden was to exercise its rights as mortgagee of Frank's properties to place a supervising manager on to *Buckingbong*, and to put Frank under pressure to sell his *Yanco*, *Colombo Creek* and *Nottingham Forest* holdings, together with his properties in Queensland and Victoria.[469]

By the late 1880s, commodity prices had not just flattened: they were shrinking. Moreover, while rural overheads remained high, land values were actually falling. Frank Jenkins, like his brother Jack, was facing a perfect financial storm.[470] In March 1886, however, Frank was able to sell 11,614 acres [about 4,700 hectares] of *Yanco* land to the Rial brothers for £33,500. In December 1886, he sold *Colombo Creek* to John and Isaac Rudd for £42,000. In May 1887, he sold some 21,000 acres [around 8,500 hectares] of *Gillenbah* to William Kiddle and Arthur Balme for £36,500. Despite these sales, the mountain of debt Frank faced continued to grow. He was forced to persist in borrowing relatively small amounts of money. According to Bill Gammage, for example, Frank wrote to Goldsbrough in January 1887 as follows:

---

466 See the *Wagga Wagga Advertiser*, Tuesday, 8 June 1880, p. 2.
467 See Gammage, *Narrandera Shire*, op. cit., p. 96.
468 Ibid. John Francis Jenkins and Frank Jenkins must have been close. The former was not only Frank's nephew but also his wife's brother-in-law: see p. 118 above.
469 See Gammage, *Narrandera Shire*, op. cit., p. 96. It might be noted that Frank's *Nive Junction* run in Queensland was in the hands of the Bank of New South Wales in October 1892. However, it is not presently known from whom or when the Bank took possession of that property: see the *Brisbane Courier*, Friday, 7 October 1892, p. 5.
470 See Merrett, op. cit., p. 410. See also pp. 87-89 above.

"I must apply to you for £1,000 to meet expenses principally for selections."[471]

However, not all of Frank Jenkins' borrowings in the late 1880s were so small. The end of that decade saw Jack Jenkins having lost what remained of his *Nangus* holdings and heavily in debt. In order to spare his older brother the ignominy of bankruptcy, Frank borrowed a further £80,000 to pay out Jack's debts.[472] Jack and Maria Jenkins subsequently moved back to *Buckingbong* to live with Frank and his immediate family until Jack's death in 1899.

---

471 See Gammage, *Narrandera Shire*, op. cit., p. 96.
472 Ibid. See also McNeill, op. cit., pp. 12-13; and p. 88 above.

Industrial Strife

In the late 1880s and early 1890s, *Buckingbong* was an epicentre for industrial action initiated by the Amalgamated Shearers' Union of Australasia in the Riverina and elsewhere. The Union, a precursor of the Australian Workers' Union, grew out of shearers' dissatisfaction generated by the cutting across Australia of shearers' rates of pay as a response to the economic pressures then faced by pastoralists. The Union demanded of employers higher piecework rates of pay and the right to work in accordance with "Union Rules". The Union backed its demands with strike action. The pastoralists responded with legal actions and the use of scab labour.[473]

The first industrial action taken by the Union on *Buckingbong* resulted in a win for the Union. On 14 August 1888, Goldsbrough's *Buckingbong* manager refused to allow the assembled shearers to work according to Union Rules and ordered all Union shearers off the run. The men then left as a body and made their way to Narrandera. Having no shearers left, the manager was compelled to send word to the shearers that he would agree to them working under Union Rules. The men then marched through Narrandera and back to *Buckingbong*.[474]

The next strike on *Buckingbong* proved to be far less successful for the shearers and for their Union. On 23 September 1890, the shearers on the property walked off part-way through shearing some 70,000 sheep after the then-manager, F W Woodbine, refused to sign an agreement allowing the shearers to finish the shearing in accordance with Union Rules. Woodbine immediately brought complaints against a total of 34 shearers, returnable in the Narrandera Police Court on 29 September 1890, and alleging misconduct on the part of each shearer in the execution of his contract.

In due course, the Court found that the shearers had indeed breached their contracts and ordered the forfeiture of the mens' accrued earnings at *Buckingbong*. The men thus suffered a loss of more than £300 in total. In making his personal views of the shearers' actions plain, Police Magistrate Donaldson observed that their conduct had been "not only clearly illegal, but scandalously dishonest".[475] Financially stretched as he was, Frank Jenkins would almost certainly have approved of the action taken by Woodbine, as Goldsbrough's manager, against the shearers.

---

473 See *Australian Trade Union Archives: Australian Shearers' Union (1886-1887)* (http://tinyurl.com/y4ymreu3) (at 3 March 2020); and *Australian Trade Union Archives: Amalgamated Shearers' Union of Australasia (1887-1894)* (http://tinyurl.com/y2fpk34x) (at 3 March 2020).

474 See the *Australian Star*, Wednesday, 15 August 1888, p. 5; and Gammage, *Narrandera Shire*, op. cit., p. 92.

475 See the *Daily Telegraph*, Tuesday, 30 September 1890, p. 5; and the *Wagga Wagga Advertiser*, Saturday, 4 October 1890, p. 4.

Industrial Strife

There seems to have been no further industrial trouble on *Buckingbong* during Frank Jenkins' lifetime until another shearers' strike on 2 September 1901.[476] The outcome of this strike appears to be unrecorded.

---

476   See *The Australasian*, Saturday, 7 September 1901', p. 10.

Final Years

In early March 1899, Frank and Bridget Jenkins celebrated their 21st wedding anniversary by hosting a dance at *Buckingbong*. The dance was attended by some 30 couples, and dancing continued until midnight. According to the *Albury Banner and Wodonga Express*:

> "The hostess had made elaborate preparations for the reception, and no trouble was spared to cater for the happiness of the visitors."[477]

Yet notwithstanding the joys associated with his happy marriage to Bridget, Frank's last years remained plagued by debt. This debt proved to be difficult for both Frank and Goldsbrough to manage. Bill Gammage has perceptively noted with respect to Frank that:

> "By 1895, his land had been reduced from 90,688 to 26,522 hectares, which Goldsbrough valued at £148,630, less the cost of converting 11,108 hectares of selected land to freehold. He owed more than that, so the company kept him on. Indeed, it had to lend him more, because the reserves which had locked up so much prime land in the 60s and 70s were now being opened under public pressure, and it was vital to secure the land."[478]

Frank's old friend, Samuel McCaughey, provided a solution to the debt problem for both Goldsbrough and Frank. In March 1900, McCaughey purchased most of Frank's accumulated debts and Goldsbrough's associated mortgage entitlements from Goldsbrough. However, exercising the spirit of generosity for which he was renowned, he allowed Frank to keep his remaining land.[479]

By 1900, Frank Jenkins was 80 years old. At a banquet given in Narrandera on 27 July 1900 in honour of Edward O'Sullivan, the New South Wales Minister for Works, the Mayor of Narrandera, Cr Fred Smith, proposed a toast to Frank's health. Frank's response to the toast was recorded in an obituary for him published in the *Narandera Argus and Riverina Advertiser* on 8 August 1902 as follows:

> "Mr Jenkins said he had been in the district since he was 12 years old, and had seen a few things that would surprise the present generation. He had come to the district before

---

477 See the *Albury Banner and Wodonga Express*, Friday, 10 March 1899, p. 31.
478 See Gammage, *Narrandera Shire*, op. cit., p. 96.
479 Ibid. See also the *Narrandera Argus*, Wednesday, 29 January 2014, p. 5.

any white man had set foot in it, and in all his experiences with black men and white men, he could say that he had never denied a man, nor had he ever sent a hungry man from his door. He required time to think before entering on his reminiscences, therefore he would only say that he had tried to live uprightly, and had always found that people had treated him kindly; for which he was very thankful."[480]

Although Frank grew frail as he approached his end, he appears to have been mobile and in good spirits until shortly before his death.[481] His physical condition a week or so prior to that death seemingly gave no cause for immediate concern. However, on Tuesday, 29 July 1902, he had a slight fall whilst arising from his bed. Soon afterwards, he lapsed into temporary unconsciousness. A doctor was called. Frank rallied slightly, and the doctor gave him "a mercury preparation". This was said to have infuriated Frank. Complaining of having been poisoned, he ordered the doctor from his house and demanded an independent autopsy if he died.[482] He subsequently again lapsed into unconsciousness. For some 50 hours prior to his death, Bridget and his surviving sons and daughters took it in turns to maintain a vigil by his bedside.[483]

Frank Jenkins died in his bed at *Buckingbong* at about 3.30 pm on Friday, 1 August 1902 at the age of 82 years. The official cause of death was recorded as "senile decay". There was no autopsy.[484]

Frank's funeral service was conducted at St. Thomas' Anglican Church, Narrandera by the Reverend G R Nobbs on Monday, 4 August 1902. To peels from St. Thomas' bells, Frank's casket was carried into the Church by four of his old friends, including Samuel McCaughey. During the service, the choir recited the 70th Psalm; apparently pursuant to a request made by Frank prior to his death.[485] As the casket was taken from the Church to the hearse, the organist played "The Dead March" from *Saul* by George Handel. The hearse then proceeded to the Narrandera Cemetery followed by some 60 horse-drawn vehicles together with numerous mounted horsemen. At the cemetery, burial prayers were offered by St. Thomas' catechist, Allan Wyrill, and Frank was then laid to rest beside his brother Jack.[486]

---

480 See the *Narandera Argus and Riverina Advertiser*, Friday, 8 August 1902, p. 2. See also the *Sydney Morning Herald*, Saturday, 28 July 1900, p. 11.

481 See **photos 34** and **35**.

482 See the *Narandera Argus and Riverina Advertiser*, Friday, 8 August 1902, p. 2; and Gammage, *Narrandera Shire*, op. cit., p.150. According to Bill Gammage:
"Frank never thought much of doctors. His remedies for sickness had been Dutch drops, porous plasters and Buckingbong brandy."
Ibid.

483 See the *Narandera Argus and Riverina Advertiser*, Friday, 8 August 1902, p. 2.

484 See *New South Wales Register of Births, Deaths and Marriages — Deaths: Francis Jenkins* (No.10226/1902); and the *Jenkins Family File*, p. 36.

485 See the *Narandera Argus and Riverina Advertiser*, Friday, 8 August 1902, p. 2; and Gammage, *Narrandera Shire*, op. cit., p. 150. In the King James version of the Bible, the first two verses of Psalm 70 read:
"Make haste, O God, to deliver me; make haste to help me, O Lord.
Let them be ashamed and confounded that seek after my soul: let them be turned backward, and put to confusion, that desire my hurt."

486 See the *Narandera Argus and Riverina Advertiser*, Friday, 8 August 1902, p. 2; McNeill, op. cit., p. 13; the *Narrandera Cemetery Heritage Walk*, p. 2; and **photo 36**.

Frank Jenkins left a Will executed by him on 10 December 1900 and a Codicil to that Will dated 15 April 1902. The Will was drafted in a convoluted manner typical of its time. By it, he appointed two of his sons, Marcus Henry Jenkins and Albert Winton Jenkins, together with one of his sons-in-law, John Ziegler Huie (the husband of Ada Mary Jenkins), to be his Executors and Trustees ("the Trustees"). All three of the Trustees had assisted in the management of *Buckingbong* over a number of years.

By his Will, Frank directed the Trustees to arrange for the payment of:
- an annuity of £200 to be paid to his widow, Bridget, for the balance of her life or until her remarriage;
- an annuity of £100 to be paid to a "Clari Richards of Buckingbong, Widow" (presumably an old servant of Frank's family);
- a lump sum of £500 to be paid to his grandson, Francis Jenkins (the son of the late Robert Jenkins and the latter's wife, Rose Jenkins);
- a lump sum of £5,000 to be paid to his daughter, Emily Grace Jenkins; and
- a lump sum of £2,000 to be paid to his daughter, Clara Florence Jenkins.

The Trustees were to arrange for payment of these bequests using income earned from Frank's interests in his remaining runs, his horses and stock and/or the sale of some of those assets. He left the residue of his interests in his runs, his horses and his stock to be shared equally between his sons, Marcus Henry Jenkins, Albert Winton Jenkins and Edwin Ridley Jenkins, and his daughter, Ada Mary Huie (the wife of John Huie), as tenants in common.

Frank further left his widow, Bridget, with:
- the use of the Buckingbong homestead, garden, watering system and adjacent land for the balance of her life or until her remarriage; and
- two pairs of horses, two ponies and two buggies and harness; and all of his furniture, household goods and personal effects, save only for his watch and chain which he left to his son, Marcus Henry Jenkins.

Next, Frank gave a life interest in his blocks of freehold land in Narrandera to his daughter, Lydia Anne Savage; with the remainder to pass on her death to her children. Finally, Frank provided by his Will that all of his other freehold land, including properties at Heathcote, Glenarres, near Melbourne, and in Queensland, together with his shares in the Wagga Wagga Building Society, be sold and that the net proceeds of such sales be divided equally between his children, Marcus Henry Jenkins, Albert Winton Jenkins, Edwin Ridley Jenkins and Ada Mary Huie.[487]

By the Codicil to his Will, Frank appointed his old friend and benefactor, Samuel McCaughey,

---

487   See the *Marr, Aitken, Watts Family Tree — Jenkins, Francis* (http://tinyurl.com/ydhcm5k2) (at 4 March 2020). The Heathcote property referred to by Frank in his Will was most likely his land at Derrinal. The location of the property referred to as being at "Glenarres" is unknown. However, it is possible that Frank was in fact referring to land at Glenaire, near to Cape Otway. The location of other properties referred to in the Will as being "near Melbourne" and in Queensland are also presently unknown: see pp. 106 and 126 above.

as a fourth Executor and Trustee alongside Marcus Henry Jenkins, Albert Winton Jenkins and John Ziegler Huie.[488]

Frank Jenkins' Will and its Codicil were granted probate in the Supreme Court of New South Wales on 15 June 1903.[489]

Frank's widow, Bridget Jenkins, never remarried following Frank's death. Nor did she live out the remainder of her life on *Buckingbong*. In November 1903, she moved to Sydney to live with relatives. Prior to Bridget leaving the Narrandera District, she was given a public farewell on 10 November 1903 attended by over 100 men and women. During the farewell, John Willans, a local solicitor and a former Mayor of Narrandera, spoke of her kindly disposition and of the hospitality she had always dispensed while living at *Buckingbong*. Isabella Spiller, the wife of a grazier from Morundah, John Spiller, presented Bridget with a diamond brooch and pendant earrings. Bridget died in the Hillington Private Hospital at Summer Hill on 16 August 1929.[490]

In the years following Frank Jenkins' death, parts of *Buckingbong* were progressively sold off. By 1906, the property had been reduced to a homestead block of around 14,800 acres [approximately 5,989 hectares].[491] By 2016, it covered an area of about 10,000 acres [some 4,046 hectares]. In July of that year, the then-owners, members of the Seidel family, sold what remained of *Buckingbong*, together with another nearby property, for about $15 million to a company controlled by Ronald and Nicola Winestock of Sydney and Anil Joshi of Melbourne.[492]

Like his brother Jack, Frank Jenkins was a truly remarkable man. In announcing his death on 5 August 1902, the *Wagga Wagga Advertiser* observed that:

> "He was a big-hearted generous man, and will be much missed in the district in which he lived."[493]

In the same vein, his friend James Gormly subsequently said of Frank:

> "He was a just and generous man, and it was his proud boast that no traveller ever passed his station without obtaining food if he needed it."[494]

---

488 See the *Marr, Aitken, Watts Family Tree — Jenkins, Francis* (http://tinyurl.com/ydhcm5k2) (at 4 March 2020).
489 Ibid.
490 See the *Albury Banner and Wodonga Express*, Friday, 13 November 1903, p. 37; the *Marr, Aitken, Watts Family Tree — Fennell, Brigid Maria* (http://tinyurl.com/y9d94rsy) (at 4 March 2020); and McNeill, op. cit., p. 13.
491 See Gammage, *Narrandera Shire*, op. cit., p. 234.
492 See the *Australian Financial Review*, Sunday, 31 July 2016 (http://tinyurl.com/y4zkh6jh) (at 4 March 2020); and *Beef Central*, Wednesday, 3 August 2016 (http://tinyurl.com/y2cxcbjd) (at 4 March 2020).
493 See the *Wagga Wagga Advertiser*, Tuesday, 5 August 1902, p. 2.
494 See James Gormly, "Exploration and Settlement in Australia", op. cit., p. 119. See also the *Gundagai Times and Tumut, Adelong and Murrumbidgee District Advertiser*, Tuesday, 5 December 1916, p. 2; and James Gormly, "Pioneering Families: The Garners & The Jenkins" in the *Narandera Argus and Riverina Advertiser*, Friday, 3 August 1934, p. 8.

There is a Jenkins family anecdote which colourfully illustrates Frank's kindness and generosity. According to his daughter, Emily Grace Parker (née Jenkins):

> "A sick rider came to Buckingbong and Francis nursed him back to health. As he was leaving, he said to Francis, 'I never told you who I am. I am Danny Morgan, the bushranger.' Francis said, 'I wish you had not told me. Now I will have to tell the police.' 'That's alright', Morgan replied, 'I'll be gone, but you and yours will never be hurt.' While stock was rustled from nearby stations, it never happened to the Jenkins."[495]

In its obituary published published on 8 August 1902, the *Narandera Argus and Riverina Advertiser*, with perhaps a little licence, wrote:

> "Gone full of years and honor, Francis Jenkins leaves in the ranks of pioneers of Australia a vacant place into which none may step. His history would fill volumes, and it would be the history of the development of the pastoral industry of Australia; for he can claim to have been the first man to devote himself exclusively to pastoral pursuits on the Murrumbidgee. Contemporary he had none when in 1832, seventy years ago, he came among the Aboriginal tribes of this part. Cattle raising was the first form of grazing that he attempted, and in spite of depredations by black and white marauders, his herd grew and flourished. The Buckingbong of his last days is a mere paddock to the miles upon miles of country over which he held sway in the 60s."[496]

Bill Gammage has noted of Frank:

> "He was the last of the Murrumbidgee pioneers. He outlived all his contemporaries save his sister-in-law, Maria, John's wife, and survived two of his three wives and seven of his fourteen children. Disease and drowning, mostly, had decimated his family, but he had battled on, against the Wiradjuri, drought, selectors and the banks.... Probably he was the model for Rolf Boldrewood's Job Claythorpe in *A Sydney-Side Saxon*, and for his great-granson, F. J. Thwaites' Francis Jenkins in *The Broken Melody*. He lived to see both the convict system and the Commonwealth of Australia, and Narrandera grow from a bush hut to a town of 2,300 people, yet he kept his pioneer values to the last.... 'Everybody knows me', he declared in 1898, 'I don't tell no lies, and nobody leaves Buckingbong with a hungry belly.' His generosity and hospitality were proverbial. He was the ideal self made man."[497]

---

495 See letter dated 4 August 2008 written by Frank's great-grandson, Ray Pugh, in the *Marr, Aitken, Watts Family Tree — Jenkins, Francis* (http://tinyurl.com/ydhcm5k2) (at 4 March 2020). "Mad" Dan Morgan was a notorious and brutal bushranger who lived between 1830 and 1865. He robbed squatters in the Riverina and beyond during the first half of the 1860s. See John McQuilton, "Morgan, Daniel (Dan) (1830-1865)" in *Australian Dictionary of Biography* (http://tinyurl.com/y62rzskx) (at 4 March 2020); and footnote 456 on p. 124 above.

496 See the *Narandera Argus and Riverina Advertiser*, Friday, 8 August 1902, p. 2.

497 See Gammage, *Narrandera Shire*, op. cit., pp. 150-151. The author of *The Broken Melody*, Frederick Thwaites, is on record as

Frank Jenkins was a man of great energy, courage and enterprise. His memory bears the stain of his likely actions as a very young man during the *Wiradjuri War*.[498] However, that stain is to an extent balanced by the kindness and generosity he extended to all in later life. His story is one of vision, tenacity and fortitude in the face of adversity. From the humblest of beginnings, he rose to great wealth only to witness his fortunes wither by his end. To adopt the words of Bill Gammage, slightly out of context, Frank Jenkins experienced during his long life "both the exhilaration of success and the misery of disaster".[499]

---

stating that the book was designed to perpetuate the memory of Frank Jenkins: see the *Muswellbrook Chronicle*, Friday, 11 May 1934, p. 1. The book became a best seller. By 1935, it was estimated to have sold 55,000 copies in Australia and 25,000 in England. By 1968, it had been reprinted 54 times and was reputed to have sold over a million copies. In 1938, Ken Hall directed a film version of *The Broken Melody* starring Lloyd Hughes. Part of the music for the film was composed by the noted Australian composer, Alfred Hill. It is interesting to note that future Australian Prime Minister, Gough Whitlam, then a Sydney University law student, appeared as an extra in an elaborate cabaret scene in the film: see *Wikipedia — The Broken Melody (1937 film)* (http://tinyurl.com/y5tdgnzt) (at 4 March 2020).

498   See pp. 55-56 above.

499   See Gammage, *Narrandera Shire*, op. cit., p. 37.

ELIZABETH JANE WILLIAMS (née JENKINS)
(1818 — 1865)

Early Days

Like all of her siblings, Elizabeth Jane Jenkins was born in Kent, England. She was christened in St. James the Great's Church, East Malling on 11 August 1818.[500] Her early years were largely spent in the Halling Workhouse with her mother, sister and brothers following her father's arrest, trial and conviction for burglary in 1820, and his subsequent transportation to New South Wales for life in 1821.[501] Those early years would no doubt have been marked by hardship and deprivation.

In 1827, Elizabeth, together with her mother and siblings, themselves arrived in New South Wales on the *Granada* to join John Jenkins; a father of whom Elizabeth could have had no recollection.[502] They were reunited with John Jenkins on James Atkinson's *Oldbury* property at Sutton Forest in late January or early February 1827. In the 1828 New South Wales Census, Elizabeth, then aged 10 years old, was recorded as being employed as a servant by James Atkinson on *Oldbury*.[503] On 11 June 1832, Elizabeth married Henry Thomas Williams in All Saints Church, Sutton Forest.[504] She was 13 years of age at the time of her marriage.

Elizabeth's husband, Henry Williams, was born in London on 7 January 1803 and baptised on 12 May 1803 in St Sepulchre-without-Newgate; an Anglican church situated almost opposite the Old Bailey. He was the son of Henry Williams Snr and the latter's wife, Sarah Williams (née Tanner), and was almost certainly raised in straightened circumstances.[505]

On 17 February 1820, the younger Henry Williams was convicted in the Old Bailey of grand larceny; having been found guilty of stealing two candlesticks, valued at 5/-, and a caddy-spoon, valued at 1/-, on 15 February 1820 from Ann Estob, of Grove-row, Mile End in London. He was sentenced to transportation for seven years.[506] On 11 August 1820, the young Henry departed England for New South Wales on the convict transport vessel *Elizabeth*. He arrived in Sydney on 31 December 1820.[507]

It is not presently known how or where Henry Williams was employed during the period he spent in New South Wales before he regained his freedom. Presumably, he secured his

---

[500] See the *Marr, Aitken, Watts Family Tree — Jenkins, Elizabeth* (http://tinyurl.com/y3popqa4) (at 4 March 2020); and McNeill, op. cit., p. 3. See also p. 9 above.

[501] See pp. 10-13.

[502] See pp. 17–18 above.

[503] See p. 20 above.

[504] See p. 25 above.

[505] See *Ancestry — Henry Thomas Williams* (http://tinyurl.com/y3j3yom9) (at 5 March 2020).

[506] See *Proceedings of the Old Bailey Online* (Ref. No. t18200217-92) (http://tinyurl.com/ydbw9fkn) (at 4 March 2020). A caddy-spoon is a small, often ornate, spoon designed to convey tea leaves to a tea pot.

[507] See *Convict Records of Australia — Henry Williams* (http://tinyurl.com/y2puaeos) (at 4 March 2020).

Certificate of Freedom at the conclusion of his seven years term of servitude in 1827. He was probably given a Ticket of Leave prior to that time. Interestingly, he does not appear to be listed in the 1828 Census conducted in New South Wales. However, it seems almost certain that he was employed as a rural labourer in the Berrima District at, and for some time prior to, his marriage to Elizabeth Jenkins.

Elizabeth and Henry Williams were to have a total of 13 children; being:
- John Henry Williams; born in 1834;
- Henry Williams; born in 1836;
- Eliza Williams; born in 1838;
- Francis Williams; born in 1839;
- Thomas Richard Williams; born in 1841;
- George Williams; born in 1843;
- James Williams; born in 1845;
- Mary Ann Williams; born in 1848;
- Helen Williams; born in 1849;
- Ridley Frederick Williams; born in 1850;
- Charlotte Williams; born in 1852;
- Robert Williams; born in 1854; and
- Rebecca Williams; born in 1855.

Of these children, it would appear that one, Helen Williams, was either stillborn or died soon after birth. The remaining children seem to have survived to adulthood.[508]

Henry Williams could well have been in the employ of the Jenkins family when he married Elizabeth. Even if that wasn't the case, he was almost certainly working for them soon afterwards. What appears to be beyond doubt is that he was managing the *Tooyal* run near Wagga Wagga for John Jenkins Snr by 1843. At some stage prior to 1850, Henry could also have worked on the Jenkins brothers' *Buckingbong* run.[509]

---

[508] See *Geneanet — Williams* (http://tinyurl.com/vna5hv9) (at 4 March 2020); *Ancestry — Elizabeth Jane Jenkins* (http://tinyurl.com/y6raf4tm) (at 4 March 2020); and *New South Wales Register of Births, Deaths and Marriages — Deaths: Elizabeth Williams* (No. 2480/1865).

[509] See *New South Wales State Archives and Records*, AONSW Reel 2748; and p. 25 above. When Francis and Thomas Williams were jointly baptised in All Saints Church, Sutton Forest on 4 September 1842, they and their parents, Elizabeth and Henry Williams, were recorded as living at "Morrumbidgee beyond the limits of the Colony": see *New South Wales Anglican Parish Registers, All Saints Parish, Camden County, 1842*, p. 8 (http://tinyurl.com/y8gqzp9q) (at 11 May 2020). This was very likely a reference to *Tooyal*.

Gol Gol

By 1850 at the latest, Henry Williams had moved with Elizabeth and their still growing family to take effective possession and control of Frank Jenkins' *Gol Gol* run on the right bank of the Murray River, nearly opposite present-day Mildura.[510] It seems that Henry and Elizabeth for the most part continued to live together on that run until Elizabeth's death in 1860.[511]

Not a great deal is known of the Williams family's life on *Gol Gol*. They appear to have used the run throughout their time on it to raise cattle. The cattle were apparently sold in both Adelaide and Melbourne. On 23 May 1914, the *Mildura Cultivator* published an interview with Elizabeth and Henry's eldest child, John Henry Williams (by then an old man), in which the latter recalled the following story of one cattle drive from *Gol Gol* to Adelaide:

> "His father and he overlanded a mob of fats from Gol Gol to Adelaide and found that capital city practically a town of women and children, the men being at the diggings. An offer of only 16/- a head was made for the cattle. Mr. Williams' father would have taken 20/-, but the son stuck out for 25/-, and, not getting it, brought the mob back to Gol Gol, losing only one animal on the entire trip. He kept them for three months, then took them to Melbourne and sold at £5.10/-."[512]

The most noteworthy incidents which occurred during the time spent by Elizabeth Williams and her family on *Gol Gol* were associated with visits to the run's homestead in September and October 1853 by passengers and crew from the paddle steamer *Lady Augusta*.

---

510   The Williams' tenth child, Ridley Williams, was seemingly born on *Gol Gol* shortly prior to 3 June 1850. It has been asserted that their seventh child, James Williams, had earlier been born on *Gol Gol* a little before 19 November 1845: see *Ancestry — Elizabeth Jane Jenkins* (http://tinyurl.com/y6raf4tm) (at 5 March 2020). This could not have been the case as Frank Jenkins did not take possession of the *Gol Gol* run until late 1847: see p. 100 above. It should be noted that although Frank Jenkins never resumed the management or active control of *Gol Gol*, he remained the registered licensee and then lessee of the run until the 1860s: see Vann, op. cit., p. 99; and Whitworth, op. cit., p. 213. See also p. 101 above.

511   It is interesting to note that the Williams' three youngest children were apparently not born on *Gol Gol*. Charlotte Williams is said to have been born in Adelaide, and Robert and Rebecca Williams in McLaren Vale: see *Ancestry — Elizabeth Jane Jenkins* (http://tinyurl.com/y6raf4tm) (at 5 March 2020). Henry Williams may have purchased or leased a property at McLaren Vale at some point in time prior to March 1852. If so, that property may have been a working farm, a holiday home or simply a base for educating at least some of the Williams' younger children: see p. 145 below. During the 1850s and 1860s, Elizabeth and Henry Williams may have spent part of their time on *Gol Gol* and part at McLaren Vale. Henry (and presumably Elizabeth) seem to have been living at McLaren Vale at the time of the marriage of their oldest daughter, Eliza Williams, to Edward William Dreyer on 29 August 1861: see *Australian Surname Group — Dreyer of South Australia* (http://tinyurl.com/yxksb8zg) (at 5 March 2020).

512   See the *Mildura Cultivator*, Saturday, 23 May 1914, p. 13. John Williams did not provide a date for this cattle drive from *Gol Gol* to Adelaide and back. However, his observation that the men of Adelaide were "at the diggings" when the Williamses and their cattle arrived strongly suggests that it occurred in or about the early to middle 1850s, when the Victorian gold rushes were at their height.

The Lady Augusta

The *Lady Augusta* was a paddle steamer built and operated by a maritime entrepreneur, Francis Cadell. Over the course of August, September and October 1853, it was engaged in an unofficial race against William Randall's paddle steamer, *Mary Ann*, to win a monetary prize offered by the South Australian Government to the owner of the first steam powered vessel to proceed up the Murray River to its junction with the Darling River and beyond. The Government's object in offering the prize was to encourage trade along the Murray, and in particular to secure wool for Adelaide merchants. Both Cadell and Randall were keen to seize as much of this trade for themselves as they could.[513]

Cadell proved to be more cunning and showy than Randall. In the first place, he named his paddle steamer after Lady Augusta Young, the wife of the South Australian Governor, Sir Henry Young. Secondly, he was successful in inviting Sir Henry, members of the latter's family, other South Australian dignitaries and two Adelaide newspaper men, James Allen Jnr, the owner and editor of the *Adelaide Times*, and Edward Andrews, the editor of the *South Australian Register*, to accompany him in the *Lady Augusta* on its maiden voyage up and down the Murray River.[514] The *Lady Augusta* left Goolwa near the mouth of the Murray with crew and passengers on 25 August 1853, shortly after the departure of the *Mary Ann* from Mannum.[515]

The *Lady Augusta* reached the *Gol Gol* homestead on its voyage up the Murray River on Thursday, 8 September 1853. James Allen recorded what then occurred as follows:

> "Reached Williams's Cattle Station at half-past ten o'clock, and eased the vessel opposite to it for a quarter of an hour, while the captain and a few of the passengers went ashore. There was a crowd of natives assembled, eagerly scanning us; some of them of them of the most extraordinary growth, regular Brobdignagians. One man must have been at least six feet three inches in height.
>
> Mrs. Williams, the wife of the owner of this station, was gallantly guarding a small piece of cannon, and using the most persevering efforts to discharge it, as a salute in honor of our arrival. A native by her side, armed with a rusty carbine, kept up a continual clicking with it, in his vain endeavours to get it to go off, but both without success.

---

513 See generally John Nicholson, *The Incomparable Captain Cadell* (2004), Chap. 9.
514 See Nicholson, op. cit., pp. 134-135. James Allen wrote of his journey in the *Lady Augusta* in a book entitled *Journey of an Experimental Trip by the "Lady Augusta" on the River Murray* first published in 1853. For his part, Edward Andrews described the journey in a series of dispatches published in the *South Australian Register* under the heading "Navigation of the Murray" and under the anonymous byline of "Our Special Correspondent": see Nicholson, op. cit., p. 134.
515 See Nicholson, op. cit., pp, 137 and 141.

The carbine and the cannon (a small boat cannon) are kept by Mrs. Williams as a valuable memento of Captain Sturt's exploratory voyage down the Murray, he having brought them with him on that occasion, as also a cutlass, mounted in a brass sheath, which are always shown as precious relics.

At a quarter to eleven we were on our way again. After proceeding about half-a-mile up the river we were gratified to hear, from a shot fired from the station to our rear, that our enthusiastic friend Mrs Williams had succeeded in discharging her refractory piece — a most memorable shot."[516]

In his shorter and less colourful account of the meeting, Edward Andrews wrote:

"We were off again before daylight, and soon after breakfast reached Mr. Williams's cattle-station on the New South Wales side of the river. He was absent at the time, and his wife endeavoured to welcome us by the discharge of a small cannon, but was unable to manage it. There are about 1,000 head of stock on the run."[517]

Yet a third version of this incident was provided by John Williams in the course of the interview with him published in 1914 in the *Mildura Cultivator*. This version went as follows:

"Other memories? A smile broke out and off went the octogenarian into the tale of that wonderful old swivel gun at Gol Gol, given to Mr. Jenkins by Captain Sturt. That gun was planted on a tree stump and was used to scare away the blacks, but one day the cook took a notion to fire it off with a real charge in it to see what it would do. He loaded it up with a pannikin of powder and a pannikin of bullets and did great havoc on the trees across the river; but the swivel gun was no longer a swivel gun: the swivel was broken by the performance.

But the Gol Gol gun was not out of commission yet. It was fixed up and charged with blasting powder to salute the first steam-boat that ever steamed up the Murray. This time there were no bullets, but the wadding was a pair of child's knickerbockers! The steamer did not arrive when expected, and when it did arrive there were no men about. Out ran Mrs. Williams and, lo, the gun would not go off at her bidding. But the lady was not to be beaten. The gun went off at last, as the steamer rounded the bend above the house, and the honour of Gol Gol was saved."[518]

Both James Allen, in his account of the *Lady Augusta*'s visit to *Gol Gol* in September 1853, and John Williams, in his 1914 interview, made reference to the cannon, which Elizabeth Williams apparently had so much trouble firing in honour of the *Lady Augusta*'s arrival, as

---

516   See Allen, op. cit., p. 28.
517   See the *South Australian Register*, Saturday, 8 October 1853, p. 2.
518   See the *Mildura Cultivator*, Saturday, 23 May 1914, p. 13. See also Nicholson, op. cit., p. 144.

having originally belonged to Charles Sturt. Allen also referred to the carbine and sword he saw at *Gol Gol* as having been Sturt's.

Yet the cannon, at least, had almost certainly not belonged to Sturt. It had been sighted on *Gol Gol* at least as early as 1848.[519] However, Sturt had made his journey down the Murray River 18 years earlier than that in 1830. As mentioned earlier, Frank Jenkins took possession of *Gol Gol* in 1847, and there is no record of either Frank or Henry Williams ever having had any contact with Sturt at any time. Moreover, an exhaustive study of relevant Sturt records by Chris Whitiker in 1978 concluded that Sturt had not carried a cannon or shot with him on his 1830 expedition.[520]

There was some speculation in the early part of the Twentieth Century to the effect that the *Gol Gol* cannon had originally belonged not to Charles Sturt but rather to Major Thomas Mitchell. This speculation was fuelled when John Williams, somewhat strangely in view of his later 1914 endorsement of the cannon's Sturt origins, agreed in 1908 with a New South Wales police trooper, George Birt, that the cannon had indeed come from Mitchell. In this regard, John is reported as having stated that:

> "Mr. Birt is quite right in saying that the cannon belonged to Major Mitchell. It was left by him with Mr. Frank Jenkins, who was then residing at Gol Gol station, on the Murray, about five miles below the present site of Mildura, but on the New South Wales side. The cannon was at the station when the Williams family went to live there. Mr. Williams forgets the history of the cannon as related by his uncle, Mr. Frank Jenkins, but remembers that it was Major Mitchell's: he had often heard his uncle talk about it. For years it lay on the bank of the river."[521]

However, Mitchell's party reached the area of *Gol Gol* in 1836, a full 11 years before Frank Jenkin's arrival. Again, there is no record of Frank having ever had any contact with Mitchell at any time. Further, according to the State Library of South Australia, Captain George Johnston, another Murray River navigator, and a cannon collector to boot, had acquired Mitchell's cannon, and had blown it up when he tried to fire it![522]

It therefore seems highly unlikely that either Frank Jenkins or Henry Williams acquired

---

519   In 1848, a 13 years old Thomas O'Shaughnessy accompanied his father on a cattle drive from the Lachlan River to Adelaide. En route, they stopped for a time at *Gol Gol*. O'Shaughnessy subsequently recalled in his Diary:
   "We travelled down the Murray River to Jenkins's station on a high bank over the river. At this station they had a small swivel gun mounted on a stump. Sometime previous the blacks were troublesome. I believe the owners had to use this gun."
   In 1857, O'Shaughnessy returned to *Gol Gol* with his wife on his way from South Australia to Cowra. He noted in his diary:
   "24 [June] Crossed the carts over the Darling in a boat and swam the horses across and went to Williams Station. We fired an old cannon off after dark."
   See Frank Murray, *My Early Pioneers and Their Lives* (http://tinyurl.com/y4zh9y5f) and (http://tinyurl.com/rguj5vu) (both at 5 March 2020).

520   See Chris Whitiker, "Captain Charles Sturt's Cannon?": (1978) 79 *Proceedings of the Royal Geographical Society of Australasia, South Australian Branch* 38-42.

521   See *The Advertiser*, Monday, 10 August 1908, p. 8.

522   See State Library of South Australia, "Did you know?: Captain Sturt's cannon" in *S A Memory: Downstream: the River Murray in South Australia* (http://tinyurl.com/y3699pmr) (at 5 March 2020).

the *Gol Gol* cannon from either Charles Sturt or Thomas Mitchell. Frank probably brought the cannon to *Gol Gol* in the late 1840s for the protection of his employees in the event of an Aboriginal attack. He may, indeed, have brought it with him in 1847 when originally searching for his Murray River run. He could have purchased the cannon on the open market: similar swivel guns were apparently readily available to buyers in the 1840s.

One further intriguing possibility as to the *Gol Gol* cannon's provenance might be suggested. Frank Jenkins' cousin, John Clark, apparently mounted a swivel gun on his *Perricoota* run near Moama on the Murray River shortly after taking up that run in 1841.[523] Frank was undoubtedly in contact with John Clark and his family from time to time over the years.[524] Could Clark have provided Frank with the swivel gun formerly located on *Perricoota* in order that Frank could take it to *Gol Gol*?

Whatever the origins of the *Gol Gol* cannon, it would appear that Henry Williams ultimately presented it before he left the *Gol Gol* run to Captain George Johnston. In 1907, Johnston's widow donated the cannon to the Royal Geographical Society of Australasia, South Australian Branch. Installed in a gun carriage constructed for it in 1971, the cannon is now on display in the South Australian Maritime Museum at Port Adelaide.[525]

On Thursday, 6 October 1853, the *Lady Augusta* stopped once more at the *Gol Gol* homestead in the course of its return journey down the Murray River. On this occasion, there was no cannon fire welcome — delayed or otherwise. Edward Andrews wrote of this second visit:

> "At a quarter to 6 we reached Mr, Williams's cattle-station on the New South Wales side of the river. He was absent when we passed before, taking his eldest daughter to school in Adelaide, and had now just returned. He has a fine family, whose bright eyes and ruddy cheeks attest the salubrity of the situation. We remained about an hour, walking through his dairy and garden, from both of which we received several welcome presents."[526]

---

523   See *The Argus*, Tuesday, 25 January 1876, p. 6; Helen Coulson, *Echuca — Moama: Murray River Neighbours* (2009), pp. 91 and 119; and Judi Hearn, *Galleries of Pink Galahs: A History of the Shire of Murray 1838-1988* (2009), p. 20. See also p. 17 above.

524   See p. 110 above.

525   See Alexandrina Library Service, *History Room News* (No. 67, February 2010) (http://tinyurl.com/y48geclq) (at 6 March 2020); State Library of South Australia, "Did you know?: Captain Sturt's cannon" in *S A Memory: Downstream: the River Murray in South Australia* (http://tinyurl.com/y3699pmr) (at 6 March 2020); and Royal Geographical Society of South Australia Inc., *Relics and Artefacts — Sturt's Cannon* (http://tinyurl.com/v4vk4nd) (at 6 March 2020). See also **photo 37**.

526   See the *South Australian Register*, Friday, 14 October 1853, p. 2. The *Mary Ann* ultimately won the unofficial race with the *Lady Augusta* on the Murray River in 1853. However, by virtue of his superior connections and showmanship, Cadell managed to ensure that he received the lion's share of the South Australian Government's prize money: see Nicholson, op. cit., pp. 153-154. See also Drawing of the *Lady Augusta* and the *Mary Ann* at Swan Hill (1853).

Looking Northwards

In or shortly prior to 1860, the Williams family turned their eyes northwards from *Gol Gol* with a view to taking up a cattle run in Queensland. In 1860, Elizabeth and Henry Williams' older sons secured such a run in the lower Warrego District of south-western Queensland, to the north of present-day Cunnamulla. They called their run *Coongoola* after the local Aboriginal name for a waterhole near where they built their homestead.[527]

Although the *Coongoola* run was taken up in the names of the Williams' older sons, some at least of their younger siblings soon joined their older brothers on the run. Henry Williams no doubt visited the property from time to time in its earliest days. However, it seems likely that he remained for the most part with Elizabeth and his youngest children on *Gol Gol* and, at times, on the Williams' McLaren Vale property.

What motivated the Williams' sons to move to the Warrego District is unknown. However, the family appears to have been close over the years to Elizabeth Williams's younger brother, Frank Jenkins. Not only did they acquire occupancy rights to *Gol Gol* from him, but some members of the family may well have dummied for Frank in his fight to beat off selectors from seeking to encroach on his Riverina runs.[528] It's known that Frank Jenkins held a Queensland run by 1876 at the latest, and that he acquired three further runs in the Warrego District a little to the north of *Coongoola* in 1887.[529] It is possible that it was Frank who sparked the Williams' interest in Queensland grazing property. However, given the dates involved, it seems more likely that it was the Williams family who inspired Frank to acquire his grazing lands in that Colony.

In their early days at *Coongoola*, the Williams brothers were touched by the ill-fated Burke and Wills expedition.

It will be recalled that Robert O'Hara Burke and William John Wills led an expedition during 1860 and 1861 organised by the Royal Society of Victoria. The object of the expedition was to cross the continent of Australia from south to north and back again; exploring the inland and pursuing scientific goals. The expedition turned out to be a disaster. Although Burke and Wills did almost reach the Gulf of Carpentaria on 9 February 1861, both died at Cooper's Creek in south-western Queensland; Burke on 28 June 1861 and Wills a day or two later.[530]

---

527 See Kenton Cameron, "Ridley Williams, Early Queensland Pastoralist" in (1960) 6(2) *Journal of the Royal Historical Society of Queensland* 342.
528 See p. 123 above.
529 See p. 106.
530 See *Wikipedia — Burke and Wills Expedition* (http://tinyurl.com/yyxme3q3) (at 6 March 2020). Burke died on 28 June 1861. The last entry in Wills' Diary was apparently written on 29 June 1861: Ibid.

According to John Williams, his younger brother, Henry Williams Jnr, having determined not to join the Burke and Wills expedition, provided its members with some sage advice and practical assistance. According to John:

> "Only Henry Williams' doubt of Burke's bushmanship had prevented him from joining their party. At his meeting with them before they started, he noted that they had water-bags of tanned leather and warned them of the folly. A trial of one of the bags was made: the water from it was of course not fit to drink and the bags were abandoned. Henry Williams then made them a water-bag from a fresh calf-skin, and for a further supply advised them to send to Wentworth for canvass, which they did."[531]

Tragically, it appears that the Williams' second and third sons, Henry Williams Jnr and Francis Williams, were not far from Burke and Wills at about the time that the latter two were dying alongside Cooper's Creek. On 22 June 1861, the two young Williams men set out on horseback from the upper Darling River, heading roughly north-west in an exploratory journey. They were accompanied by another young pastoralist, John Neilson, who had settled on a cattle run a few kilometres to the north of *Coongoolla*.[532] Their object was probably to spy out new grazing land. The three men turned back to begin their return journey on 28 June 1861: the day John O'Hara Burke died. In a letter Neilson wrote to William Landsborough on 22 May 1862 describing the route he and the Williams brothers had taken, Neilson described their position when they turned back:

> "I consider our position to be within about thirty-five miles [about 56 km] of Cooper's Creek."[533]

The three men would, of course, have been totally unaware at the time of the men expiring about a day or two's ride from them.

By 21 May 1862, the Williams brothers were aware that the bodies of Burke and Wills had recently been discovered by a Victorian search party led by Alfred Howitt.[534] On 21 May 1862,

---

[531] See the *Mildura Cultivator*, Saturday, 23 May 1914, p. 13. It is not likely that Henry Williams Jnr had his meeting with the Burke and Wills party in Melbourne prior to the party's departure. Canvas for water bags would have been readily available in Victoria's capital. It is more likely that the meeting took place in Swan Hill, or perhaps, Menindee, as the expedition moved north.

[532] See the *Queensland Times, Ipswich Herald and General Advertiser*, Thursday, 28 January 1864, p. 3; and *Pugh's Queensland Almanac* (1867), pp. 190-191 (http://tinyurl.com/yynlc2zo) (at 6 March 2020).

[533] See William Landsborough, *Journal of Landsborough's Expedition From Carpentaria In Search of Burke and Wills* (1862), p. 122. See also the *Mildura Cultivator*, Saturday, 23 May 1914, p. 13; Australian Stockman's Hall of Fame, *Ridley Williams: Detailed Report* (No. USH 00063); and Leslie Jenkins, *A Brief History of Quilpie Shire* (2001), p. 9. William Landsborough was born in Scotland in 1825 and migrated to New South Wales in 1841. After engaging in an unsuccessful search in 1851 for traces of the missing explorer Ludwig Leichhardt, he was engaged in 1861 by the Victorian and Queensland Colonial Governments to search for Burke and Wills from the Gulf of Carpentaria southwards. He later served as a Member of the New South Wales Legislative Council, as a Police Magistrate, as a surveyor and as an alluvial tin miner. He died in 1886: see Gwen Trundle, "Landsborough, William (1825-1886)" in *Australian Dictionary of Biography* (http://tinyurl.com/n7x9tu68) (at 6 March 2020).

[534] See *Wikipedia — Burke and Wills Expedition* (http://tinyurl.com/yyxme3q3) (at 6 March 2020).

one of the brothers, whose first name is presently unascertained, was able to advise Landsborough of Howitt's melancholy discovery. At the time, Landsborough was leading a Queensland search party and making his second unsuccessful attempt to locate Burke and Wills. Following the Warrego River in a south-easterly direction, he and his party eventually arrived at *Coongoola*. In his Journal, Landsborough described his arrival and reception as follows:

> "This morning we followed down the river for about two and three-quarter miles in a south and by east direction, and reached the station occupied by Mr. Williams, where we were received in a most hospitable reception and learnt the unfortunate fate of Burke and Wills. Here I took sights and made the meridian altitude of the sun A. H. 83 degrees 85 minutes. The latitude is by that observation 27 degrees 38 minutes."[535]

The following day, 22 May 1862, Landsborough sold his party's surplus supplies to Williams and purchased extra rations from him.[536] Landsborough left *Coongoola* on 23 May 1862. He described his departure in his Journal thus;

> "As the road was indistinct, Messrs. Williams kindly accompanied us to the stage, about two and a half miles this side of the station, where they showed us the tree marked by Mr Kennedy K XIX. The horsemanship and bushmanship displayed by these young Australians were very remarkable. A large portion of my life has been spent in the bush, yet dray-tracks that I could only follow at a few places, they evidently considered at all places a plain road."[537]

At the time when the Williams brothers took it up, *Coongoola* was an isolated cattle run. The

---

535 See Landsborough, op. cit., pp. 61 and 118. See also Leslie Jenkins, op. cit., p. 8.

536 See Landsborough, op. cit., p. 118. In his Journal, Landsborough detailed these transactions in the following manner:
"Today we made preparations for proceeding to the Darling River. I sold to Mr. Williams the following articles: Carbine 4 pounds; Enfield rifle 3 pounds; revolver (Colt) small size 4 pounds 10 shillings; cartridges for revolver 12 shillings; steelyards [straight-beam balances] 5 shillings; pick and shovel 5 shillings; 2½ pounds of powder 10 shillings; cartouche box [ammunition box] 5 shillings; shoeing tools 15 shillings; four sets horseshoes 8 shillings; spokeshave [a tool used to shape and smooth cart wheel spokes] etc. 4 shillings; 1¼ boxes gun caps 9 shillings; three powder flasks (one damaged) 3 shillings; cleaning rod for gun etc. 4 shillings; three boxes gun caps (broken) and pistol cleaning rod 6 shillings; 6 yards canvas (damaged) 6 shillings; nine saddle-girths (partly damaged) 14 Shillings; 6 pound nails and screws at 1 shilling and 6 pence; medicine 10 shillings; frying pan 2 shillings; two packsaddles (broken) 2 pounds; crupper [a strap attached to the back of a saddle and looped under a horse's tail to prevent the saddle from sliding forward on the horse's back] 4 shillings and 6 pence. Total 19 pounds 13 shillings and 6 pence. And bought the following supplies: 100 pounds of flour 2 pounds 10 shillings; 24 pounds of sugar 18 shillings; 3 pounds of tea 12 shillings; one bar of soap 4 shillings. Total 4 pounds 4 shillings. The money Mr Williams gave for stores was a higher amount than would have been obtained at a township by public auction. Neither did he purchase them so much because he wanted them as to oblige me. He also supplied us with as much beef and butter as we requested to take with us, and would not accept payment for any supplies that were raised by themselves."
Landsborough, op. cit., pp. 118-119.

537 Landsborough, op. cit., p. 119. Edmund Kennedy was a Guernsey-born explorer in the mid-Nineteenth Century. As an Assistant Surveyor in New South Wales, he was directed in 1847 by the Surveyor General, Major Thomas Mitchell, to lead an expedition to determine whether or not Mitchell's "Victoria" River (now the Barcoo River) flowed into the Gulf of Carpentaria. Having ascertained that it did not, and instead joined Cooper's Creek flowing south-westwards into Lake Eyre, Kennedy led his party along the Warrego River for some distance on his return journey: see Edgar Beale, "Kennedy, Edmund Besley (1818-1848)" in *Australian Dictionary of Biography* (http://tinyurl.com/s47zyme) (7 March 2020); and *Wikipedia — Edmund Kennedy* (http://tinyurl.com/ujue9tr) (7 March 2020). During this expedition, Kennedy must have incised a survey mark on the tree shown by the Williams brothers to Landsborough.

brothers secured their supplies from Bourke in New South Wales, over 300 km to the south. In turn, those supplies were brought up the Darling River by barge to Bourke.[538] With a frontage on the left bank of the Warrego River, *Coongoola* was said to have a carrying capacity of 2,000 head of cattle.[539] By 1864, the brothers were also occupying a smaller outstation which they named *Teckulman*. Like *Coongoola*, this run was located on the Warrago River. It lay some 35 km to the south of *Coongoola* and was said to be capable of carrying over 500 head of cattle in its own right.[540]

It is presently unclear which of the Williams brothers were lessees of *Coongoola,* and *Teckuman*. It seems likely that Henry Williams Jnr and Francis Williams, at least, were lessees from the outset.[541] John Williams may have been as well. However, the names of the lessees almost certainly changed from time to time over the years of the Williams family's occupancy of the runs. It may also be that John Neilson was an early, if short-lived, co-lessee of *Coongoola*.[542]

---

538 See Cameron, op. cit., p. 342.

539 See the *Queensland Times, Ipswich Herald and General Advertiser*, Thursday, 28 January 1864, p. 3; and *Pugh's Queensland Almanac* (1867), p. 191 (http://tinyurl.com/yynlc2zo) (at 7 March 2020). In 1875, the Williams brothers were able to ship 350 head of cattle from *Coongoola* to Adelaide: see the *Sydney Mail and New South Wales Advertiser*, Saturday, 25 September 1875, p. 390.

540 See the *Queensland Times, Ipswich Herald and General Advertiser*, Thursday, 28 January 1864, p. 3; and *Pugh's Queensland Almanac* (1867), p. 191 (http://tinyurl.com/yynlc2zo) (at 7 March 2020).

541 See p. 147 above.

542 Ibid.

Last Days and Descendants

On 15 August 1865, Elizabeth Williams died whilst under medical care in Wentworth. On her Death Certificate, her cause of death was said to "abscess of the liver" from which she had suffered for some seven months prior to her death. She was just 47 years old when she died. Elizabeth was buried on 17 August 1865 in the cemetery on *Gol Gol*.[543]

Following the death of his wife, it seems that Henry Williams moved with his younger children to live on *Coongoola* with his older sons. He would have been around 62 years of age at the time of this move, and he likely lived in semi-retirement on the run. At some point in time in the late 1870s, he moved from *Coongoola* to live with his eldest daughter, Eliza Dreyer (née Williams) and her family in their home on Wright Street West in Adelaide.[544] He died there on 12 March 1879, aged 76 years old. He was interred two days later in the West Terrace Cemetery in Adelaide.[545]

Following the death of his sister, Elizabeth Williams, and the departure of most, if not all, of her family to south-western Queensland, Frank Jenkins sold his leasehold interest in the *Gol Gol* run to the brothers Frederick and George Peppin.[546] A few years later, the Peppins onsold their interest in *Gol Gol* to a Robert Patterson. He greatly enlarged the run, so that it came to incorporate Lake Mungo and more of the remaining Willandra Lakes. This vastly enhanced *Gol Gol* run was finally broken up in 1921.[547]

Elizabeth and Henry Williams were the progenitors of a large Williams family line. Perhaps putting things more accurately, they were the progenitors of a number of large Williams family lines. They were survived by numerous children, and now have a legion of descendants. The exploits of some of their children, and in particular of their tenth child, Ridley Williams, will be explored in some detail below.

---

543 See *New South Wales Register of Births, Deaths and Marriages — Deaths: Elizabeth Williams* (No. 2480/1865).

544 As earlier noted, Eliza Williams married Edward Dreyer on 29 August 1861: see footnote 511 on p. 141 above. The marriage took place at Eliza's parents' house in McLaren Vale. Eliza and Edward had a total of eight children together: see *Geni — Eliza Williams* (http://tinyurl.com/svwalpb) (at 7 March 2020); and *Geni — Carl Edward William Dreyer* (http://tinyurl.com/u6s4vp2) (at 7 March 2020). Edward was born Karl Eduard Wilhelm Dreyer in Hannover, Germany in 1834. He emigrated from Bremen to Adelaide with his parents and siblings on the *Heloise* in 1847. In Adelaide, he initially worked as a hairdresser before becoming a publican. Over time, he was the licensee of a number of Adelaide hotels. These included the *Prince Albert* (1852-1865), the *Crown* (1866), the *Ship Inn* (1868-1871), the *Golden Fleece* (1871), the *Ship Inn* again (1873-1875) and the *Prince Albert* again (1875-1876): see Reg Butler, "South Australian Publicans — Carl Dreyer" in *Localwiki: Adelaide Hills*; and the *South Australian Register*, Tuesday, 13 March 1866, p. 3. On 27 July 1866, Edward joined the South Australian Volunteer Force Cavalry on a part-time basis: see the *South Australian Register*, Friday, 3 August 1866, p. 3. Edward died in Adelaide on 26 September 1876: see *Geni — Carl Edward William Dreyer* (http://tinyurl.com/u6s4vp2) (at 7 March 2020); and Eliza Dreyer on 18 August 1897, also in Adelaide: see *The Advertiser*, Thursday, 19 August 1897, p. 4; and *Geni — Eliza Williams* (http://tinyurl.com/svwalpb) (at 7 March 2020).

545 See the *South Australian Advertiser*, Saturday, 15 March 1879, p. 4; the *Express and Telegraph*, Saturday, 15 March 1879, p. 3; and the *South Australian Chronicle and Weekly Mail*, Saturday, 22 March 1879, p. 6.

546 See Jane Lennon, *Pastoral Australia: Fortress, Failures and Hard Yakka: An Historical Overview* (2010), p. 70.

547 See New South Wales Parks and Wildlife Service, *Mungo: 1788-1901*, at p.15 (http://tinyurl.com/yxg79g9g) (at 7 March 2020).

RIDLEY FREDERICK WILLIAMS
(1850 — 1922)

Early Days in Queensland

As mentioned earlier, Ridley Williams, the tenth child of Elizabeth and Henry Williams, was born on *Gol Gol* shortly prior to 6 March 1850.[548] It seems likely that he was taken by his father to his older brothers' *Coongoola* run in Queensland shortly after his mother's death in 1865. Ridley apparently thrived in outback Queensland. He grew up to be both a fine horseman and a superb bushman.

Between 1865 and 1876, a number of the Williams brothers, ultimately including Ridley, acquired leasehold interests in a total of 18 further pastoral properties to the north-west of *Coongoola*. These properties, which were in essence contiguous, were acquired as follows:

- Fairlie Plains: taken up on 15 August 1865 (about 130 square kilometres);
- Fairlie Plains West: taken up on 7 October 1865 (about 130 square kilometres);
- Bierbank: taken up on 20 February 1867 (about 130 square kilometres);
- Haredean East: taken up on 23 February 1868 (about 130 square kilometres);
- Injuringa: taken up on 13 November 1868 (about 130 square kilometres);
- Yarron Plains: taken up on 18 November 1868 (about 120 square kilometres);
- Haredean West: taken up on 8 December 1868 (about 130 square kilometres);
- Quilberry: taken up on 19 January 1869 (about 130 square kilometres);
- Maroochoo: taken up on 19 January 1869 (about 130 square kilometres);
- Bierbank East: taken up on 23 January 1869 (about 130 square kilometres);
- Wokolena: taken up on 12 November 1874 (about 75 square kilometres);
- Yeatman: taken up on 15 November 1874 (about 70 square kilometres);
- Bierbank West: taken up on 3 January 1875 (about 65 square kilometres);
- Munberry North: taken up on 12 August 1876 (about 166 square kilometres);
- Munberry South: taken up on 12 August 1876 (about 110 square kilometres);
- Altanau: taken up on 18 October 1876 (about 272 square miles);
- Avron: taken up on 18 December 1876 (about 115 square kilometres); and
- The Cool: taken up on 30 December 1876 (about 65 square kilometres).[549]

In all, these 18 additional pastoral blocks, centred on the Beechal Creek (a tributary of the Paroo River), covered a vast area of around 2,228 square kilometres. Together with their *Coongoola* and *Teckulman* runs, the Williams brothers came to occupy over 3,000 square kilometres

---

[548] See *Ancestry — Elizabeth Jane Jenkins* (http://tinyurl.com/y6raf4tm) (at 7 March 2020). See also note 510 on p. 141; and photo **38**.

[549] See Jenkins, op. cit., p. 22.

of Warrego District land.[550] However, the total area they occupied was reduced in 1878 when they sold their interests in *Coongoola* (and, presumably, in its outstation, *Teckulman*) to a client of the London Chartered Bank.[551] It is not presently known why the brothers sold their interests in these properties. It may have been to raise capital to assist in the development of their remaining properties. More likely, the sale proceeds may have been used to buy out one or more of the brothers who wished to move elsewhere.

If the Williams brothers had one abiding recreational interest whilst they lived and worked in the Warrego District, it was horse racing. As Kenton Cameron put it:

> "Being all horse lovers, they were keen racing men and were regarded as true sportsmen. Their horses competed at all the local race meetings: Charleville, Cunnamulla, Adavale, Thargomindah and as far distant as Bourke, New South Wales. Jim Williams was the most noted and successful in this field."[552]

Not all of Elizabeth and Henry Williams' children moved to south-western Queensland. Their oldest child, John Henry Williams, married Marion Wilson in Willunga, South Australia on 1 April 1858.[553] It is likely that he brought Marion back to live on *Gol Gol*. However, in 1865, and probably following his mother's death, John moved with his wife and children to a property on the Murray River at Curlwaa near Wentworth which they named Williamsville. John developed the first orchard in the district on that property.[554] John and Marion Williams subsequently moved to Melbourne, where John died on 10 October 1922.[555]

As earlier mentioned, Elizabeth and Henry Williams' eldest daughter, Eliza Williams, married Edward Dreyer on 29 August 1861 in McLaren Vale.[556] Dreyer may well have partnered the Williams brothers from the outset in their acquisition of Queensland runs. He is certainly on record as having been a co-lessee of the *Bierbank* run.[557] However, with his hotel interests in Adelaide, it is doubtful whether he or his wife Eliza ever lived on one of the Queensland properties. Dreyer's interests in the runs may have simply been those of an investor.[558]

Others among Ridley Williams' siblings did not live foe long on the family's remote Warrego

---

550   See *Wikitree — Ridley Frederick Williams (1850-1922)* (http://tinyurl.com/y4f2sxh3) (at 8 March 2020).

551   See Cameron, op. cit., p. 343.

552   Ibid.

553   See *Wikitree — John Henry Williams (1833-1922)* (http://tinyurl.com/y33q5zjr) (at 8 March 2020).

554   See Shire of Wentworth, *Heritage Study: Williamsville Homestead (No. 55)* (http://tinyurl.com/y3bsrh3c) (at 8 March 2020).

555   See *Wikitree — John Henry Williams (1833-1922)* (http://tinyurl.com/y33q5zjr) (at 8 March 2020).

556   See footnote 511 on p. 141 and footnote 544 on p. 150, both above.

557   In a Queensland Land Board Notice dated 21 March 1887, Edward William Dreyer, together with Francis Williams, Thomas Williams, George Williams, Ridley Williams and Robert Williams, are recorded as being the lessees of the *Bierbank* run; this notwithstanding that Dreyer died in 1876: see *Queensland State Archives* ("*QSA*"), Series 218 Pastoral Holdings Files, Item 437408. It is not presently known which of the Williams brothers named in the Notice, other than Ridley and Robert Williams, and perhaps Thomas Williams, were still physically occupying *Bierbank* in 1887: see Jenkins, op. cit., p. 23. Robert Williams died on the run on 22 August 1900: see footnote 655 on p. 178 below.

558   See *Roots Web — Eliza Williams* (http://tinyurl.com/y2afez82) (at 8 March 2020). It might be noted that all eight of Eliza and Edward Dreyer's eight children were born in Adelaide: Ibid. Moreover, Henry Williams moved in the late 1870s to live with Eliza and her family at their home in Adelaide: see p. 150 above.

properties; either moving away or dying. Henry Williams Jnr, for one, died in Brisbane on 7 March 1869.[559] He was barely 33 years old when he died.

In 1880, all 18 of the Williams brothers leased properties in the Warrego District were consolidated into one. Initially known as *Ingringbar*, the consolidated pastoral land was subsequently renamed *Bierbank*. Following this consolidation, Ridley Williams appears to have become the chief manager of the property.[560]

Towards the middle of 1882, Ridley Williams instructed a Charleville land agent, T. S. Sword, to make application on his behalf to the Queensland Government for the purchase of two blocks of vacant Crown land in the small village of Adavale to the north of *Bierbank*. Each of the two blocks, Allotment 9 of Section 4 and Allotment 8 of Section 9, was 2 roods [0.5 of an acre or 0.2 of a hectare] in area. Sword lodged the applications on 19 July 1882.[561] They were approved on 1 September 1882. Ridley paid £5.14.2 for each block. It appears that no building was ever constructed on either block, and it is not presently known when or to whom Ridley ultimately disposed of the blocks of land.

The Williams brothers stocked *Bierbank* with prime Shorthorn cattle. However, by the early 1880s, cattle raising in Australia was proving to be not particularly profitable. In the words of Kenton Cameron:

> "The overseas frozen beef trade had not been developed and was yet only a pleasant fancy. Cattle numbers were rapidly increasing, and stations were becoming overstocked, with no means of the owners disposing of them."[562]

For pastoralists in the Warrego District, whose markets were chiefly in Victoria, the long distances involved in servicing those markets with meat on the hoof made life even more difficult.

Notwithstanding Ridley's purchase of the Adavale properties, he and his brothers were apparently sufficiently disheartened by their economic prospects on *Bierbank* towards the end of 1882 that they sought to sell their interest in the run. Through agents in Adelaide, W. Gordon & Co., an auction of the property, together with 10,000 head of cattle, was held at the Adelaide Town Hall Exchange Room on 24 November 1882. The auction was not a success and the property was passed in.[563] No further attempt seems to have been made by the Williams' brothers to sell *Bierbank*.

---

[559] See the *Queenslander*, Saturday, 13 March 1869, p. 1.

[560] See Cameron, op. cit., p. 343. It might be of interest to note that one of Australia's rarest birds, the night parrot (Geopsittacus occidentalis), is likely to be found living elusively on *Bierbank* land. A pair of the birds were apparently sighted nearby in 1972: see A. C. Cameron, "Possible Sight Record of the Night Parrot *Geopsittacus Occidentalis*" in (1972) 8(4) *The Sunbird* 87. See also Penny Olsen, *Night Parrot: Australia's Most Elusive Bird* (2018), p. 237.

[561] See *QSA*, Series 14078 Sale of Crown Lands after Auction, Items 78292 and 78293.

[562] See Cameron, op. cit., p. 343. See also p. 125 above.

[563] See the *South Australian Register*, Wednesday, 22 November 1882, p. 7.

The Barrow Creek Cattle Drive

Late 1882 also witnessed the genesis of an epic cattle drive directed by Ridley Williams from *Bierbank* in south-western Queensland to Barrow Creek in what was then the Northern Territory of South Australia. An astute businessman as well as being at home in the saddle in outback Australia, Ridley negotiated a contract for sale and delivery of 2,000 head of cows to Andrew Wooldridge, David Murray and John Brodie Spence, of the Barrow Creek Pastoral Company, for £2.10.0 a head. Wooldridge, Murray and Spence had established their *Barrow Creek Station* on some 51,800 square kilometres of land which they had leased from the South Australian Government. The run was centred on the Barrow Creek, about 300 km to the north of present-day Alice Springs. At the time, it was the largest property held by any person, persons or company in Australia.[564]

Ridley Williams' Barrow Creek cattle drive was to take him away from *Bierbank* for around 22 months in all. The cows were driven over more than 2,500 km of territory only partially explored by Europeans. They were taken through the Channel Country and across land to the immediate north of the Simpson Desert. The cattle and their drovers were faced with crossing stony ranges and stretches of deep sand. Today, the Donohue Highway in Queensland and the linked Plenty Highway in the Northern Territory, both in the main still unsealed tracks, trace a substantial portion of the route taken.

Undoubtedly, the largest problems faced by Ridley, his drovers and his cattle were scarcity and unreliability of water. The cattle were frequently kept for days, sometimes weeks and on occasions months, at reliable watering points whilst Ridley either explored ahead for more sources of water or waited for rain to fill waterholes in ephemeral rivers and creeks.

According to the diary Ridley kept of the cattle drive, he divided the cows at *Bierbank* into two mobs of 1,000 cows each. He placed Charles ("Charlie") Lowe in charge of one of the mobs and Charlie's brother, Frederick ("Fred") Lowe in charge of the other. Each was allocated five men (including a cook), a dray loaded with rations and supplies, draught horses and saddle horses.[565]

---

[564] See *The News* (Adelaide), Monday, 2 March 1925, p. 9; and Cameron, op. cit., p. 344. At £2.10.0 per cow, the contract with Wooldridge, Murray and Spence for the sale and delivery of 2,000 head was potentially worth £5,000 to the Williams brothers' *Bierbank* partnership. In present-day Australian dollars, that would be the equivalent of over $644,500: see Thom Blake, *How Much Is It Worth* (http://tinyurl.com/y2w86obz) (at 8 March 2020). However, as will be seen later, Ridley Williams was ultimately unable to deliver the full 2,000 cows to the Barrow Creek Pastoral Company. The total price paid by the company for the cows is unknown.

[565] Ridley Williams left a hand-written diary containing a vivid account of his epic cattle drive to Barrow Creek. At some unknown point in time, this passed into the hands of Estella Grace Margherita ("Grace") Bignell (née Williams), who was a daughter of Ridley's brother, James Williams. In about 1958, Grace Bignell apparently provided the diary to Robert Purvis, of *Woodgreen Station* to the north-east of Alice Springs. Robert Purvis and his wife, Adela Viola Purvis (née Zimmerman), were both keen local historians; with Adela Purvis being the founder of the National Trust of Australia (Northern Territory). Robert Purvis typed a copy of Ridley Williams' diary. His transcript is now to be found as part of Book 2 of an unpublished collection of documents compiled by Adela Purvis and entitled *Heroes Unsung* ("*Ridley Williams' Diary*"). This is to be

The drovers set off with both mobs of cattle in April 1883. They were accompanied by a herd of bulls under the charge of a stockman, Richard Batton. Like the Williams brothers' cows, Batton's bulls were bound for the *Barrow Creek Station*. It seems that Batton had his own contract with Wooldridge, Murray and Spence to move the bulls from Queensland to the Northern Territory.[566] During the drive, the bulls were allowed to run with the cows. In the result, a number of calves were born en route. These calves were routinely killed by the drovers so that the movement of the cattle was not impeded.

Ridley Williams did not initially accompany the drovers on the Barrow Creek cattle drive. He was held back by his need to muster a further 500 head of cattle on *Bierbank* for consignment to Sydney. However, in early June 1883, he received word from Charlie Lowe that the cattle had reached the *Diamantina Lakes Station* in the Channel Country, but that "pleuro" (contagious bovine pleuropneumonia) had broken out in the herd. Ridley, together with a station hand, Richard ("Red Dick") Hadlow, left *Bierbank* on 17 June 1883 with vaccine to inoculate the cattle.[567]

Ridley and Hadlow travelled roughly north and then west towards the *Diamantina Lakes Station*.[568] They apparently found the weather trying. Ridley noted that:

> "My companion remarked at times when we were crossing the downs to the west of Jundah, where the wind blew fit to almost freeze us in the mornings, that a man could enjoy himself here with nothing on but a pair of spurs or a pair of spectacles.... At other times, he would remark that this would be a nice place to be on a summer's day with a dry waterbag and under the shade of a wire fence; which, by the way, were very scarce in these parts...."[569]

On reaching the *Diamantina Lakes Station*, Ridley was given permission by the Manager, A. E. Shaw, to erect and occupy a yard on the Mayne River to inoculate the cattle. After about three weeks, he was able to move the herd onwards in a north-westerly direction to the Burke River below Boulia. Leaving the cattle at that River and its water. Ridley rode westwards with Hadlow to explore for more water and the best way forward. Travelling up the Georgina

---

found in the Alice Springs Library. Shortly before her death in about 1975, Adela Purvis published an article in the *Journal of the Royal Historical Society of Queensland* (Vol. 9(3), 1972, p. 107) entitled "Concerning The Meeting Of The Ross And Mills Parties North Of Alice Springs March 18, 1871". In footnote 32 on p. 134 of the article, she noted:

"The original Ridley Williams Diary is in the possession of the writer, destined for inclusion in the proposed Historical Library of the Alice Springs Municipal Council. Copy in Commonwealth Archives, Canberra, A. C. T."

As mentioned above, the Alice Springs Library has the typescript copy of *Ridley Williams' Diary*. However, it does not possess the original, hand-written document. Following Adela Purvis' death, her papers were deposited with the National Archives in Canberra. Enquiries have revealed that the papers were subsequently transferred to the Northern Territory Archives Service in Darwin. They remain there; as yet unexamined and uncatalogued under the name of "Adela Viola Zimmerman". In the extracts from *Ridley Williams' Diary* that follow, some corrections to spelling and punctuation have been made to assist with readability. Ridley's preparation for the cattle drive are recorded at p. 50 of *Ridley Williams' Diary*. See also Cameron, op. cit., p. 344.

566 See the *Border Watch*, Thursday, 12 May 1927, p. 2.
567 See *Ridley Williams' Diary*, p. 50.
568 What was once the *Diamantina Lakes Station* is now largely part of the *Diamantina National Park*.
569 See *Ridley Williams' Diary*, p. 50.

River, the pair eventually reached Lake Idamea and the nearby homestead on *Glenormiston Station*.[570]

Leaving *Glenormiston Station*, Ridley and Hadlow rode in a north-westerly direction up the Linda Creek. This took them into the Toko Gorge in the Toko Range, and ultimately up on to the tablelands at the top of that Range. As they explored the area, they found a number of small waterholes. On seeing a tree near one of these waterholes which had been engraved with the inscription "CB/81", Ridley named the waterhole "Potjostler Waterhole" in tribute to William ("Potjostler") Carr-Boyd, who had explored the area in 1881.[571]

As Ridley and Hadlow travelled, they supplemented the food which they had brought with them with ducks, pigeons, and galahs which they shot. These they either grilled over the coals of fires or stewed in boiling water.[572]

After exploring for a while longer, Ridley decided to return to the cattle at the Burke River and bring them up to the head of the Linda Creek and the tablelands and waterholes on top of the Toko Range. He and Hadlow took about a week to get back to the herd. Moving the cattle towards the Toko Range, Ridley received permission from the Manager of the *Herbert Downs Station*, Jerome Walford, to spell the animals on that run for a further week. Ridley and Hadlow used this time to explore further west in an attempt to find water for the herd towards the head of the Mulligan River. They arrived at the *Sandringham Station* homestead on that River on the same day as did the surveyor and explorer, Charles Winnecke, who was travelling north on a survey which had commenced in the Flinders Ranges of South Australia. Winnecke was able to provide Ridley with some useful insights as to what he could expect after he had entered the Northern Territory.[573]

Ridley and Hadlow continued riding up to the head of the Mulligan River. Finding that the watering points to be found there were inferior to those near the head of the Linda Creek, they made their way back to the *Herbert Downs Station*. There, Hadlow left Ridley and his party and returned east. Ridley immediately moved the herd up to the head of the Linda Creek. Utilising the stock watering points available there, he established a camp which he called "Depot No. 1".[574]

At Depot No. 1, Ridley paid off a few of his drovers who he deemed to be no longer required for the cattle drive. He then made a number of further exploratory trips on his own through surrounding areas. After a time resting back at Depot No. 1, he set out again to look for reliable

---

570 Ibid.

571 See *Ridley Williams' Diary*, p. 52. Ridley was correct in concluding that the tree had indeed been marked by William Carr-Boyd; an explorer, prospector and raconteur who was widely referred to as "Potjostler". Carr-Boyd had explored in and around the Toko Range in 1881: see Mary Durack, "Carr-Boyd, William Henry James (1852-1925)" in *Australian Dictionary of Biography* (http://tinyurl.com/y6mkl4vt) (at 9 March 2020).

572 See *Ridley Williams' Diary*, p. 52. Like many others in inland Australia then and now, Ridley referred to these pigeons as "topknot pigeons". However, given that topknot pigeons only have a coastal distribution, it appears likely that the pigeons were in fact crested pigeons: see "Topknot Pigeons" in *Birds in Backyards* (http://tinyurl.com/y3hlnnqk) (at 9 March 2020); and "Crested Pigeons" in *Birds in Backyards* (http://tinyurl.com/y3j2j5e7) (at 9 March 2020).

573 See *Ridley Williams' Diary*, p. 53. See also Sidney Pearson, "The South-West Corner of Queensland" in (October 1940) 3(2) *Journal of the Royal Historical Society of Queensland* 100, at pp. 118-122.

574 See *Ridley Williams' Diary*, pp. 52-53.

water for the cattle. On this exploratory trip, he was accompanied by Richard Batton. The two rode in a generally west-north-west direction from Depot No. 1 for a number of days, finding little good water until they came across a large waterhole. Ridley christened this waterhole "Cockroach Lagoon" after his saddle horse, "Cockroach".[575]

On the evening of the day that they first encountered Cockroach Lagoon, Ridley and Batton did not camp beside its waters. Rather, they moved to a point about 2½ km away. The reason for this distance was fear of the local Aborigines. As Ridley put it:

> "I was afraid the blacks, should they be camped near about, may frighten our horses during the night.... We were safer away from the water for they were not to be trusted at night. I never was the least afraid of them in daylight, but at night they could throw their spears and one would not know where they were coming from."[576]

If the need to find scarce water for the cattle was Ridley's primary concern during his cattle drive, then fear of being attacked by hostile Aborigines must have followed as a close second. He likely would have had significant contact with Aborigines on both *Gol Gol* and *Bierbank*. Whether that contact involved any hostile actions, on the Aborigines' part or on his, is not known. Ridley's view of Aborigines was probably one shared by most of his contemporaries of European extraction in Australian frontier areas. He was clearly fearful of being attacked by them. At the same time, he almost certainly saw the Aborigines he encountered as lesser beings and figures of amusement. At times, these negative views were, as will be seen below, tempered by measures of both pity and kindness.

Two days after he and Batton had moved on from Cockroach Lagoon, Ridley came across the first local Aborigines he acknowledged in his Diary as having met on the cattle drive. On this occasion, his reaction evidenced amusement, pity and kindness. Ridley observed:

> "We came suddenly on a lot of gins and piccaninnies who, on seeing us, fled in all directions. I let my horse go and cantered around them, and here and there in the bushes there were gins and piccaninnies with their heads hidden and all the rest of their bodies in full view....
>
> On rounding a hill we saw a dog and, on going to where the dog was, we found 2 gins and 4 piccaninnies up a tree. After a good lot of persuasion, we made them understand we wanted them to show us were we could get water. They all seemed to be very thirsty, and in the camp their waterbags were all dry. However, we found they called waterbags here Goothiea, and they pointed north west and made signs that it was over there and, as we thought, close handy. But we travelled about a mile [1.6 km] and [saw] no sign of it. I suggested we should have a drop out of our bags, which we did, a half pint each, and we

---

[575] See *Ridley Williams' Diary*, p. 53. Situated immediately to the south of the Plenty Highway in the Northern Territory, and roughly 100 km to the west of the Queensland border, Ridley Williams' "Cockroach Lagoon" is now officially known as "Cockroach Waterhole": see the *NT Place Names Register — Cockroach Waterhole* (http://tinyurl.com/y6lfghec) (at 9 March 2020). Cockroach Waterhole's geographic coordinates are Latitude 22° 32′ 29″ S, Longitude 137° 09′ 53″ S.

[576] See *Ridley Williams' Diary*, p. 54.

gave the two gins a lot each. I was much amused to see them trying to drink. They had no idea of putting the bottle between their lips, as we would do, but tried to put their mouths inside the top; trying to avoid spilling a drop of it. The poor wretches were very thirsty. However, after this, they seemed to have more confidence in us, and pushed on till we came to a small waterhole which they had covered with bushes. There were not more than 3 or 4 buckets of water in all. I let them have a billy can, which they dipped in and drank away until we filled our bags.... We gave them an old pocket knife and a jam tin. After our horses had drunk up all the water we had left in the hole, we parted from them and went our way and let them go their own way."[577]

Ridley and Batton continued on exploring for a few more days; riding first to the west, then to the north and finally to the south. Camping for the night in an area timbered with gidgee wattle, Ridley found the site chosen anything but conducive to rest. In his words:

"After tea we went to bed as usual. About midnight, the wind blew rather strong and started the roly polies rolling about. Suddenly, I felt something not very pleasant crawling up the leg of my trousers. On drawing my leg up suddenly, and getting up at the same time, I saw a large brown snake within a foot of my face with its head flattened out, as they always do when savage and about to bite. I threw the blankets towards him and jumped to my feet. But he disappeared before I could get a stick to kill it."[578]

Needless to say, both Ridley and Batton shifted their sleeping places for the balance of the night after this incident.

The following day, and not finding more water, the two men returned to Cockroach Lagoon. Ridley's sleep that night was also a disturbed one. However, the cause of his unrest on this occasion was not a snake but rather ants. He wrote:

"I tried to have a sleep but the black ants were so numerous that sleep was impossible. So we walked about the greater part of the night. Here we had to spell for a day to let our horses recover from the last journey. So to beat the ants, I built a bank near the water by

---

[577] See *Ridley Williams' Diary*, pp. 54-55. There is no indication in the Diary that Ridley gave any thought to the impact of allowing the horses to drink the small waterhole dry might have had on local Aboriginals.

[578] See *Ridley Williams' Diary*, p. 55. The roly polies being blown about were likely prickly saltwort or tumbleweed (Salsola australis), a species of bushes found throughout Central Australia. Dead plants break off at ground level and are easily moved by wind: see Western Australian Department of Primary Industries and Regional Development, *Roly poly* (http://tinyurl.com/y66n7c78) (at 9 March 2020).

Identifying the species to which Ridley's "large brown snake" belonged is not easy. One large brown snake which inhabits the area where Ridley and Batton were likely to be camping is the inland taipan or fierce snake (Oxyuranus microlepidotus); the snake with the world's most toxic venom. However, inland taipans are rarely encountered by humans. Moreover, members of the species are diurnal and do not flatten their heads when aroused: see University of Melbourne Biomedical Sciences Department, *Australo-Papuan Taipans* (http://tinyurl.com/y6a8k4g5) (at 9 March 2020). A more likely candidate for the snake in question is the king brown or mulga snake (Pseudechis australis), This species is widespread across inland Australia, is active day and night and does flatten its head and neck when threatened: see Australian Museum, *Mulga Snake* (http://tinyurl.com/yxsezwmj) (at 9 March 2020).

putting in the ground 4 forks in which I placed sticks across and grass on top.... [I dug] holes around the forks which I filled with water to block the ants crawling up them."[579]

The next night, although not bothered by snakes or ants, Ridley again woke at about midnight; on this occasion to a noise. He immediately thought that he and his companion were in the process of being attacked by Aborigines. He stated:

"I saw distinctly some black object in the grass and, putting my hand on my rifle, which was a 380 Martini-Henry, I pulled it shut. I always slept with it at my side, and my revolver also. On shutting, it clicked.... Out jumped 2 emus from amongst the grass and trees, and scooted past us at a great rate. It was quite a relief to find that they were not blacks as I at first supposed."[580]

The following morning, Ridley and Batton began their journey back to Depot No 1 and their cattle on the tablelands near the head of the Linda Creek. On Christmas Day 1882, Ridley dined on duck which he had shot and roasted. After four days, they reached the herd. Conscious of the lack of water for the cattle to his west, Ridley decided to graze them locally until sufficient rain had fallen to fill waterholes and allow the cattle drive to progress onwards. In the meantime, Ridley, Batton and the drovers moved the cattle from waterhole to waterhole around the top of the Linda Creek; establishing as they did successive camps which they called "Depot No. 2" and "Depot No. 3". They also called Depot No. 3 "Bumble Camp".[581]

From time to time while the cattle were left to graze around the waterhole near the head of the Linda Creek, Ridley and Batton made further reconnaissance forays, but could find no useful water. However, after good falls of rain in early March 1883, they rode out to Cockroach Lagoon and found it full of water. They hurriedly returned to the tablelands at the head of the Linda Creek to collect the cattle. On arriving back with the herd, they found that "Charlie", a young Aboriginal boy who Charlie Lowe had brought on the drive with him, was dying of consumption. Ridley noted:

"We found the poor little blackboy Charlie dying. He was unable to speak and passed off the next day. So we buried him close to the camp on rising ground."[582]

After the cattle were mustered and shifted to Cockroach Lagoon, Ridley and Batton again rode off exploring to westwards. This exploratory trip was to be a particularly long one. For a time, they were accompanied by another exploring party, led by a Mr Buttfield, which they had met near the head of the Linda Creek. The combined group travelled to the north of the

---

579   See *Ridley Williams' Diary*, p. 56.
580   Ibid.
581   See *Ridley Williams' Diary*, pp. 56-58.
582   See *Ridley Williams' Diary*, p. 58.

Tarlton Range and out into sandy spinifex country immediately to the north of the Simpson Desert. After crossing a dry Arthur Creek and reaching the Jervois Range, where they intended to camp, they again encountered a group of Aborigines. Of this encounter, Ridley wrote:

> "There were two gins and two piccaninnies here, and one of the gins had a coolamon full of grass seeds, an iguana, a lizard or two and some native cucumbers, all together in the one vessel. N.B. A coolamon is a wooden vessel cut out of wood; generally taken from a bended tree or elbow and cut out till it is very thin. Some of them will hold over a bucket of water.
>
> When these gins saw us, they got such a fright that the one carrying the coolamon dropped it and spilled a lot of the contents. But when they saw we did not intend to hurt them, they started to pick it all up again; almost crying at the loss of the seed, which was very fine.
>
> We gave them a little bread to help make up for their loss when they went off to their camp on the hill, where we could see a number of heads watching us. We took turn about and watched for the night in case the niggers may make a raid on us...."[583]

Ridley and Batton continued riding westwards until they struck the Marshall River, which Ridley described as "a dry, sandy, waterless, barren channel".[584] Here, Buttfield and his exploring party left them. Ridley and Batton travelled north-west up the Marshall River for a little under 20 km and then cut to the south to intersect the Plenty River. Having done so, they travelled further west up that River to a point where they were able to dig in the river's bed and find good water. They later learned that Charles Winnecke had named this reach of the Plenty River "Plenty Wells". Ridley and Batton continued riding up the Plenty River towards its head in the Harts Range. From that head, they crossed the Range and found a good waterhole in the bed of the Waite River near its source. Being very short of food, they dined that evening on pigweed and an emu which Ridley had shot.[585]

The following day, the heavens opened as Ridley and Batton were riding through sandy desert country. Ridley observed:

> "We were caught in a thunderstorm. So, [we] hurried to get our packs off and covered up before the swags got wet. The storm only lasted about 20 minutes, but it fell very heavy and water was running down a flat near where we were camped three or four inches deep. But in an hour, there was not a drop to be seen anywhere, and we had to fill our pots for supper out of the billy we had collected while it was raining. I dug a few holes

---

583   See *Ridley Williams' Diary*, p. 59. The native cucumber (Cucumis melo ssp. Agrestis) is widespread in Central Australia
584   Ibid.
585   See *Ridley Williams' Diary*, p. 60. The pigweed eaten by Ridley and Batton was almost certainly *Portulaca oleracea*, otherwise commonly known by an Aboriginal name, Munyeroo. All parts of the plant can be eaten raw or cooked. Pigweed is reputed to have been the indigenous vegetable most widely eaten by early European colonists and inland explorers. The tiny seeds of this plant were harvested by Central Australian Aborigines, ground to a paste and cooked before being consumed: see Attila Kapitany, *Australian Pigface and Pigweed* (2013), pp. 15 and 22; and Australian Native Plants Society, *Portulaca Oleracea* (http://tinyurl.com/y559h9z6) (at 10 March 2020). The fine seeds spilled from the coolamon by the Aboriginal woman who had earlier been surprised by Ridley and Batton might well have been pigweed seeds: see this page above.

with the shovel, but five minutes after the rain stopped, there was not a drop of water in the holes: the ground was like a sieve."[586]

After the rain, Ridley walked to the top of a nearby hill with a map in order to see whether he could spy a prominent peak marked as Mount Byrne to his west. He had no difficulty in identifying the peak. He knew that it lay to the west of the Overland Telegraph Line connecting Port Augusta in the south with Darwin in the north. He was therefore able to determine that he and Batton were only some 15 miles [around 24 km] to the east of the Telegraph Line, and that the country in between was relatively flat.[587] The two had nothing but pigweed and sugarless tea for supper and for breakfast the succeeding morning.[588]

The next day, Ridley and Batton set out for the Telegraph Line. Ridley rode ahead, with Button following up driving their packhorses. After riding for about four hours, Ridley came across a track. Looking around, he spotted the Telegraph Line. Ridley waited for Batton to catch him up with the packhorses, and then the two men set off along the track in what they thought was the direction of the Alice Springs Telegraph Station. They stopped for a time to secure water at Burt's Well. In due course, they came upon a hut and a sheep yard. Ridley recorded their reception at the hut as follows:

> "On reaching the hut, two men came out and, after saying the usual 'Good Morning', the first question was 'which way have you come? We did not hear of you coming down the line. This is the only road in [these parts]'.
>
> When I told them we had come through from Queensland, they were somewhat astonished and asked if we were some of Williams' party. When I told them I was the man himself, they told me that a party with camels had been out three weeks to look for us and had given us up as lost.... They thought that we must all [have] perished or been killed by the blacks."[589]

Having been fed and housed for the night at the hut, Ridley and Batton continued on to the Alice Springs Telegraph Station. On reaching it, Ridley was able to send a wire to Elder, Smith and Co., the stock agents for Wooldridge, Murray and Spence, advising that he had "got through". He sent another telegram to inform family and friends that he had "got across". A third wire was sent to Mr Bill Benstead, the Manager of the *Barrow Creek Station* to let him know of the situation. In consequence, Benstead brought down two fresh packhorses and rations from the run for Ridley and Batton to take back with them to the drovers at Cockroach Lagoon.[590]

Ridley and Batton then made their way back to the herd at Cockroach Lagoon. Finding water

---

586 See *Ridley Williams' Diary*, p. 60.
587 Ibid.
588 See *Ridley Williams' Diary*, p. 61. Ridley, a non-smoker, noted that Batton was as concerned about having run out of pipe tobacco as he was about having little food. As Ridley put it, tobacco was for Batton "a sort of Job's comforter": Ibid.
589 See *Ridley Williams' Diary*, pp. 61-62.
590 See *Ridley Williams' Diary*, p. 62. See as to Benstead generally, Peter Bridge and Ian Murray (eds.), *William Benstead: Pioneer of Alice Springs and Coolgardie* (2019).

very scarce, they dug three wells along the way. They also came across an emu nest with nine eggs in it. These they took with them to supplement their rations.[591] The drovers at Cockroach Lagoon would no doubt have been relieved to see the returning men.

Ridley started out for the Telegraph Line from Cockroach Lagoon with about 360 of the strongest cattle. He was assisted in driving them by Charlie Lowe and an Aboriginal youth from the Georgina River area. Fred Lowe and Richard Batton followed up with the horses. A drover, W. A. Martin, together with another Aboriginal youth, were left behind to tend to the remaining cattle at Cockroach Lagoon.[592]

Ridley was aware that the route his party and the cattle would take westwards would be very dry at least as far as the Harts Range. However, he expected to find water in that Range. As he put it:

> "I was confident there was plenty of water to be found in the Harts Range, although I had not seen it, by the number of black cockatoos along the head of the Plenty which used to fly straight across to the range every evening for water. These birds, and the bronze wing pigeons, were my principal guides, and water was always to be found in the direction they fly near sundown.... Where these birds are not seen, there is little hope of finding water. The smaller birds will guide a person when near a water, but many of these hang about the water for the best part of the day if the weather is at all hot."[593]

In the event, the cattle relied in large measure on eating parakeelya until the party reached good water at the Waite River.[594]

At the Waite River, it was decided that Batton would ride on to the Alice Springs Telegraph Station, contact Benstead and see whether he would supply a man or men to assist with driving the cattle. At the same time, Ridley, with Fred Lowe, would return to Cockroach Lagoon and bring the remainder of the herd across to the Waite River. Charlie Lowe and the Aboriginal youth were left to look after the cattle already at the Waite River until Batton returned from the Alice Springs Telegraph Station.[595]

On their way back to Cockroach Lagoon, Ridley and Fred Lowe camped one evening at a small soakage. Numerous Aboriginal tracks around the area left them wary. Depositing their equipment and personal belongings at the soakage, they led their horses away from it for the evening. In the course of doing so, Ridley looked around and saw Aborigines raiding their equipment and belongings at the soakage. He noted:

---

591 Ibid.
592 Ibid.
593 See *Ridley Williams' Diary*, p. 64.
594 See *Ridley Williams' Diary*, pp. 63-64. Parakeelya (Calandrinia balonensis) is a succulent herb native to Central Australia. It provided the cattle with both food and sufficient moisture to get by in dry conditions: see Australian National Herbarium, *Calandrinia balonensis* (http://tinyurl.com/y4yghrnd) (at 10 March 2020); and *Wikipedia — Calandrinia balonensis* (http://tinyurl.com/yy5494dy) (at 10 March 2020).
595 See *Ridley Williams' Diary*, p. 64.

"I looked back and there was one nigger with my swag in his arms, the other with Fred's saddlecloth. He was afraid to touch [Fred's] swag as the rifle was lying across it. Here was a nice go! All the clothes, except the ones we had on, and the blankets we were possessed of,[596] were in those two swags, and there was mine in the arms of a nigger just in the act of making off with it. I called to Fred to catch a horse quick while I made all speed on foot, revolver in hand, which I discharged a couple of times and frightened the nigger, who dropped the swag after carrying it a few yards. Fred caught the first horse and in his hurry threw the reins over the horse's head, which were crossed under his neck, jumped on barebacked and, revolver in hand, set sail at full gallop.... [He] just got opposite the camp, where there were a lot of rat holes, and, trying to pull the horse away from the holes, he pulled him right into them.... The horse] turned a somersault and sent Fred sprawling in the sand, where, it is needless to say, the chase ended.... As the niggers had dropped everything they were taking, we did not trouble further with them."

Soon after they reached Cockroach Lagoon and the rest of the cattle, Ridley and Fred Lowe were joined by Charlie Lowe and the Aboriginal youth who had remained at the Waite River with the latter. They had been relieved of their cattle-minding duties after Batton's return to the River with a drover and another Aboriginal youth assigned for the purpose by Benstead.[597]

The party at Cockroach Lagoon set off for the Waite River with the remainder of the herd. Ridley calculated that they would have to face driving the cattle over about 130 km without water before reaching "the parakeelya country", a further 80 km from there to the Plenty Wells and then about another 113 km to the Waite River.[598]

Moving almost continuously by day and night, the cattle reached the parakeelya country in a parched condition; not having had access to any water since leaving Cockroach Lagoon. The parakeelya quenched their thirst and enabled the drive to continue on to the Plenty Wells.[599]

At Plenty Wells, Ridley went off by himself searching for strays which had fallen behind the herd. Of his efforts in that regard, he wrote:

"On reaching the Plenty Wells, there were 6 or 7 away one morning and I went back for them, having to go back nearly 30 miles [about 48 km] for two of them. I got them all and started back to catch the cattle.... When travelling along on the tracks, driving those through some spinifex country about midnight, it was bitterly cold. So I let them camp

---

596 See *Ridley Williams' Diary*, pp. 64-65.
597 See *Ridley Williams' Diary*, p. 65.
598 Ibid.
599 Ibid. In a brief article relating to Ridley Williams' journey published in the *South Australian Advertiser* on 5 January 1885, the anonymous author wrote:
"Incredible as it may appear to anyone not acquainted with the country passed through, the cattle were at one time no less than eighteen days without a drink. This is explained by the fact that the country they were travelling through abounded in parakillia [sic]. A peculiar plant, much like "pigface" in appearance, having solid leaves, apparently containing nothing but water. This plant grows only on poor sandy soil, and nothing else will grow where it is. Cattle eat it greedily, and it is both food and drink to them."
See the *South Australian Advertiser*, Monday, 5 January 1885, p. 5. See also footnote 585 on p. 162 above.

for a few minutes and set fire to some bundles of spinifex to have a warm. I could see some of them and thought they were alright. But after having a warm, I went to start on again with them and found I was three short.... I could not find them in the dark after looking around for some time. I decided not to be beaten, so I left the ones I had and rode back about 5 miles along the tracks and camped till daylight.... [I] then rode across the tracks for some distance on each side but saw no [cattle] tracks going back. So I drove them on, picked up two more that had been dropped and caught the cattle at the head of the Plenty just at sundown. Both my horse and myself were not sorry for a rest. The horse had not had the saddle off him for 36 hours, and during the whole of that, I had been on his back with the exception of about two hours...."[600]

Ridley and his party found the country between the Plenty Wells and the Waite River to be very dry. On arriving at that river, they found that the cattle already there had nearly exhausted all of the available pooled surface water. In order to enable the recombined herd to drink, Ridley saw to the digging of a well in the river bed and the erection of a makeshift cattle trough; the latter incorporating a tarpaulin which he had earlier prepared for the purpose whilst still at Cockroach Lagoon.[601]

Ridley described how he went about watering the cattle as follows:

"I rigged the trough by putting in two forks about 30 feet [around 9 metres] apart a good depth in the sand, then a long rail to reach from one to the other which was about 3 feet [a little under 1 metre] high. Then I put a good thick butt of a log on the inside of each fork about 4 feet [approximately 1.2 metres] long. I cut a notch in each of these and put two more long rails, one on each side of the fork. Then I put the tarpaulin over this and tucked it under the rails and banked the sand upon either side to hold the tarpaulin in its place. By this means, it held about 70 or 80 buckets of water. I had two men continually bailing water, and we cut the cattle off the mob which we kept close by, in about 40 in each lot, and brought them down to the creek to the trough.... After they had taken a drink, we started them out on the other side of the creek. We kept this up all day till about 9 pm, when we got them all watered.... There were only a few of them that did not drink by this means. We watered during the day nearly 1,200 head of cattle."[602]

Ridley's party found the land between the Waite River and the hut and sheep yard near the Alice Springs Telegraph Station to be even drier than the country between the Plenty Wells and the Waite River. They covered the distance by driving the cattle by night as well as by day; allowing them only about three hours rest at a time. The herd ended up being strung out

---

600 See *Ridley Williams' Diary*, pp. 65-66.
601 See *Ridley Williams' Diary*, p. 66. At Cockroach Lagoon, Ridley had cut the tarpaulin in two and sewn the two separate ends together so as to be able to use it to construct a long trough: see *Ridley William' Diary*, p. 63.
602 See *Ridley Williams' Diary*, p. 66.

over a long distance and a number of the cattle died of thirst. Those remaining were able to find water near the hut.[603]

Ridley and his drovers rested with the cattle at the hut for a few days. During this period, Ridley rode to the Alice Springs Telegraph Station to contact Benstead. It was agreed that all cows with calves, together with all of the weakest cows, would be moved for agistment to the *Barrow Creek Station*'s outstation, the *Simpsons Gap Station*, located about 40 km to the south-west of the Telegraph Station. The remaining cattle were then to be driven to the location where the *Barrow Creek Station*'s main herd were currently grazing, roughly 200 km to the north-west of the Telegraph Station.

Approximately half of the cattle in Ridley's charge were successfully taken to the *Simpsons Gap Station* and left there by Ridley in the care of a young Aboriginal man. Ridley and his party then set out to deliver the remaining cows at the hut, together with Button's bulls, to Benstead on the *Barrow Creek Station* proper.[604] This cattle drive took them first to the Annas Reservoir. The Reservoir is in fact a waterhole on the Wickstead Creek, approximately 150 km to the north-west of the Alice Springs Telegraph Station.

Early in 1884, Bill Benstead had overseen the construction of a three-roomed stone house, together with a blacksmith's hut, at the Annas Reservoir. The house was intended to be the homestead for the *Barrow Creek Station*. However, in August 1884, local Anmatyerre tribesmen, who had earlier been spearing the Station's cattle, attacked the homestead. Only Harry Figg, the *Barrow Creek Station*'s head stockman, and Thomas Coombes, a cook, were present at the homestead at the time of the attack. Both were gravely wounded.[605]

Ridley and his drovers arrived at the Annas Reservoir soon after the Anmatyerre attack. Ridley provided the following description of what he had been told had occurred:

> "There was a good little house built at this reservoir, but the blacks had burned the roof. They had stuck up the stockman, Henry Figg, and the cook; the Manager being away from home. They first tackled the cook, who slept near the kitchen part of the house, and had speared him 8 different times. They then tackled the stockman, who had been awakened by the row, and had got his revolver ready for action. He opened the door and a shower of spears met him. He fired several shots, wounding some of the blacks.... They set fire to the roof, which was a thatched one.... After the shirt was on fire on his back, [he was] forced to rush out of the house. He fired his revolver four or five times at the blacks and they scattered. He got one spear in his shoulder, but he pulled it out and

---

603 See *Ridley Williams' Diary*, pp. 66-68. The waterhole near the hut and sheep yard might have been the waterhole, currently known as "Wigley's Waterhole", in the bed of the Todd River a short distance to the north of the Alice Springs Telegraph Station. Whether or not there was a hut and sheep yard close to the Wigley Waterhole has not been ascertained to date. However, in view of the surrounding landforms and local surface hydrology, an association between the hut and sheep yard and Wigley Waterhole appear to be highly likely.

604 See *Ridley Williams' Diary*, p. 68.

605 See Parks and Wildlife Commission of the Northern Territory, *Annas Reservoir Conservation Reserve* (http://tinyurl.com/y4gpymzf) (at 11 March 2020). The Annas Reservoir attack was probably precipitated by Anmatyerre anger at the European incursion on Anmatyerre country, and in particular the negative impact of that incursion on scarce local water supplies. It would also seem that the Annas Reservoir was an Anmatyerre sacred site: Ibid.

rushed towards them when they fled. He then stood out in the open. The light of the house burning made everything as clear as day for some time.... To his astonishment, the old cook crawled out from his room, covered with blood from his spear wounds and very weak. The stockman managed to get a horse and [harness] to the cart and drive the cook and himself to the camp where we were now about to take the cattle. I saw them both when we reached there, and they were both in a fair way [to] recovery from the burns and spear wounds."[606]

From the Annas Reservoir, the cattle were driven in a north-westerly direction for some 50 km to join the *Barrow Creek Station*'s herd. Conditions were very dry and the cattle thirsty. Ridley and his drovers had to move them over a very rough, stony hill. They were then met by Benstead and one of his men, who piloted the party and their cattle over the last stretch to the *Barrow Creek Station*'s herd. Having delivered the cattle, Ridley and his drovers rested for a few days with Benstead and his men. They then headed back to the Alice Springs Telegraph Station.[607]

---

[606] See *Ridley Williams' Diary*, p. 68.
[607] See *Ridley Williams' Diary*, pp. 68-69.

Alice Springs Interlude

At or near to the Alice Springs Telegraph Station, Ridley Williams paid off the two Lowe brothers and all the other men with the exception of the drover, W. A. Martin, and an Aboriginal youth known to Ridley and Martin only as "Billy". The men paid off planned in due course to follow the Overland Telegraph Line south towards Adelaide. It was Ridley's intention to retrace his steps back to *Bierbank* in company with Martin and Billy. However, neither they nor Fred Lowe began their respective journeys immediately.[608]

Back at the Alice Springs Telegraph Station, Ridley met with a Mr Willoughby; one of the three lessees of the *Bond Springs Station*, some 15 km to the north. Willoughby informed him that local Arrernte Aborigines had been killing a lot of the cattle which Ridley and his party had left at the *Simpsons Gap Station*. Ridley and Fred Lowe were persuaded to join a party of volunteers, under the command of a local South Australian policeman, Mounted Constable Daer, formed to hunt down and hopefully capture the perpetrators of the cattle killings.[609]

Daer's party traced the Aborigines for two days before catching up with them in hilly terrain to the east of Simpsons Gap in the MacDonnell Ranges to the south of the Alice Springs Telegraph Station. On spying their pursuers, the Aborigines took flight. Due to the rocky nature of the country, the members of Daer's party spread out, dismounted and chased their quarries on foot. Of this chase, Ridley wrote:

> "We heard a shot away behind and we saw two niggers going over the next hill about a quarter of a mile [a little less than 390 metres] away. The black-trackers we had had hunted them out and they were practising at them at about 8 or 9 hundred yards [about 730 to 820 metres].... [They had about as much chance of hitting one of them as they had of flying. These two trackers were very anxious to catch some of this tribe as a few days before they killed the cattle at Simpsons Gap, they had killed one of [the trackers'] tribe near Alice Springs, and the two tribes were bitter enemies."[610]

---

608 See *Ridley Williams' Diary*, p. 69.

609 Ibid. In a telegram published on 19 September 1884 in the *Port Augusta Dispatch and Flinders Advertiser*, Daer reported:
"Traced natives to East Simpsons Gap, where I found they had been killing cattle within the last week, several head having been killed wantonly, and no meat being taken away. Have obtained warrants and will try to execute them. Have formed a party of volunteers. The cattle are the property of [Wooldridge], Murray, Spence & Co. This will be the same party who attacked the native shepherd about a mile from the Alice on the 12th."
See the *Port Augusta Dispatch and Flinders Advertiser*, Friday, 19 September 1884, p. 2.

610 See *Ridley Williams' Diary*, pp. 69-70. At least one of the Arrernte Aborigines being chased was wounded. In a subsequent telegram sent to an Inspector Besley and also published in the *Port Augusta Dispatch and Flinders Advertiser* on 19 September 1884, Daer wrote:
"Returned to-day, having tracked the natives to Simpson's Gap. Came on them on the 15th inst. In the ranges, but was unable to effect any captures, owing to the roughness of the country. The natives escaped into inaccessible ranges. Called on them

Following this confrontation, Daer and his party gave up the chase. They spent the night at an unnamed outstation hut where, according to Ridley:

> "Mr Willoughby and I chattered over the trip we had with the cattle. He was never tired of listening and asking questions, and talking himself of Darwin's theory of the origination of man."[611]

---

to surrender, which they refused to do. We fired, wounding Youlla, one of the ringleaders. Was forced to return, as the members of the party could not remain out any longer. The party consisting of Messrs Willoughby and Williams, squatters, F. Lowe and W. Gordon, two black-trackers, and myself."
See the *Port Augusta Dispatch and Flinders Advertiser*, Friday, 19 September 1884, p. 2.

611 See *Ridley Williams' Diary*, p. 70.

Journeying Back to Bierbank

Ridley Williams, Martin and Billie set off from the Alice Springs Telegraph Station for *Bierbank* on about 18 September 1884. They took with them at least 20 horses, some of which they hitched in rotation to a dray containing supplies, food and casks of water. After two long days, they reached and camped at the Waite River. Ridley's first night at that River on his return journey was a disturbed one. He wrote of it:

> "As the tracks of blacks were plentiful about, I did not sleep too much that night. I was lying down close to the well. We let the fire go out on purpose.... Something passed over me with a "whis", and I drew my revolver quickly and let drive. The report echoed again, and a curlew flew with a screech from close beside me. However, I was not at all satisfied. So the next morning, I had a good look around the direction the curlew came from and saw the tracks of a nigger where he had run for all he was worth on the sound of the revolver. He had evidently been sneaking behind a big gum tree to have a look at what he could see and had startled the bird when it flew across where I was lying. The bird no doubt was wanting water, which it did not get that night. I never mentioned to Martin or the blackboy about the track but cautioned them always to be on the look out as there were plenty of blacks about."[612]

Ridley and his companions spent three days at the Waite River. While camping there, Ridley shot numerous pigeons to supplement their food supplies. The manner in which he went about shooting the birds exemplified both his bush skills and his resourceful nature. He first constructed a water trough. Of its construction, he noted:

> "I stripped a long sheet of bark off a gum sapling about 9 inches [about 23 cm] thick and plugged up the ends with antbed, which I had to ride about two miles [around 3.2 km] to find. I then put short sticks across it to prop it open and buried it level with the sand. Then I filled it with water."[613]

The next morning, he hid behind some bushes in line with the trough. As he anticipated,

---

612   Ibid.
613   See *Ridley Williams' Diary*, p. 71.

pigeons flew down "in a shower" to drink from the trough. Firing his gun at the flock at short range, he bagged 19 pigeons — with no ammunition being wasted.[614]

It was around 130 km from the Waite River to the Plenty Wells. Ridley, Martin and Billy found no water along the way. They relied on water from the casks in the dray and on their own water bags. A good part of the journey was conducted at night to avoid the worst of the heat of the day. Fortunately, they found ample water in the well which Ridley's party had previously dug at Plenty Wells.[615]

With the reluctant assistance of an Aboriginal man and woman, Ridley was able to find water again some 120 km onwards by digging a well in the sandy bed of the Marshall River. He lined his well with flattened strips of bark to keep the sand back. It was apparently easy to use this well to water the horses as the water table was only a metre or so below the surface of the sand.[616]

Leaving Martin and Billy at the Marshall River, Ridley next set off for Cockroach Lagoon to ascertain whether or not it still held water. He found it hard going riding through heavy sand and spinifex almost all the way. On reaching the Lagoon, he found that it was holding water. He also saw signs of Aborigines in the area. Ridley secured water from the Lagoon for himself and his horses and then, wary of being attacked, camped "about a mile" [about 1.6 km] away. The following morning, he returned to the Lagoon for more water and surprised a group of Aborigines. They scattered when they saw him.[617] With respect to one of these Aborigines, Ridley noted:

> "I saw one old nigger hopping on one leg and stick. He had one leg off about half way between the knee and the ankle. He was out of sight in a few minutes."[618]

Ridley returned to his companions at the Marshall River. Together, they made their way back to Cockroach Lagoon. There, they found "lots of blacks" camped. They also found a stray and crippled cow. This they shot and skinned, using the hide "to bind false spokes in one of the wheels on the dray, which was very shaky". Ridley left Billy to butcher the carcass and give the meat to the Aborigines, who then dispersed.[619]

By the time they had reached Cockroach Lagoon, Ridley had decided to try and catch two small Aboriginal boys if he could in order to take them back with him to *Bierbank* — almost certainly to work in a labouring capacity on the run.[620]

It has been estimated that in 1899, more than 2,000 Aboriginal workers were employed in

---

614 Ibid.
615 See *Ridley Williams' Diary*, pp. 71-72.
616 See *Ridley Williams' Diary*, p. 72.
617 See *Ridley Williams' Diary*, pp. 72-73.
618 See *Ridley Williams' Diary*, p. 73.
619 Ibid. Presumably, the men strengthened the defective spokes on the wheel by using strips of the hide to bind lengths of suitable local timber to them as splints.
620 See *Ridley Williams' Diary*, p. 74.

the southern reaches of Queensland alone, and that Aboriginal child workers constituted one-fifth of all male Aboriginal workers in the Colony.[621] Shirleene Robinson has observed that:

> "There were four overlapping economic and social factors that drew employers to Aboriginal child labour [in Queensland]. First, settlers employed Aboriginal children because of the shortage of other workers in the colony, and later the state. Secondly, these servants represented the most inexpensive form of labour available in the region. Thirdly, settlers were aware that Aboriginal children were easier to control than Aboriginal adults. Finally, settlers argued that Aboriginal children could be civilised and the indigenous threat disbanded if Aboriginal children were made to perform labour for Europeans."[622]

Tellingly, it would seem that over the course of the second half of the Nineteenth Century, Aboriginal boys in Queensland were mainly employed as pastoral workers.[623] Most pastoral runs had many Aboriginal workers, including child workers.[624] Perhaps even more tellingly, Ridley Williams' plan to abduct the boys was abhorrent, but it was anything but an unusual event. Shirleene Robinson has noted:

> "In the period before the passage of the *Aboriginals Protection and Restriction on the Sale of Opium Act 1897* (Qld), European employers predominantly obtained Aboriginal child workers through kidnapping."[625]

Indeed, it would appear that the kidnapping of Aboriginal children for employment purposes reached its peak in Queensland in around 1890.[626]

Ridley also planned to abduct an Aboriginal girl or young woman as a "bride" for Billy. In Ridley's words:

> "Billy, our blackboy, was very anxious to get a gin. So, when these blacks had cleared out and we had got the wheel patched up, Martin and I arranged with Billy that we would go out to look for the blacks and if we found them, we would bring a gin with the boys if he would stay in the camp and look after the dray and other things while we were away."[627]

---

621 See Shirleene Robinson, *'Something like slavery?' The Exploitation of Aboriginal child labour in Queensland, 1842-1945* (PhD Thesis, University of Queensland, 2003) (http://tinyurl.com/wph3j7n) (at 23 March 2020), p. 463.

622 See Robinson, op. cit., p. 451. According to Shirleene Robinson:
"The majority of these child workers were not paid for their labour and were not provided with an education or the basic essentials of life. Furthermore, the racial structure that was extant in Queensland during the nineteenth and twentieth centuries meant that European employers were predisposed to treat these children as inferiors in every sense."
See Robinson, op. cit., pp. iv-v.

623 See Robinson, op. cit., p. 4.

624 See Robinson, op. cit., p. 67.

625 See Robinson, op. cit., p. iv. See also Robinson, op. cit., pp. 126 and 452.

626 See Robinson, op. cit., p. 129.

627 See *Ridley Williams' Diary*, p. 74.

There is nothing to suggest that either Ridley or Martin harboured any moral concerns regarding these proposed abductions. Clearly, they saw the Aborigines they encountered as lesser beings; without the human rights of Europeans; and as men, women and children whose feelings could very largely be ignored.

Leaving Billy at Cockroach Lagoon, Ridley and Martin rode out eastwards towards the Tarlton Range for their continued journey home. At a small creek, they found "a little black-boy" sitting on his own beside a cooking fire. Ridley caught the boy when he attempted to flee. After consuming a meal, the two men placed the boy on the back of a packhorse and the party rode on until they encountered more Aborigines. Ridley described what then occurred in the following terms:

> "After some time we came to some blacks. Here was a mixture. There was one gin about 14 or 15 years old. The rest were all old.... [There was] one... grey headed old thing who could not walk at all by the look of her, and evidently the others used to carry her.
>
> We picked the young gin up and put her on the packhorse behind the boy, intending to take her back for Billy if we saw nothing better. She was not a very charming looking creature. But we thought she might suit Billy, who was about as ugly a boy as one could find in any camp of blacks."[628]

About a kilometre further on, Ridley and Martin captured a second Aboriginal boy and brought him with them.[629]

Near to where they caught the second Aboriginal youth, Ridley and Martin came upon a well which the local Aborigines had cut through rock; evidently to access a permanent water supply. In the well, Ridley found a number of discarded Aboriginal water bags

> "all made out of kangaroo skins. They prepared them by tanning them on the flesh side with bark so that they can carry water in them for days without it going bad, as it would if the skins were not tanned."[630]

At the well, Ridley and Martin came across a number of Aboriginal women and girls. In relation to this encounter, Ridley wrote:

---

628 Ibid.

629 Ibid.

630 Ibid. In its brief article relating to Ridley Williams' cattle drive, published in the *South Australian Advertiser* on 5 January 1885, the anonymous author wrote of this Aboriginal well:
"Mr. Williams states that the only permanent water on the track, as far as he could judge, was a native well about five miles [about 8 km] east by south of the northern end of the Tarlton Range, in some broken hills. He found there a large heap of natives' kangaroo waterbags, thrown away. The well is about 12 feet [some 3.6 metres], apparently sunk through solid rock. However the natives sunk it with their rude appliances is a mystery. About fifty miles [around 80 km] north-west from the north end of the same range is another well, 30 feet [approximately 9 metres] deep, and sunk in a peculiar manner. The shaft goes down about 5 feet [about 1.5 metres], then there is a short drive of about 2 feet [around 0.6 of a metre], then shaft another 5 feet, then another drive, and so on to the bottom, making the well resemble a staircase."
See the *South Australian Advertiser*, Monday, 5 January 1885, p. 5. See also the *Brisbane Courier*, Saturday, 27 December 1884, p. 5. In possible contrast to Ridley's comments regarding the tanned kangaroo hide water bags, see p. 147 above.

> "We saw more gins here; mostly young…. There was one amongst them who was by far the best looking of the lot. She was, I should say, about 18 years old; not a bad style. Of course, they were all naked and there was nothing to hide their limbs. So we could judge them the same as we would a horse or any other beast…. We decided to leave the first one and take this one as Billy's bride. So, with the two boys and the gin, we started back to our camp; the gin and one of the boys riding on the packhorse and the other behind me on my horse. I led the packhorse and Martin brought up the rear carrying the rifle: a good picture for Punch we would have made. We did not get back to the campsite until late that night…. When we got back, we had to keep our eyes on them, our captives…. [We] left Billy to camp near them to make up the fire for them if they got cold. Billy was very proud of his bride, but he dare not lose sight of her for fear she would clear out."[631]

The next morning, Ridley and his expanded party left Cockroach Lagoon. They reached Potjostler Waterhole without incident. From there, they set out for the waterhole near where Ridley had established his Depot No. 2 in the Toko Range. As they made their way towards that waterhole, the defective wheel on the dray finally gave way.[632] Ridley noted of this incident:

> "In a rough, stony creek we had to cross, the wheel of the dray gave way…. Every spoke broke. So we had to camp…. We had to take our horses on about two miles [some 3.2 km] for water, and pack water back for our own use the next morning. I started to cut timber for spokes out of what is known as Minnirichi timber, which is very tough wood…. While [I was] fitting these into the nave of the wheel, Martin was doing some cooking and Billy and the gin were pounding some Mulligan salt, which is very coarse, to get it ready to salt a beast when we could see one. The two boys were playing about the camp. Billy was supposed to be keeping his eye on them. But suddenly they had disappeared and, as the country near the camp was very stony, there was no hope of tracking them."[633]

Once the dray wheel was repaired, Ridley and his diminished party continued on their way to the Depot No. 2 waterhole, and from there down the Linda Creek. After about five days, they reached the *Glenormiston* homestead near Lake Idamea. Here, Ridley left the Aboriginal girl — presumably to return to her people. With respect to her release, Ridley wrote:

---

631 See *Ridley Williams' Diary*, p. 75.
632 See p. 171 above.
633 See *Ridley Williams' Diary*, p. 75. The wood from which Ridley cut the new spokes for the dray wheel was probably derived either from the Eucalyptus minniritchi tree or from the Round-leaved Mallee tree (Eucalyptus orbifolia): see *Wikipedia — Eucalyptus minniritchi* (http://tinyurl.com/y7mdu76b) (at 11 May 2020); and (Australian Native Plants Society, *Eucalyptus orbifolia* (http://tinyurl.com/y5l34xfl) (at 11 May 2020). In either case, the tree or trees used would probably have been located at or close to the far eastern limit or limits of its or their occurrence. Mulligan salt would have been salt obtained locally from deposits in the bed of the nearby Mulligan River.

> "As the blackboy Billy had not watched the boys better, I told him I would not take the gin for him."[634]

From the *Glenormiston* homestead, Ridley, Martin and Billy made their way towards Boulia. Close to the latter hamlet, Ridley was able to provide water to three European men on foot who appeared to be dying of thirst.[635] At Boulia, he gave a rough plan of his journey to the local Sergeant of Police. Billy left Ridley and Martin in Boulia and ultimately joined an Aboriginal police detachment. Before departing the village, Ridley was able to sell some of his horses, harnesses and the dray.

Leaving Boulia. Ridley and Martin broke their journey home at both the *Diamantina Lakes Station* and the *Connemara Station*. They also stopped overnight at Adavale. Ridley observed:

> "On passing Adavale, I called at Mr. Alfred Skinner's store to get a few things.... When I walked into the store, Mr. Skinner asked: 'Is that you or your ghost. I heard you had perished, and by jove I am glad to see you back again.' We had a bit of a jollification at the Hotel there that night."[636]

From Adavale, it was a comparatively short journey back to *Bierbank*. Of his arrival home, Ridley wrote:

> "We got home about the first week in February 1885 and found the country very dry: grass was very scarce on the run. Everybody was very pleased to see us back, and I was very glad to be home again, and not very anxious for another trip like it."[637]

The Alice Springs and Central Australian historian, Adela Purvis, whose husband had typed the manuscript of *Ridley Williams' Diary*, was very taken with that diary and with the journey it recounted. In the Introduction she wrote for the typescript, she stated:

> "Those bushmen and pioneers who have had the privilege of perusing the Diary declare [Ridley Williams'] records as 'as accurate to the last waterhole'."[638]

According to Purvis, Ridley Williams' was known to at least some of his contemporaries by the nickname "Wigley".[639] It was Purvis' contention that three geographical features near the Alice Springs Telegraph Station were named after "Wigley" Williams: Wigley Big Hill (located

---

634 See *Ridley Williams' Diary*, p. 76.
635 Ibid.
636 See *Ridley Williams' Diary*, p. 77.
637 Ibid.
638 See Adela Purvis, *Heroes Unsung* (1971), Book 2, p. 49. See also footnote 565 on pp. 156-157 above.
639 See Adela Purvis, "Concerning The Meeting Of The Ross And Mills Parties North Of Alice Springs March 18, 1871", op cit., p. 134.

about 3 km north of the Telegraph Station on the original road north); Wigley Gorge (a small gorge formed by the Todd River and running through part of the Chewings Range approximately 4 km to the north of the Telegraph Station); and Wigley Waterhole (a waterhole in the bed of the Todd River at the northern end of Wigley Gorge).[640]

It should, however, be pointed out that Purvis' ascription of Ridley's asserted nickname to Wigley Waterhole and Wigley Gorge (together, presumably, with Wigley Big Hill) is contested. According to the *NT Place Names Register*, these features were in fact named after William Wigley, a solicitor and Member of the South Australian Parliament prior to 1886.[641]

In any event, it might be noted that Ridley Williams' name is commemorated on a plaque located on the Central Australian Pioneers Memorial in Trevor Reid Park, Alice Springs.[642]

---

640 Ibid, and also at p. 135. See also Adela Purvis, "This Township Named Stuart, Now Alice Springs" in [1947] *Proceedings of the Royal Geographical Society of Australasia, South Australian Branch* 54, at pp. 58 and 74; Adela Purvis, *Our Alice Springs: A Brief History From Its Earliest Times To The Present* (1952), pp. 91ff; footnote 603 on p. 167 above; and **photos 39** and **40**.

641 See the *NT Place Names Register — Wigley Gorge* (http://tinyurl.com/yy6xh2bw) (at 12 March 2020).

642 See **photos 41** and **42**.

Ridley Williams on *Bierbank* following the Cattle Drive

It is not presently known how many head of cattle Ridley Williams was able to deliver to the Barrow Creek Pastoral Company, nor how much Ridley and his *Bierbank* partners would have earned from the transaction. It might be recalled that the he contract he struck with Wooldridge, Murray and Spence in late 1882 was for the sale and delivery of 2,000 cows at £2.10.0 a head.[643] What is known is that by the time all the cattle reached the Waite River, the 2,000 cows which had started out had been reduced to "nearly 1,200" head.[644] An unknown number of the cattle who had made it that far died of thirst on the ensuing leg of the drive from the Waite River to the Overland Telegraph Line.[645] If, say, 1,100 head of cattle were ultimately delivered to the Barrow Creek Pastoral Company, then, at £2.10.0 a head, Ridley and his partners would have received £2,750 (worth around $153,280 in present-day Australian dollars).[646] Of course, significant sums from that amount would have to have been deducted for wages and the costs of supplies.

As welcome as the cattle drive monies would have been to the Williams brothers on *Bierbank* in early 1885, it seems likely that the remainder of the 1880s and the 1890s would have been economically challenging for them. The depressed beef prices which confronted them in 1882, and which probably contributed to the brothers' unsuccessful attempt to auction off *Bierbank* in November of that year, remained a problem.[647] The 1890s depression only exacerbated the matter.

On 1 March 1887, around a quarter of the *Bierbank* land then under lease to Ridley and his brothers was resumed by the Queensland Government under the provisions of Part III of the *Crown Lands Act 1884* (Qld).[648] The resumed land was made available by the Government for selection with the object of securing closer rural settlement. Pending any such selection, the Williams partners were entitled, upon payment of an annual fee, to continue depasturing their cattle on the resumed land. In accordance with the Act, they were apparently granted

---

643 See p. 156 above.
644 See p. 166 above.
645 See pp. 166–167 above.
646 See Thom Blake, *How Much Is It Worth* (http://tinyurl.com/y2w86obz) (at 14 March 2020).
647 See p. 155 above.
648 See 48 Vic. No. 28 (Qld). This Act, known as "the Dutton Act"), had its parallel in New South Wales in the contemporaneous *Crown Lands Act 1884* (NSW): see p. 124 above.

a 15 years lease of the non-resumed land.⁶⁴⁹ It is not currently known whether any part of the resumed land was in fact selected in consequence of the division.

Due to the increasing numbers of travellers passing by or through *Bierbank*, a hotel, known as the *Bierbank Hotel* and located on the right bank of Beechal Creek to the south of the *Bierbank* homestead, was constructed on the run. According to Leslie Jenkins:

> "The hotel was 75 feet [about 23 metres] long and 32 feet [around 10 metres] wide. It was made of round mulga plastered with antbed and had a wooden floor. The Bierbank Hotel also included a store, kitchen, dining room, bathroom, wash house, meat house, stable and a yard which was topped off with a picket fence around the hotel garden."⁶⁵⁰

Ridley's link with the *Bierbank Hotel*, which came to serve as a local community focal point, may well have been one factor contributing to his appointment as a Justice of the Peace by the Queensland Government on 1 January 1889.⁶⁵¹

In 1891, *Bierbank* appears to have been caught up in the great Shearers' Strike of that year. On 9 May 1891, the *Warwick Examiner and Times* reported that a wagon and associated harness belonging to Ridley Williams were burned on the Charleville road; almost certainly by striking shearers.⁶⁵² Why *Bierbank* or Ridley should have been so singled out by shearers is unclear as *Bierbank* carried no sheep; only cattle and horses. In the event, this brush with striking shearers might explain Ridley's later decision to join the Warrego Pastoralists' Association. In January 1893, he was elected to the Committee of that Association.⁶⁵³

Ridley's involvement in Warrego community affairs extended beyond his involvement with the Pastoralists' Association. In January 1898, he entertained the Governor of Queensland, Lord Lamington, for lunch at *Bierbank* whilst the Governor was touring the south-western districts of the Colony.⁶⁵⁴ Further, on 16 January 1901, Ridley was elected to the Committee of Subscribers to the Charleville Hospital.⁶⁵⁵

As the 1890s depression intensified, the Williams brothers' earnings from *Bierbank* diminished. By the mid-1890s, the brothers faced a mounting debt owed to the Commercial Banking Company of Sydney.⁶⁵⁶ However, it was prolonged drought between 1894 and 1902 which

---

649 See "In the Matter of the Division of the Run known as Bierbank, situated in the Pastoral District of Warrego, in the Colony of Queensland": *QSA*, Series 218 Pastoral Holdings Files, Item 437408.

650 See Jenkins, op. cit., p. 23. See also **Plan of Part of the Bierbank Run in 1902**, showing the homestead and the *Bierbank Hotel*.

651 See *The Telegraph* (Brisbane), Tuesday, 1 January 1889, p. 5.

652 See the *Warwick Examiner and Times*, Saturday, 9 May 1891, p. 2.

653 See *The Queenslander*, Saturday, 4 February 1893, p. 226.

654 See *The Week* (Brisbane), Friday, 28 January 1898. It might be recalled that both Ridley's mother and his father had entertained the Governor of South Australia, Sir Henry Young, on *Gol Gol* in September and October 1853: see pp. 142-143 and 145 above.

655 See the *Charleville Times*, Saturday, 19 January 1901, p.3. In addition to his community activities, Ridley was also filling a responsible role in his own family's affairs. On 22 October 1900, he was appointed by the Supreme Court of Queensland to be the Administrator of the estate of Bridget Williams, the wife of his brother, Robert Williams, who had died at *Bierbank* on 22 August 1900: see *The Telegraph*, Monday, 12 November 1900, p. 2.

656 See Jenkins, op cit., p. 24.

delivered the fatal blow to Ridley Williams' occupation of *Bierbank*. By the middle of 1902, things had got so bad that he found himself forced to abandon the run.[657] By this point in time, Ridley appears to have been the last of the Williams brothers still in occupation of the property. The year 1902 would have seen the expiration of the 15 year lease of the non-resumed *Bierbank* land granted by the Queensland Government to the brothers in 1887.[658] Clearly, Ridley was not minded to seek a further term from the Government. On 13 April 1904, the run was formally forfeited to the Crown. [659]

In an interview published in *The Advertiser* on 30 June 1903, Ridley described the events leading up to his departure from *Bierbank* in the following terms:

> "Not a decent season has been experienced since 1894 until the present year. We lost over 11,000 head of cattle and 150 horses. Not a blade of feed was to be seen on the station for two years, and all the adjoining country was in the same deplorable state. Cattle were kept alive on dead leaves and mulga. Fortunes were spent in cutting mulga for them, and even then the stock died. Vast areas of mulga and bushes have died off, and so have the gum trees, even along the creeks. The *Bierbank* station comprises 869 square miles [about 2,227 square kilometres] of country, and when the drought occurred we were carrying only one head of cattle to one square mile and a half, and although we cut mulga and scrub for them, they died in a wholesale way. They cannot be kept alive on mulga alone for a long time. I found that it was advisable to give the stock plenty of salt with the mulga. The saltbushes have died right out on many of the stations. Some, however, are left on the Bulloo and between Warrigal and Bulloo, where once there were miles upon miles of nothing but saltbush country....
>
> The grass is [now] growing luxuriantly. From the beginning of 1902 to November 25 of the same year, only 2.42 in. of rain fell, but from the latter date to the end of the year nearly 7 in. was recorded....
>
> The country must, however, be given a spell, and if an attempt is made to stock it at the present time, it will take years and years to recover. The risk is too great to restock the country at present. After the disappearance of the annual grasses, there will not be old bushes and deep-rooted grasses to fall back upon, as was the case in times past. This is the reason I have left the country; Bierbank station, with its improvements, has been abandoned."[660]

---

657   Ibid. See also the *Brisbane Courier*, Friday, 15 August 1902, p. 3.
658   See pp. 177-178 above.
659   See the *Queensland Government Gazette*, Saturday, 16 April 1904.
660   See *The Advertiser*, Tuesday, 30 June 1903, p. 9. According to Kenton Cameron:
       "Beechal Creek, the principal water supply on Bierbank, possessed few good waterholes and these dried up during the long dry years....
       Bierbank was in 1906 secured by tender from the Lands Department by H. B. Coward of Lyssington Station, New South Wales, who paid the bank a few hundreds of pounds for the improvements, put down an artesian bore, and stocked it with sheep. Today [1959], with resumptions, its area is reduced to about 350 square miles [approximately 906 square kilometres]. The small township of Cheepie on the Quilpie-Charleville railway stands to-day on part of the former lease."
See Cameron, op. cit., p. 351. Cheepie is now uninhabited.

Ridley Williams' Last Years

Following his departure from *Bierbank*, Ridley Williams moved from Queensland to South Australia, where he very likely maintained family connections. At some presently undetermined time, either before or after he moved, he purchased a farming property at Hackham to the immediate south of Adelaide. The homestead on the property, known as *Hackham House*, was built by Edward Castle in the 1850s.[661] Having moved into the building, *Hackham House* was to be Ridley's principal residence for the remainder of his life. It is unclear at this point how he farmed his land, but his farming activities were said in 1904 to be "on a large scale".[662]

On 1 November 1905, Ridley married Alice Sophia Forsyth in St. Saviour's Anglican Church, Glen Osmond.[663] At the time of the marriage, Ridley was 55 years old. His bride was 24 years of age. Ridley and Alice had a total of five children; these being:

- Phyllis Ada Williams; born on or shortly prior to 18 August 1906;
- Marjory Elizabeth Williams; born on or shortly before 10 November 1907;
- Lorna Mabel Williams; born on or shortly prior to 7 December 1909;
- Reginald Ridley Williams; born on or shortly before 29 December 1911; and
- Maxwell Henry David Williams; born on or shortly prior to 18 June 1913.[664]

Ridley Williams' life on his *Hackham House* farm seems to have been largely uneventful. A dispute over rates with the Noarlunga Council took him successfully to the Willunga Local Court in 1906.[665] Later in that year, he place an advertisement in an Adelaide newspaper offering a reward for the return of two missing horses.[666] Whether he ever recovered the horses is unknown.

However, it is clear the Ridley's horizons and interests extended well beyond *Hackham House* and its environs. In 1911, he successfully applied to the Victorian Government to lease Allotment 44 in the Parish of Mulcra.[667] This lot was located in the Victorian Mallee close to the South Australian town of Pinnaroo. It would appear that Ridley cropped wheat on the land. Although his principal residence continued to be *Hackham House*, it is likely that he closely supervised operations on his Mulcra farm, and that he was reasonably active in local Mulcra

---

661 See City of Noarlunga, *Noarlunga Heritage Study* (1979), p. 14.
662 See *The Register*, Monday, 26 December 1904, p. 3.
663 See *Ancestry — Ridley Williams* (http://tinyurl.com/yxorop76) (at 14 March 2020). See also **photo 43**.
664 See *Ancestry — Ridley Williams* (http://tinyurl.com/yxorop76) (at 14 March 2020).
665 See *The Advertiser*, Monday, 20 August 1906, p. 9; and the *The Chronicle* (Adelaide), Saturday, 25 August 1906, p. 38.
666 See the *Express and Telegraph*, Saturday, 29 December 1906, p. 10.
667 See the *Pinnaroo and Border Times*, Friday, 24 November 1911, p. 5; and *The Argus*, Monday, 14 August 1911, p. 8.

affairs; being a member of the Mulcra Branch of the Victorian Farmers Union. In March 1917, he was appointed a Commissioner for Taking Affidavits by the Victorian Government.[668]

Ridley Williams died in Adelaide on Friday, 1 December 1922. He was 72 years of age.[669] He was buried in the Morphett Vale Scotch Cemetery, located a short distance from *Hackham House*.[670] It appears that his death did not give rise to any obituaries published in the press. Ridley lived a rich and challenging life. Adela Purvis observed that his cattle drive from *Bierbank* in Queensland to the *Barrow Creek Station* in the Northern Territory:

"must go down in early Central Australian history as the most daring attempt at crossing semi-arid country with a large number of cattle and horses...."[671]

In retrospect, that feat must be seen as stained by Ridley's illegal and immoral abduction of the four young Aboriginals taken by him as he and Martin made their way home from the Northern Territory. That stain properly acknowledged, Adela Purvis' description of him as "a man of experience, grit and determination" remains apposite.[672]

The son and grandson of convict transportees, Ridley Williams used his ingenuity and acumen to successfully carve out an interesting and rewarding life for himself which extended over wide swathes of Australia.

---

668 See the *Pinnaroo and Border Times*, Friday, 16 March 1917, p. 3.
669 See *The Journal* (Adelaide), Saturday, 2 December 1922, p. 8; *The Register*, Monday, 4 December 1922, p. 6; and *Ancestry — Ridley Williams* (http://tinyurl.com/yxorop76) (at 14 March 2020).
670 See **photo 44**.
671 See Adela Purvis, *Heroes Unsung* (1971), Book 2, p. 49.
672 Ibid.

Conclusion

Transportation to New South Wales proved to be the making of John Jenkins Snr. Spared the noose following his conviction for burglary in 1820, he was also spared a likely life of economic privation and social immobility in rural Kent. In Australia, his geographic, economic and perhaps social horizons expanded beyond any which he could have reasonably imagined whilst a young man in England. After squatting on a large expanse of fine grazing land near Wagga Wagga, replete with valuable cattle, he ended his days in an imposing stone house in Berrima.

John lived long enough to see his children, and indeed at least some of his grandchildren, build upon his achievements in New South Wales so as to acquire vast tracts of land and great wealth. While his step-son, Thomas Jenkins, may not have been as successful in life as his other children, he certainly appears to have lived a worthy life which brought him at least a fair measure of rewards.

John's elder daughter, Mary Ann, together with her husband, James Garner, occupied a small grazing property, *Ploughed Ground*; and later also *Ulong*, a much larger run with a Murrumbidgee River frontage. They subsequently acquired and successfully ran a hotel, the *Gap Inn*, at Jerrowa near Yass; together with a grazing property, *Walgrove*, to the south-east of Yass. One of Mary Ann's great-grandsons, Walter Merriman, was knighted in 1954 for his services to the wool industry.

However, John Jenkins' two sons, Jack and Frank, proved to be the most successful of his children. Jointly, and then severally, the two brothers came to squat on very large runs in and around the Riverina. By supplying beef cattle to the hungry miners on the Victorian gold fields, they each acquired wealth which would have been utterly unattainable, or even imaginable, for them in England given their parents' stations in life.

Although always at heart graziers, both Jack and Frank turned their seemingly boundless energies and ambitions to additional pursuits. In Jack's case, he purchased and built hotels and commercial premises in Gundagai, and constructed flour mills in both Spring Flat and North Wagga. His most ambitious, and likely least successful, venture was probably the paddle steamer *Nangus*, which Jack had constructed for transporting rural produce on the middle reaches of the Murrumbidgee River.

Jack Jenkins appears to have been somewhat less successful than his brother Frank in his speculative business ventures. Although Frank, too, built hotels and acquired urban commercial premises in Narrandera, Wagga Wagga and elsewhere, he concentrated his energies on the acquisition and exploitation of grazing properties in New South Wales, Victoria and

Queensland. Although thwarted in his attempt to gain a depasturing licence over the land on which Mildura now stands, Frank was able to establish the *Gol Gol* run on the opposite bank of the Murray River.

Soon after taking up the *Gol Gol* run, Frank Jenkins effectively transferred it to his second sister, Elizabeth, and her husband, Henry Williams. They, and their multitude of children, successfully ran the property until Elizabeth's untimely death in 1865.

By the time of Elizabeth Williams' death, a number of her sons had left *Gol Gol* and the south-west of New South Wales for south-western Queensland. There, they came to occupy and graze a consolidated run known as *Bierbank* which covered literally thousands of square kilometres of outback land centred on the Beechal Creek in the Warrego District. The most prominent, and perhaps the most successful, of Elizabeth's sons was Ridley Williams. The latter led a daring and monumentally challenging cattle drive in and between 1882 and 1884 from *Bierbank* to Alice Springs and Barrow Creek in the Northern Territory. In doing so, he amply demonstrated his skills as an astute businessman, a great horseman and a superb bushman.

At least some of John Jenkins' children and grandchildren came to enjoy wealth and the trappings of wealth. Like their father, Jack and Frank both occupied fine rural homesteads which now enjoy heritage classifications — Jack on *Nangus* and Frank on *Buckingbong*. At one point during the gold rushes, Jack was apparently able to shoe at least one of his horses with golden horseshoes. It was not for nothing that he was known locally as "Roaring Jack". For his part, Frank saw fit to secure the services of an expert from France to make both his own wine and his own brandy for him.

However, it must be acknowledged that the pastoral expansions of John's children and grandchildren contributed to the disaster which fell upon the original inhabitants on the lands on which John's descendants came to graze. Jack and Frank, in particular, were at the cutting edge of the European conquest of Aboriginal territories, and of the effective dispossession of the original inhabitants. Arriving at *Buckingbong* as very young men during the *Wiradjuri War*, Jack and Frank almost certainly participated in the slaughter of Aboriginal men, women and children on Massacre Island in the Murrumbidgee River in late 1840 or early 1841. Frank may also have been responsible, or partly responsible, for subsequent deaths of local Aborigines on the evocatively named Poisoned Waterholes Creek.

In their treatment of Aborigines, Jack and Frank Jenkins were probably no worse nor better than the great majority of their European neighbours. They almost certainly saw their involvement in the *Wiradjuri War* in existential terms — a case of kill or be killed, of survival of the fittest. They likely would have seen themselves as biologically superior to local Aborigines, and as entitled as much by nature as by law to the lands on which they squatted. They very likely saw their actions as being necessary and justifiable, rather than as wicked or cruel.

The fundamental contempt which both Jack and Frank probably held for the Aborigines with whom they contested control of land was also probably a contempt which the Jenkins brothers shared with their nephews. It was certainly a contempt which thoroughly imbued the attitudes and actions of their nephew, Ridley Williams. It was no doubt that contempt, grounded in a perception that Aborigines were lesser human beings, which coloured Ridley's feelings when he abducted the four Aboriginal youngsters on his return journey from Barrow Creek to *Bierbank* in 1884. Like his Jenkins uncles, Ridley was probably an instinctive believer in Social Darwinism without ever being formally acquainted with the theory.[673] Again like his uncles, Ridley was probably no worse and no better in his attitude towards, and treatment of, Aborigines than most of his local European contemporaries.

Although Jack and Frank Jenkins enjoyed great wealth for much of their respective lives, it seems that neither died wealthy. In the end, circumstances substantially beyond their control brought them down. The principal causes of their downfalls were undoubtedly the costs associated with their efforts to defend their lands from the inroads of selectors and would-be selectors coupled with the economic turbulence and upsets of the late 1880s and 1890s. Poor investments probably also contributed to Jack's ultimate failure.

Ridley Williams was no doubt affected badly by the economic problems at the end of the Nineteenth Century. However, it is clear that it was primarily prolonged drought which saw him off *Bierbank*.

Squatting on Australia's pastoral frontiers was an inherently risky business. To some, it was the foundation of rural empires. However, there is little doubt that more squatters ultimately failed than succeeded. Yet although they may have finally come to grief as pastoralists, the children and grandchildren of John Jenkins whose lives are traced above led rich and eventful lives. It is striking that Elizabeth Williams, the daughter of one transportee and the wife of another, came to entertain the Governor of South Australia on *Gol Gol* (albeit briefly), and that her son, Ridley Williams, similarly entertained the Governor of Queensland on *Bierbank*.

In the final analysis, the Jenkins family, at the least, present us with a microcosm of a substantial portion of the men and women who were at the forefront of the European conquest and settlement of rural Australia over the course of the Nineteenth Century.

---

673   Although see p. 170 above.

Genealogical Charts

John Jenkins

Proximate Family Tree

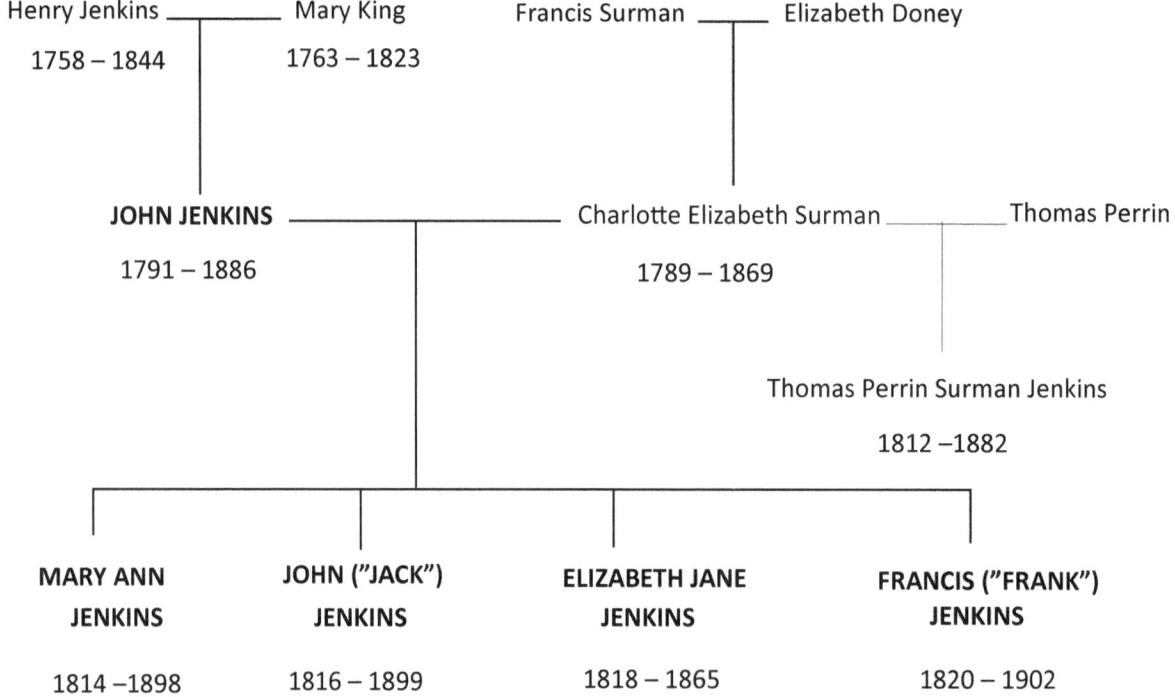

Thomas Perrin Surman Jenkins

Proximate Family Tree

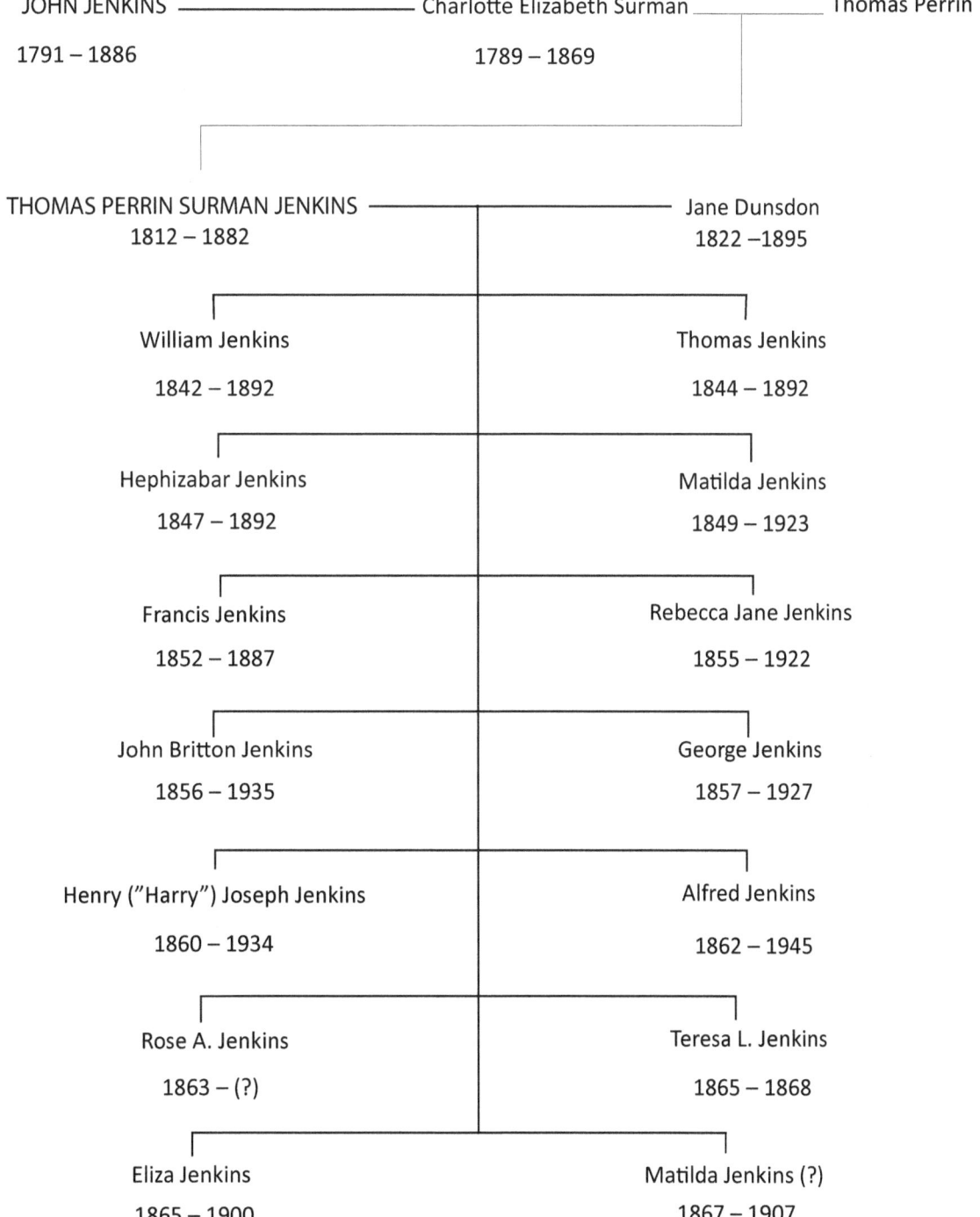

Mary Ann Garner (née Jenkins)
Proximate Family Tree

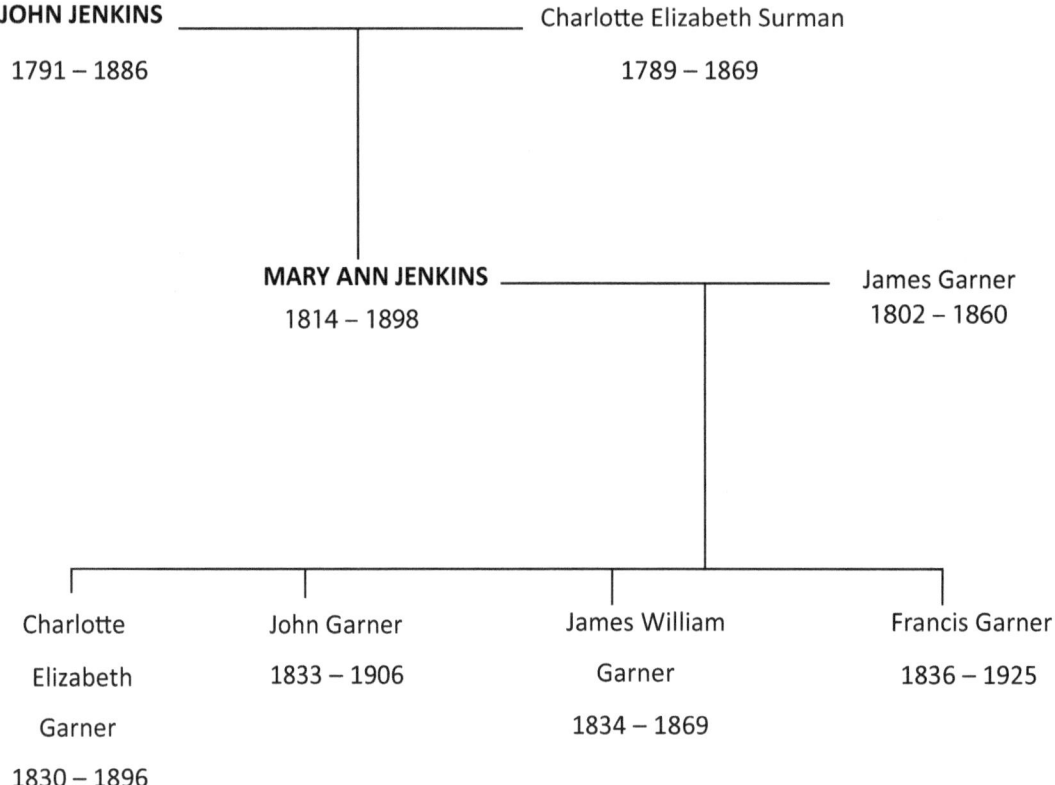

John ("Jack") Jenkins Junior
Proximate Family Tree

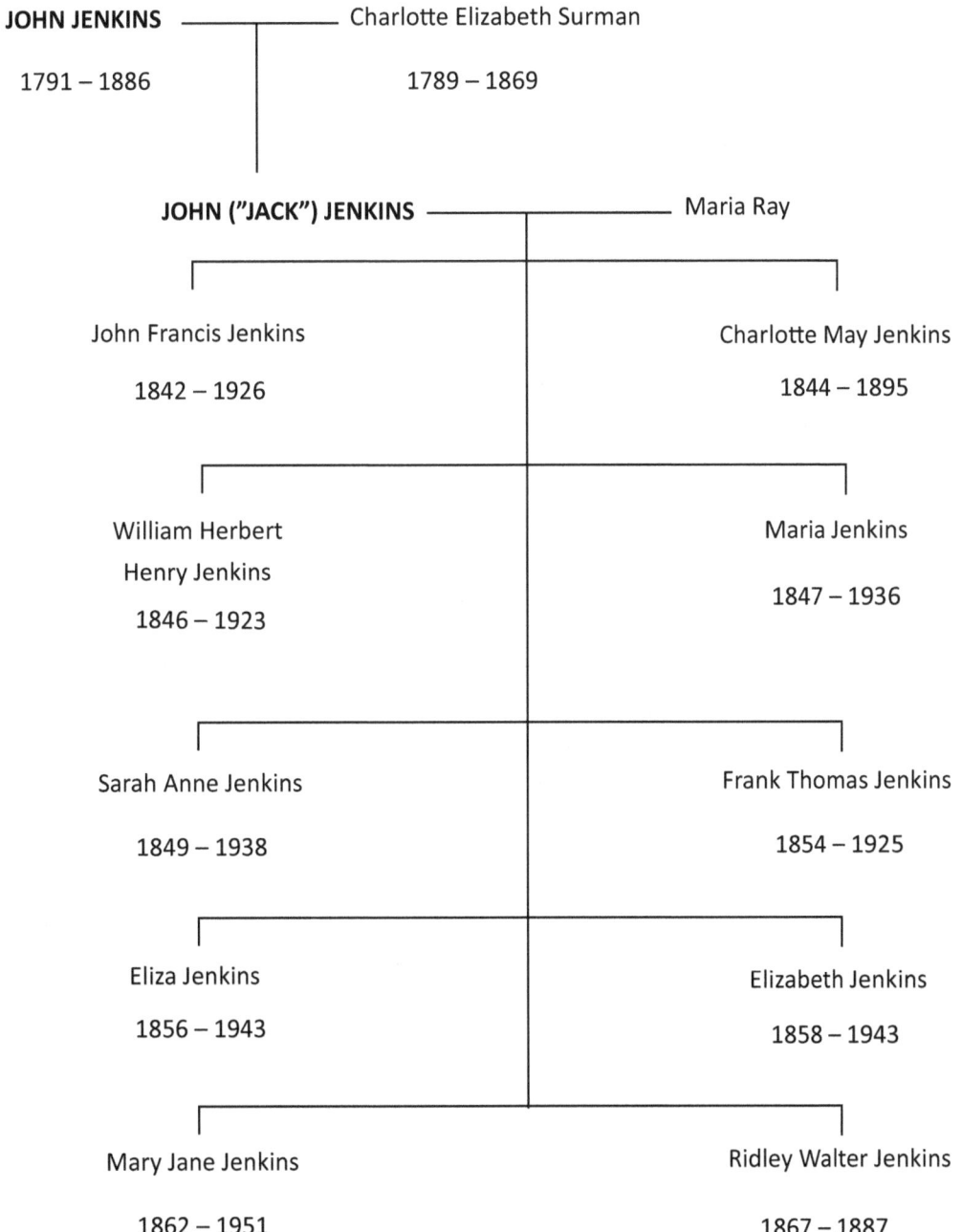

Francis ("Frank") Jenkins
Proximate Family Tree

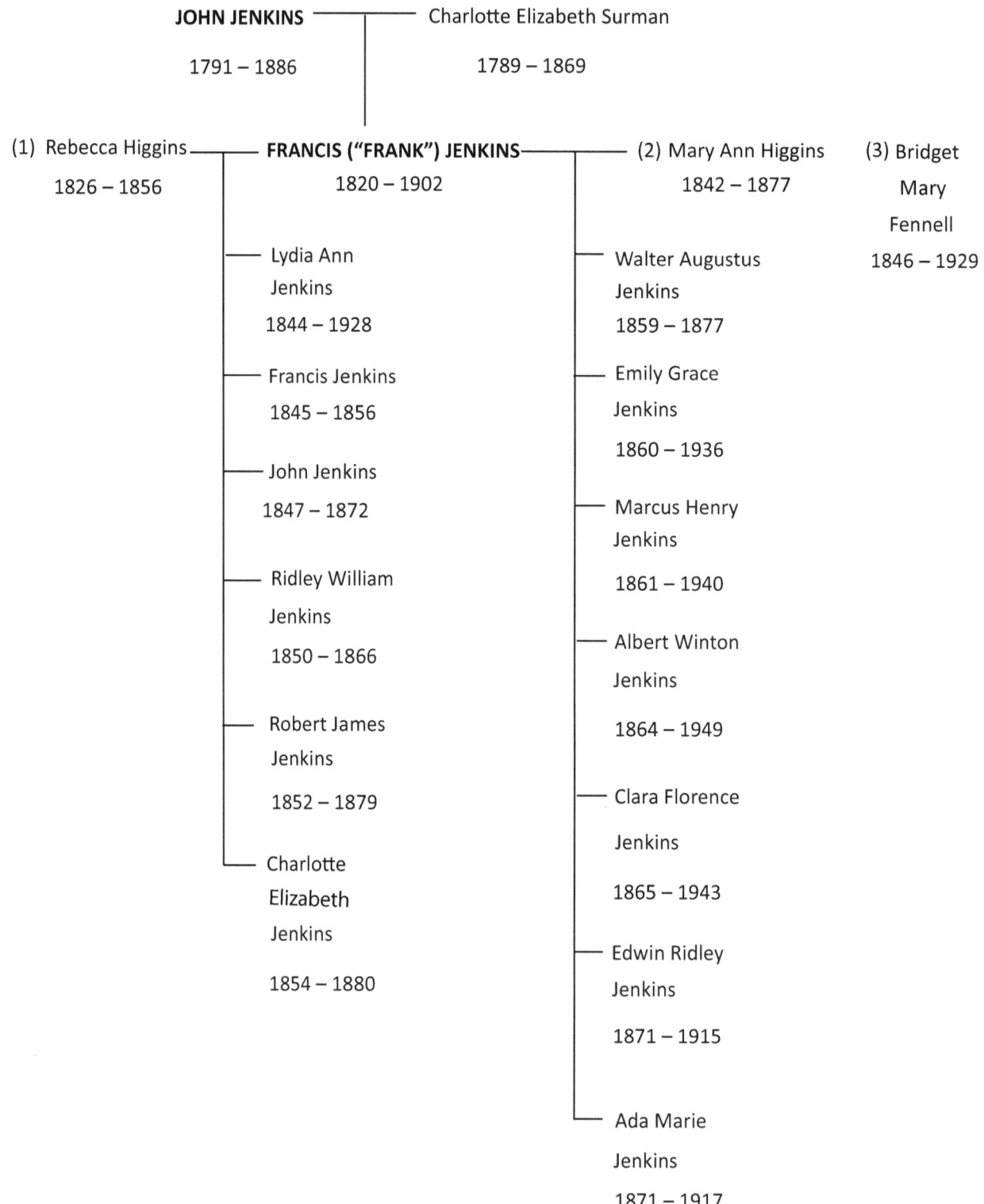

Elizabeth Jane Williams (née Jenkins)
Proximate Family Tree

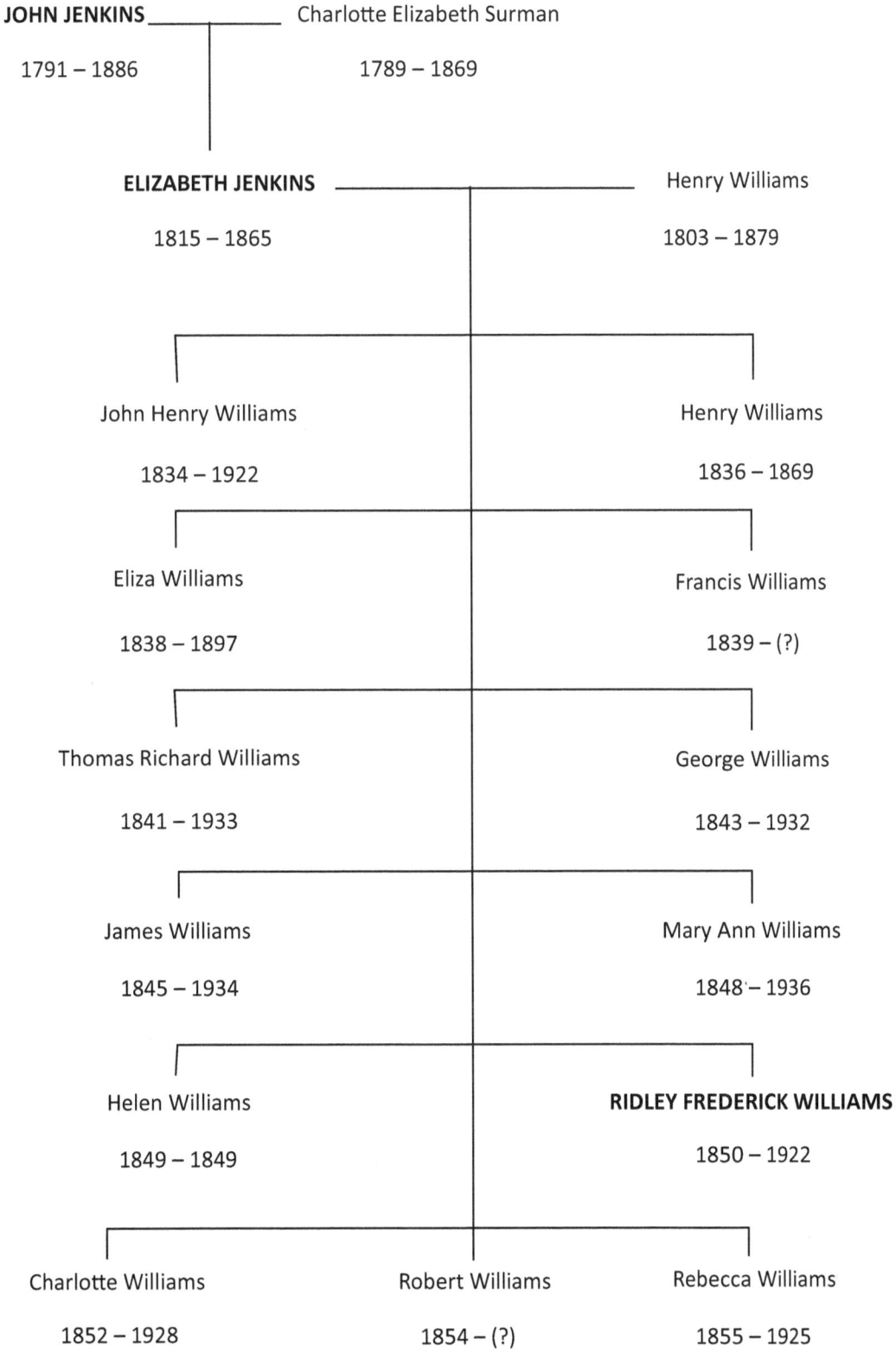

Ridley Frederick Williams
Proximate Family Tree

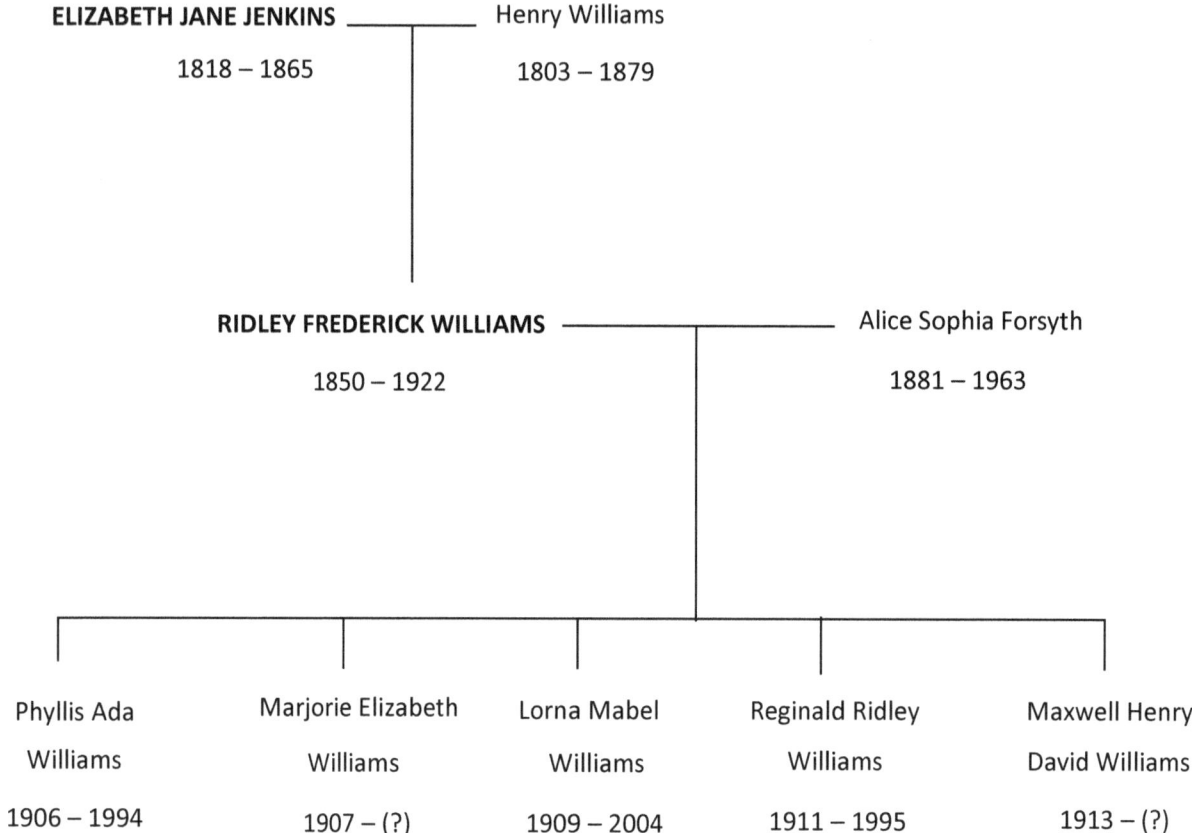

Maps and Plans

Medway River Valley Map. The parishes of East Malling, West Malling, Waterbury and Bredhurst are highlighted on a white background.

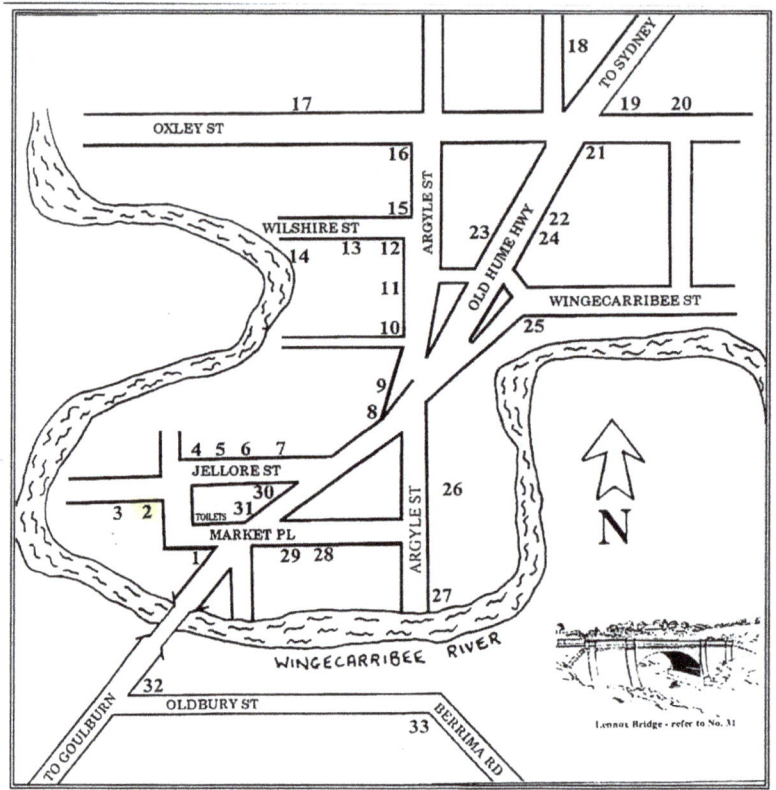

Historic Berrima Plan — see footnote 102 on p. 28.

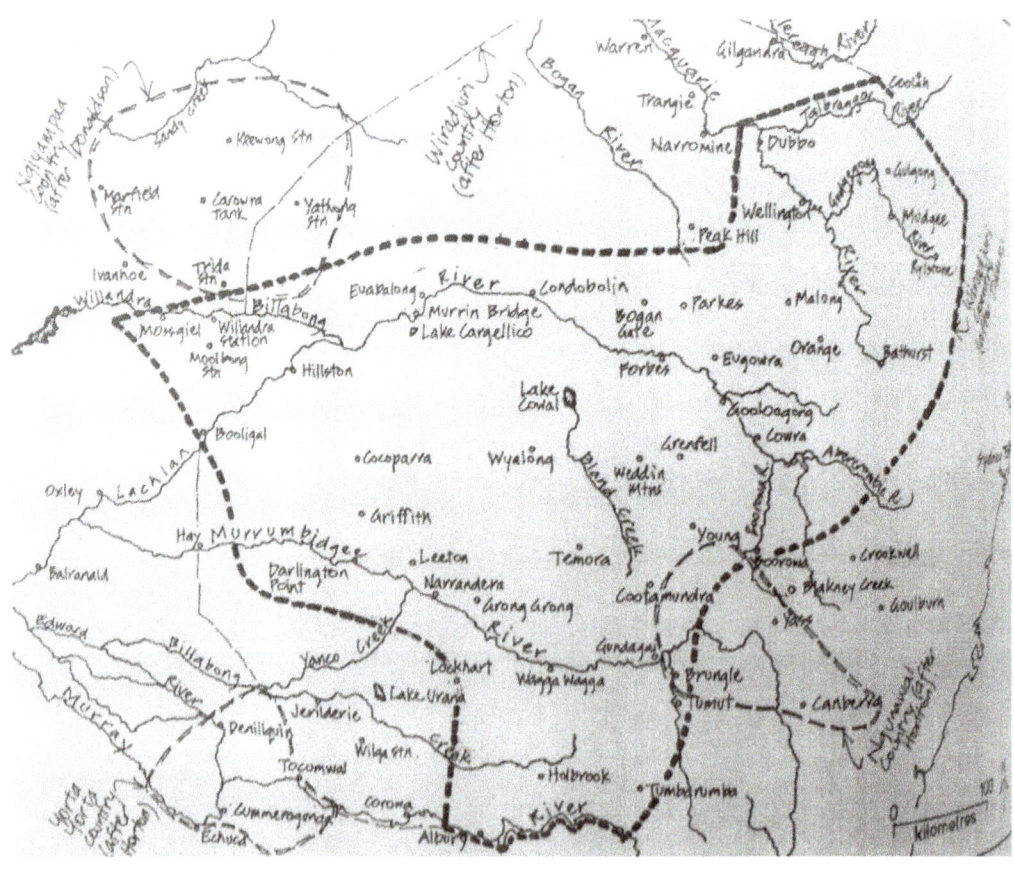

Wiradjuri Country Map — see footnote 173 on p. 51.

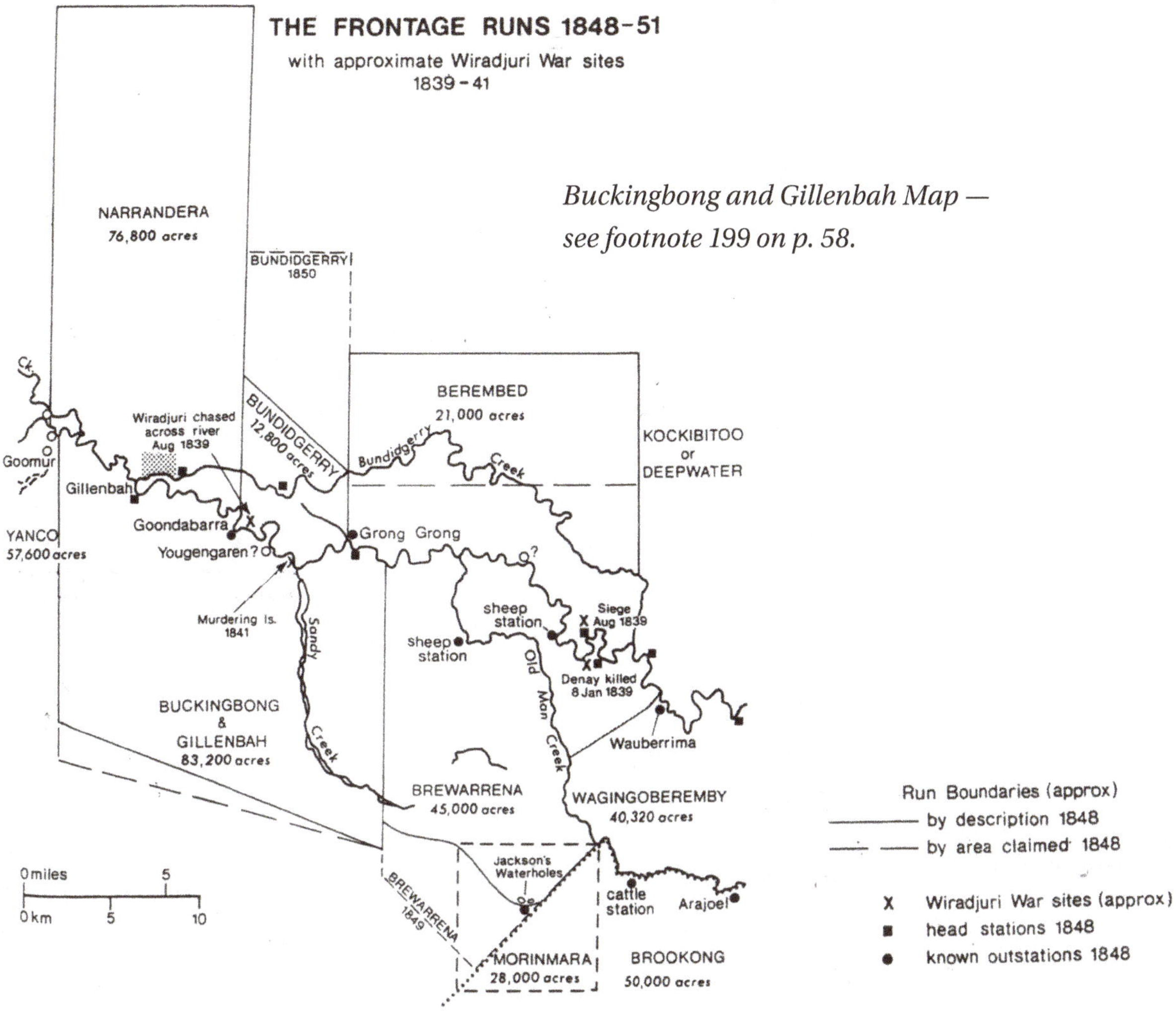

*Buckingbong and Gillenbah Map —
see footnote 199 on p. 58.*

North Wagga Flour Mill Site Plan — see footnote 249 on p. 70.

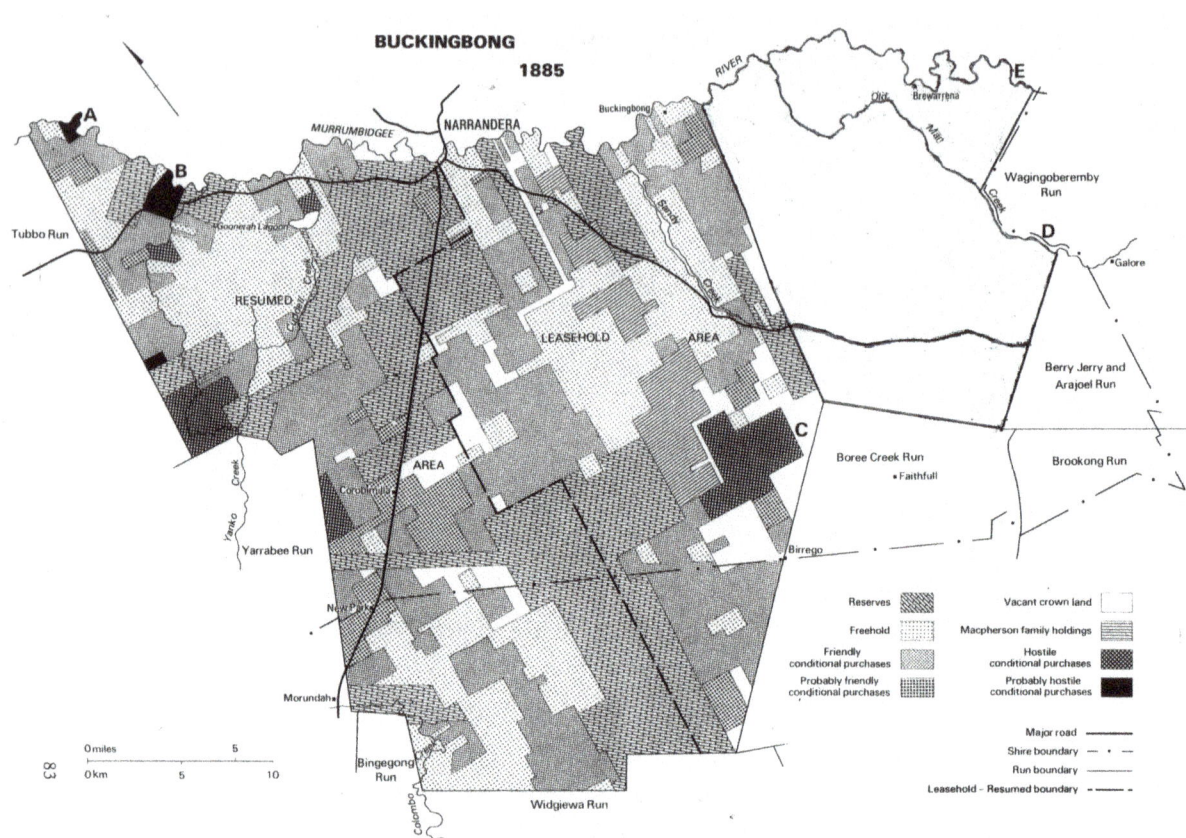

Buckingbong in 1885 – see footnote 459 on p. 124.

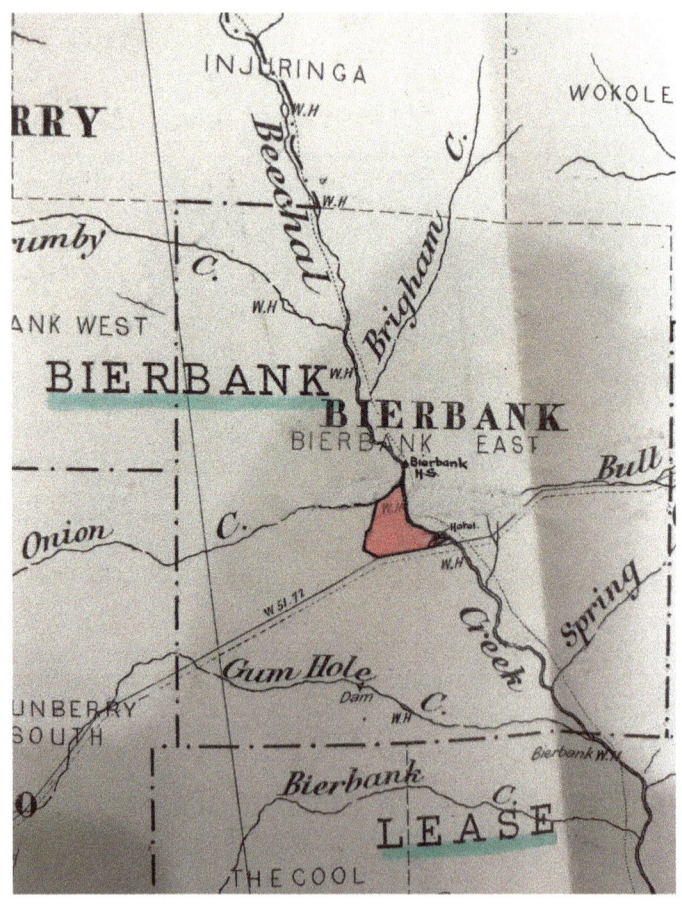

Plan of Part of the Bierbank Run in 1902 – see footnote 650 on page 179.

Drawings

Drawing of the Retribution — see footnote 30 on p. 11.

Drawing of the North Wagga Flour Mill — see footnote 241 on p. 70.

*Drawing of Auburn-villa at the time of its subdivision and sale in 1925
— see footnote 432 on p. 117.*

*The Lady Augusta (left) and the Mary Ann (right) at Swan Hill in September 1853
— see footnote 526 on p. 145.*

Bibliography

Books

Allen, James: *Journey of an Experimental Trip by the "Lady Augusta" on the River Murray* (1853)

Anon.: *St. Paul's Nangus: Centenary 1878-1978* (1978)

Atkinson, James: *An Account of the State of Agriculture and Grazing in New South Wales* (1826)

Australian Heritage Commission: *The Heritage of Australia: The Illustrated Register of the National Estate* (1981)

Baylis, James: *Early History of the Murrumbidgee-Wagga Wagga* (1914)

Beddoe, Noel: *The Yalda Crossing* (1912)

Billis, Ralph and Kenyon, Alfred: *Pastoral Pioneers of Port Phillip* (2nd ed., 1974)

Boldrewood, Rolf: *A Sydney-Side Saxon* (1891)

Boyce, James: *!835: The founding of Melbourne and the Conquest of Australia* (2011)

Bride, Thomas (ed.): *Letters from Victorian Pioneers* (Republished 1983)

Bridge, Peter and Murray, Ian (eds.), *William Benstead: Pioneers of Alice Springs and Coolgardie* (2019)

Campbell, J. F.: *Squatting on Crown Lands in New South Wales* (1968)

Cantlon, Maurice: *Homesteads of Southern New South Wales: 1830-1900* (1981)

City of Boroondara Municipal-Wide Heritage Gap Study (2019), Vol. 6

City of Noarlunga: *Noarlunga Heritage Study* (1979)

Coulson, Helen: *Echuca-Moama: Murray River Neighbours* (2009)

Featherstonhaugh, Cuthbert: *After Many Days* (1917)

Ferguson, James: *Squatting: Romance and Reality* (2017)

Freeman, Peter: *The Homestead: A Riverina Anthology* (1982)

Gammage, Bill: *Narrandera Shire* (1986)

Gammage, Bill: *The Biggest Estate on Earth: How Aborigines Made Australia* (2011)

Gilmore, Mary: *Old Days, Old Ways: A Book of Recollections* (1934)

Gormly, James: *Exploration and Settlement in Australia* (1921)

Grant, Stan: *Talking to my Country* (2016)

Hanson, William: *The Pastoral Possessions of New South Wales* (1889)

Hearn, Judi: *Galleries of Pink Galahs: A History of the Shire of Murray 1838-1988* (2009)

Historical Records of Australia: Series 1, Vols. 1, 18 and 21

Ireland, William: *England's Topography: or a New and Complete History of the County of Kent* (1829), Vol. 3

Irvin, Eric (ed.): *Letters from the River* (1959)

Jenkins, Leslie: *A Brief History of Quilpie Shire* (2001)

Kabaila, Peter: *Wiradjuri Places: The Murrumbidgee River Basin* (1995), Vol.1

Kapitany, Attila: *Australian Pigface and Pigweed* (2013)

Kiddle, Margaret: *Men of Yesterday* (1980)

King, Cecil: *An Outline of Closer Settlement in New South Wales, Part 1: The Sequence of Land Laws, 1788-1956* (1957)

Landsborough, William: *Journal of Landsborough's Expedition from Carpentaria in Search of Burke and Wills* (1862)

Lennon, Jane: *Pastoral Australia: Fortress, Failures and Hard Yakka: An Historical Overview* (2010)

Lindner, W. Benjamin: *Waltzing Matilda: Australia's Accidental Anthem: A Forensic History* (2019)

Main, George: *The Regeneration of Rural Place* (2005)

Macklin, Robert: *Hamilton Hume: Our Greatest Explorer* (2016)

Macquarie, Lachlan: *Lachlan Macquarie, Governor of New South Wales: Journals of his Tours in New South Wales and Van Diemen's Land* (1956)

McGowan, Barry: *Tracking the Dragon* (2015)

McWilliam, Gwen: *Hawthorn Street Index: A Brief History of the Streets of Hawthorn* (2004)

Mitchell, Thomas: *Three Expeditions into the Interior of Eastern Australia* (1838), Vo. 2

Morris, Sherry: *Wagga Wagga: A History* (1999)

Nicholson, John: *The Incomparable Captain Cadell* (2004)

Narrandera Cemetery Heritage Walk

Olsen, Penny: *Night Parrot: Australia's Most Elusive Bird* (2018)

Parsons, Robert: *Ships of the Inland Rivers* (1st ed., 1987)

Parsons, Robert: *Ships of the Inland Rivers* (3rd revised ed., 1996)

Press, Kate and Thompson, Valerie: *West Limerick Families Abroad* (2001)

Pugh's Queensland Almanac (1867)

Purvis, Adela: *Our Alice Springs: A Brief History From Its Earliest Times To The Present* (1952)

Purvis, Adela: *Heroes Unsung* (1971), Book 2

Roberts, Stephen: *History of Australian Land Settlement* (1924)

Smith, L. R.: *The Aboriginal Population of Australia* (1980)

Spreadborough, Robert and Anderson, Hugh: *Victorian Squatters* (1983)

Stone, Barry: *The Squatters* (2019)

Sturt, Charles: *Two Expeditions Into The Interior Of Southern Australia* (1834), Vol. 1

Thornton-Kemsley, Colin: *Kentish Kemsleys and Their Descendants* (1980)

Thwaites, Francis Joseph: *The Broken Melody* (1930)

Vann, John: *The Squatting Directory for New South Wales* (1865)

Vaux, James Hardy: *Memoirs of James Hardy Vaux* (1819), Vol. 2, Chap. 9

Walker, Thomas: *A Month in the Bush in New South Wales* (1838)

Westwood, Joseph: *The Journal of Joseph Westwood* (1865)

Whitworth, Robert: *Bailliere's New South Wales Gazetteer and Road Guide* (1866)

Articles

Abbott, G. J.: "Merriman, James (1816-1883)" in *Australian Dictionary of Biography* (http://tinyurl.com/qn3p5nd)

Alexandrina Library Service: *History Room Service (No. 67, February 2010)* (http://tinyurl.com/y48geclq)

Anon.: "Census 'snapshot' of Berrima in 1841" in (July, 2014) 463 *Berrima District Historical and Family History Society Newsletter* 1, p. 6 (http://tinyurl.com/sdc7jql)

Anon.: *Measuring Worth* (http://tinyurl.com/y5kpae96)

Anon.: *The Family Hotel* (http://tinyurl.com/yxnggxqg)

Answers: What is Extra History of Hawthorn? (http://tinyurl.com/y58hpz5n)

Australian Museum: *Mulga Snake* (http://tinyurl.com/yxsezwmj)

Australian National Herbarium: *Calandrinia balonensis* (http://tinyurl.com/y4yghrnd)

Australian Native Plants Society: *Eucalyptus orbifolia* (http://tinyurl.com/y5134xfl)

Australian Native Plants Society: *Portulaca oleracea* (http://tinyurl.com/y559h9z6)

Australian Stockman's Hall of Fame: *Ridley Williams — Detailed Report* (No. USH 00063)

Australian Trade Union Archives: *Amalgamated Shearers' Union of Australasia* (http://tinyurl.com/y2fpk34x)

Australian Trade Union Archives: *Australian Shearers' Union (1886-1887)* (http://tinyurl.com/y4ymreu3)

Australasian Underwater Cultural Heritage Database — Nangus [1314] (http://tinyurl.com/yyqvntq9)

Barnard, Alan: "Mort, Thomas Sutcliffe (1816-1876)" in *Australian Dictionary of Biography* (http://tinyurl.com/y3poz9bn)

Bassett, Judith: "The Faithfull Massacre at the Broken River 1838" in (2009) 13(24) *Journal of Australian Studies* 18.

Bateson, Charles: "Reid, David (1777-1840)" in *Australian Dictionary of Biography* (http://tinyurl.com/y7gblxem)

Baylis, James: "The Murrumbidgee and Wagga Wagga" in (1927) 13(4) *Journal and Proceedings of the Royal Historical Society* 253

Beale, Edgar: "Kennedy, Edmund Besley (1818-1848)" in *Australian Dictionary of Biography* (http://tinyurl.com/s47zyme)

Bean, Christine: *From Tradesman to the Poor House (Gransden Family Website)* (http://tinyurl.com/y7z2xkx4)

Blake, Thom: *How Much Is It Worth* (http://tinyurl.com/y2w86obz)

Brown, Richard: "Unlocking the Land" in *Looking at History (2013)* (http://tinyurl.com/lqrhu7v)

Butler, Reg: "South Australian Publicans — Carl Dreyer" in *Localwiki: Adelaide Hills*

Buxton, Gordon: "Gormly, James (1836-1922)" in *Australian Dictionary of Biography* (http://tinyurl.com/uq5k8hc)

Cameron, A. C.: "Possible Sight Record of the Night Parrot *Geopsittacus Occidentalis*" in (1972) 8(4) *Sunbird* 87

Cameron, Kenton: "Ridley Williams, Early Queensland Pastoralist" in (1960) 6(2) *Journal of the Royal Historical Society of Queensland* 342

City of Wagga Wagga — Wagga Bridge (http://tinyurl.com/yxopezzu)

Clark, Richard: "Letter dated 1 December 1865" in (2008) 12(1) *Snodland Historical Society Newsletter* 3 (http://tinyurl.com/j26229j)

Crockett, Roger: *The Early History of Bredhurst Manor* (2012) (http://tinyurl.com/jtgzunk)

"Crested Pigeons" in *Birds in Backyards* (http://tinyurl.com/y3j2j5e7)

Durack, Mary: "Carr-Boyd, William Henry James (1852-1925)" in *Australian Dictionary of Biography* (http://tinyurl.com/y6mkl4vt)

Ellis, William: "Mill Street" in *The Street Names of Wagga Wagga* (http://tinyurl.com/yxe63kuo)

Fenby, Claire and Gergis Joëlle: "Rainfall variations in south-eastern australia part 1 — consolidating evidence from pre-instrumental documentary sources, 1788-1860" in (2012) 33(14) *International Journal of Climatology* 2956 (http://tinyurl.com/y4g2to8m)

Francis, Charles: "Stawell, Sir William Foster (1815-1889)" in *Australian Dictionary of Biography* (http://tinyurl.com/yyxf5695)

Gammage, Bill: "The Wiradjuri War of 1838-1840" in (1983) 16 *The Push From The Bush: A Bulletin Of Social History* 3

Gibbney, H. J.: "Sturt, Charles (1795-1869)" in *Australian Dictionary of Biography* (http://tinyurl.com/3qhcu76)

Gormly, James: "Exploration and Settlement on the Murray and Murrumbidgee" in (1906) 2(2) *Journal of the Australian Historical Society* 34

Griffin, Carl J.: "Parish Farms and the Poor Law: A Response to Unemployment in Southern England" in (2011) 59 *Agricultural History Review* 176

Hohnen, Peter: "McCaughey, Sir Samuel (1835-1919)" in *Australian Dictionary of Biography* (http://tinyurl.com/yxdtw4bc)

McQuilton, John: "Morgan, Daniel (Dan) (1830-1865)" in *Australian Dictionary of Biography* (http://tinyurl.com/y62rzskx)

Merrett, David: "The Australian Bank Crashes of the 1890s Revisited" in (2013) 87 *Business History Review* 407

Merryvale Stud — History (http://tinyurl.com/y7a3olck)

Micalong Swamp Flora Reserve No. 70 Working Plan (http://tinyurl.com/y3z9zxp8)

Mildura & District Genealogical Society Inc.: "The Naming of Mildura" in (2008) 8(2) *The Grapeline* 6

Mitchell, Jessie: *'Country Belonging to Me': Land and Labour on Aboriginal Missions and Protectorate Stations, 1830-1850* (http://tinyurl.com/86mrrvw3)

Murray, Frank: *Mangles Indent* (http://tinyurl.com/y494jtaq)

Nairn, Bede: "Robertson, Sir John (1816-1891)" in *Australian Dictionary of Biography* (http://tinyurl.com/y42edrrq)

New South Wales Office of Environment and Heritage — Berrima House (http://tinyurl.com/yaxzhq8c)

New South Wales Government State Archives and Records: *Land Grants Guide, 1788-1856: Historical Background* (http://tinyurl.com/y9dnpq8j)

New South Wales Parks and Wildlife Service: *Mungo: 1788-1901* (http://tinyurl.com/yxg79g9g)

Open Houses 2019: St. Joseph's School Hawthorn: Fairmount House, East Hawthorn (http://tinyurl.com/y3zvhe7b)

Parks and Wildlife Commission of the Northern Territory: *Annas Reservoir Conservation Reserve* (http://tinyurl.com/y4gpymzf)

Parliament of New South Wales: *Mr Robert Pitt Jenkins (1814-1859)* (http://tinyurl.com/y32cpgat)

Pearson, Sidney: "The South-West Corner of Queensland" in (October 1940) 3(2) *Journal of the Royal Historical Society of Queensland* 100

Perry, T. M.: "Atkinson, James (1795-1834)" in *Australian Dictionary of Biography* (http://tinyurl.com/y7mdupxz)

Popper, Robert: "History and Development of the Accused's Right to Testify" in [1962] *Washington University Law Review* 454

Purvis, Adela: "Concerning The Meeting Of The Ross and Mills Parties North Of Alice Springs March 18, 1871" in (1972) 9(3) *Journal of the Royal Historical Society of Queensland* 107

Purvis, Adela: "This Township Named Stuart, Now Alice Springs" in [1947] *Proceedings of the Royal Geographical Society of Australasia, South Australian Branch* 54

Rathbone, R. W.: " Flood, Edward (1805-1888)" in *Australian Dictionary of Biography* (http://tinyurl.com/yxwf462u)

Royal Geographical Society of South Australia Inc.: *Relics and Artefacts — Sturt's Cannon* (http://tinyurl.com/v4vk4nd)

Seymour, George: "Days of Cheap Sheep" in *My Heritage — George Seymour* (http://tinyurl.com/yxdpz6kv)

Shaw, A. G. L.: "Victoria's First Governor" in (2003) 71 *The Latrobe Journal* 85 (http://tinyurl.com/k4pcovb)

Sherratt, Tim: *SRNSW — Index, Data, Depasturing Licences, CSV* (http://tinyurl.com/qtw9no7)

Shire of Wentworth: *Heritage Study — Williamsville Homestead (No. 55)* (http://tinyurl.com/y3bsrh3c)

State Library of South Australia: "Did you know?: Captain Sturt's cannon" in *S A Memory: Downstream: the River Murray in South Australia* (http://tinyurl.com/y3699pmr)

Stephenson, John: *Richard Morris Rivers — West Blowering Station* (http://tinyurl.com/y6nx7o3z)

Thompson, Chris: "No. 11 of Berrima 1841 — John Jenkins, Jellore Street" in *The 36 Households: Harper's Mansion, Berrima* (http://tinyurl.com/y3azfpw2)

Thompson, Valerie: "Men of the Mangles, 1822" in (Winter, 2002) *The Old Limerick Journal* 36

"Topknot Pigeons" in *Birds in Backyards* (http://tinyurl.com/y3hlnnqk)

Trundle, Gwen: "Landsborough, William (1825-1886)" in *Australian Dictionary of Biography* (http://tinyurl.com/n7x9tu68)

University of Melbourne Biomedical Sciences Department: *Australo-Papuan Taipans* (http://tinyurl.com/y6a8k4g5)

Walsh, G. P.: "Merriman, Sir Walter Thomas (1882-1972)" in *Australian Dictionary of Biography* (http://tinyurl.com/w98td9z)

Western Australian Department of Primary Industries and Regional Development: *Roly poly* (http://tinyurl.com/y66n7c78)

Whitiker, Chris: "Captain Charles Sturt's Cannon?" in (1978) 79 *Proceedings of the Royal Geographical Society of Australasia, South Australian Branch* 38

Wikipedia — Bathurst War (http://tinyurl.com/yb9cksd4)

Wikipedia — Berrima House (http://tinyurl.com/ycrq286a)

Wikipedia — Berrima, New South Wales (http://tinyurl.com/y94mcnun)

Wikipedia — Bleeding Diathesis (http://tinyurl.com/y47qfwaj)

Wikipedia — Bloody Code (http://tinyurl.com/y4mql8lf)

Wikipedia — Bredhurst (http://tinyurl.com/hwqzuck)

Wikipedia — Burke and Wills (http://tinyurl.com/yyxme3q3)

Wikipedia — Calandrinia balonensis (http://tinyurl.com/yy5494dy)

Wikipedia — Capital Punishment in the United Kingdom (http://tinyurl.com/zps5zmh)

Wikipedia — Edmund Kennedy (http://tinyurl.com/ujue9tr)

Wikipedia — Firestick Farming (http://tinyurl.com/tfqrc54)

Wikipedia — Granada (1810 ship) (http://tinyurl.com/yxg3upgr)

Wikipedia — Gundagai (http://tinyurl.com/mybx35s)

Wikipedia — Gundagai: Riverboat Trade (http://tinyurl.com/y6ond7hn)

Wikipedia — Jack Cade's Rebellion (http://tinyurl.com/yyc46onf)

Wikipedia — Jarijari (http://tinyurl.com/y4zx5bhz)

Wikipedia — Nineteen Counties (http://tinyurl.com/y9pany9e)

Wikipedia — Oldbury Farm (http://tinyurl.com/vzlpjdn)

Wikipedia — Ticket of Leave (http://tinyurl.com/y8ouhjwp)

Wikipedia — The Broken Melody (1937 film) (http://tinyurl.com/y5tdgnzt)

Wikipedia — Tumblong, NSW (http://tinyurl.com/y6n2x6n5)

Wikipedia — Warren Hastings (1789 ship) (http://tinyurl.com/y72zgums)

Wikipedia — William Macarthur (http://tinyurl.com/y9ka9vjv)

Genealogical Materials

Ancestry — Geoffrey Ward Family Tree: Elizabeth Jane Jenkins (http://tinyurl.com/y6raf4tm)

Ancestry — Geoffrey Ward Family Tree: Henry Thomas Williams (http://tinyurl.com/y3j3yom9)

Ancestry — Geoffrey Ward Family Tree: Ridley Williams (http://tinyurl.com/yxorop76)

Ancestry — Stokes Family Tree: Jane Dunsdon (http://tinyurl.com/tgr2o7d)

Ancestry — Stokes Family Tree: Thomas Perrin Surman Jenkins (http://tinyurl.com/yyz89ncq)

Australian Royalty — Charlotte Elizabeth Surman (1789-1869) (http://tinyurl.com/y9l39tt7)

Australian Royalty — Rebecca Higgins (1826-1856) (http://tinyurl.com/y6ak9wbh)

Australian Surname Group — Dreyer of South Australia (http://tinyurl.com/yxksb8zg)

Convict Records of Australia — Dick voyage to New South Wales Australia in 1820 with 141 passengers (http://tinyurl.com/y97ct7p2)

Convict Records of Australia — Henry Williams (http://tinyurl.com/y2puaeos)

Convict Records of Australia — James Garner (http://tinyurl.com/yd585zsk)

Convict Records of Australia — Speke voyage to New South Wales, Australia in 1820 with 156 passengers (http://tinyurl.com/ya7cazmc)

Convict Records of Australia — Thomas Dillon (http://tinyurl.com/y5du7qe6)

Convict Records of Australia — William Garner (http://tinyurl.com/y7bppbg2)

East Malling Burials, 1570-1924 — Mary Jenkins 1823 (http://tinyurl.com/v4kyrnk)

Free BDM — Henry Jenkins (http://tinyurl.com/y3jb63ql)

Geneanet — Williams (http://tinyurl.com/vna5hv9)

Geni — Carl Edward William Dreyer (http://tinyurl.com/u6s4vp2)

Geni — Eliza Williams (http://tinyurl.com/svwalpb)

Marr, Aitken, Watts Family Tree — Fennell, Brigid Maria (http://tinyurl.com/y9d94rsy)

Marr, Aitken, Watts Family Tree — Fennell, Daniel (http://tinyurl.com/y6s2zeej)

Marr, Aitken, Watts Family Tree — Garner, James (http://tinyurl.com/y8ruqna5)

Marr, Aitken, Watts Family Tree — Higgins, Mary Anne (http://tinyurl.com/yaefjg2f)

Marr, Aitken, Watts Family Tree — Higgins, Rebecca Charlotte (http://tinyurl.com/r4tmd9e)

Marr, Aitken, Watts Family Tree — Jenkins, Charlotte Elizabeth (http://tinyurl.com/utgxldy)

Marr, Aitken, Watts Family Tree — Jenkins, Elizabeth (http://tinyurl.com/y3popqa4)

Marr, Aitken, Watts Family Tree — Jenkins, Francis ("Frank") (http://tinyurl.com/ydhcm5k2)

Marr, Aitken, Watts Family Tree — Jenkins, Francis (http://tinyurl.com/ybnw7zam)

Marr, Aitken, Watts Family Tree — Jenkins, Henry (http://tinyurl.com/yxchu65f)

Marr, Aitken, Watts Family Tree — Jenkins, John ("Jack") (http://tinyurl.com/ya5ohz7a)

Marr, Aitken, Watts Family Tree — Jenkins, John (http://tinyurl.com/y6vxa6ly)

Marr, Aitken, Watts Family Tree — Jenkins, John Francis (http://tinyurl.com/y38fe4h8)

Marr, Aitken, Watts Family Tree — Jenkins, Mary Ann (http://tinyurl.com/y9ekyfez)

Marr, Aitken, Watts Family Tree — Jenkins, Robert James (http://tinyurl.com/y4v4l78q)

Marr, Aitken, Watts Family Tree — Jenkins, Thomas Perrin Surman (http://tinyurl.com/y796tfl4)

Marr, Aitken, Watts Family Tree — Kemsley, Adam (http://tinyurl.com/yxoyu77g)

Marr, Aitken, Watts Family Tree — Kemsley, Ann (http://tinyurl.com/y4ylf7v6)

Marr, Aitken, Watts Family Tree — Kemsley, Elias (http://tinyurl.com/y67tetbl)

Marr, Aitken, Watts Family Tree — Kemsley, John (1) (http://tinyurl.com/ycm5amxx)

Marr, Aitken, Watts Family Tree — Kemsley, John (2) (http://tinyurl.com/yysqfjsw)

Marr, Aitken, Watts Family Tree — Kemsley, Robert (1) (http://tinyurl.com/y6073amd)

Marr, Aitken, Watts Family Tree — Kemsley, Robert (2) (http://tinyurl.com/yxkpzhar)

Marr, Aitken, Watts Family Tree — Kemsley, Stephanus (http://tinyurl.com/yxpfb2dj)

Marr, Aitken, Watts Family Tree — Kemsley, Stephen (http://tinyurl.com/y4oke7zu)

Marr, Aitken, Watts Family Tree — Kemsley, Thomas (http://tinyurl.com/yxeo5rvg)

Marr, Aitken, Watts Family Tree — Kemsley, William Gregory (http://tinyurl.com/yyk5hutf)

Marr, Aitken, Watts Family Tree — King, Mary (http://tinyurl.com/yyrfo6dv)

Marr, Aitken, Watts Family Tree — Parker, Walter Robert (http://tinyurl.com/uaj4bg4)

Marr, Aitken, Watts Family Tree — Ray, Maria (http://tinyurl.com/t7svxda)

Marr, Aitken, Watts Family Tree — Stories, Buckingbong Station (http://tinyurl.com/y23c4p65)

Marr, Aitken, Watts Family Tree — Surman, Charlotte Elizabeth (http://tinyurl.com/y8zfn83x)

Marr, Aitken, Watts Family Tree — Williams, Henry (http://tinyurl.com/y4x6qkja)

Mary Wade Family Website — Charlotte Jenkins (http://tinyurl.com/y2hmhxpe)

Murray, Frank, *My Early Pioneers and Their Lives* (http://tinyurl.com/y4zh9y5f) and (http://tinyurl.com/rguj5vu)

My Heritage — George Merriman (1820-1860) (http://tinyurl.com/ycozudp7)

My Heritage — Thomas Jenkins (http://tinyurl.com/sva4hee)

RootsWeb — AUS — VIC — NE — Clark Family, Wangaratta (No. 16) (http://tinyurl.com/tjx2t2d)

RootsWeb — Eliza Williams (http://tinyurl.com/y2afez82)

RootsWeb — Re Gundagai (http://tinyurl.com/y27s5dk6)

William Duncombe/Mary Haughton Family Website — Henry Smithers Hayes [2227] (http://tinyurl.com/rgbuhnz)

William Duncombe/Mary Haughton Family Website — William Hamilton Hayes [2229] (http://tinyurl.com/se7bz3t)

Wikitree — Charlotte Elizabeth Gardner (1830-1896) (http://tinyurl.com/y6wxlkqo)

Wikitree — George Merriman (1820-1860) (http://tinyurl.com/sua7o3o)

Wikitree — John Henry Williams (1833-1922) (http://tinyurl.com/y33q5zjr)

Wikitree — Louis Edward A. Margules (1819-1896) (http://tinyurl.com/yazcwqbk)

Wikitree — Louis Margules (1860-1949) (http://tinyurl.com/y9gmvczl)

Wikitree — Ridley Frederick Williams (1850-1922) (http://tinyurl.com/y4f2sxh3)

Wikitree — Thomas Dillon (1774-1852) (http://tinyurl.com/y6sqytoj)

Document Collections and Unpublished Works

Berrima District Historical and Family History Society: *File of Jenkins Family-related documents* ("the *Jenkins Family File*")

Dredge, James: *Diaries, Notebook and Letterbook, ?1817 to 1845* (State Library of Victoria, MS 11625)

McNeill, Ian: *In Search of our Colonial Heritage: A Story of John Jenkins and his Family* (monograph held in the possession of the Berrima District Historical and Family History Society)

Morris, Sherry: *Biographical Notes — John Jenkins ("Johnny")* (monograph held in the possession of the Wagga Wagga City Library)

Ridley Williams' Diary (manuscript typed from a hand-written original by Robert Purvis and incorporated by Adela Purvis in Book 2 of a bound but unpublished collection of essays entitled *Heroes Unsung* held in the Alice Springs Library)

Gormly, Richard: *Early History of Nangus Station* (1961) (monograph held in the files of the Heritage Council of New South Wales)

Architectual Conservation Consultants: *Nangus Station Homestead: Report to Accompany an Application to the Heritage Council of New South Wales for Financial Assistance* (1981) ("*Nangus Station Homestead Report*") (report held in the files of the Heritage Council of New South Wales)

The Family Hotel History Notice Board (affixed to the front of *The Family Hotel* in Gundagai)

Baylis, James: "Notes on Buckingbong Station" in *Recollections of the Murrumbidgee District* (manuscript held in the Mitchell Library, Sydney: 1832-1888: Ab 139/1)

Henry Campey: *H. and J. Campey Papers* (documentary collection held in the Mitchell Library, Sydney: MS 1380/1)

Black, Niel: *Journal, 30 September 1839 — 8 May 1840* (manuscript held in the State Library of Victoria: MS 11519, Box 99/1)

Mayrick, Henry Howard: *Letters, 1840-1847* (copies held in the State Library of Victoria: MS 7959

Theses

Perrott, Jennifer: *For the Moral Good? The Government Scheme to Unite Convicts with their Families* (Master of Humanities Thesis, University of Tasmania, 1994)

Read, Peter John: *A History of the Wiradjuri People of New South Wales 1883-1969* (PhD Thesis, Australian National University, 1983)

Robinson, Shirleene: *"Something like slavery?" The Exploitation of Aboriginal child labour in Queensland 1842-1945* (PhD Thesis, University of Queensland, 2003)

Newspapers and Magazines

Albury Banner and Wodonga Express (Albury, New South Wales)
Australian Financial Review (Sydney, New South Wales)
Australian Star (Sydney, New South Wales)
Australian Town and Country Journal (Sydney, New South Waales)
Beef Central (Brisbane, Queensland)
Bell's Life in Sydney and Sporting Review (Sydney, New South Wales)
Border Watch (Mount Gambier, South Australia)
Bowral Free Press (Bowral, New South Wales)
Bowral Free Press and Berrima District Intelligencer (Bowral, New South Wales)
Brisbane Courier (Brisbane, New South Wales)
Canberra Times (Canberra, Australian Capital Territory)
Charleville Times (Charleville, Queensland)
Cootamundra Herald (Cootamundra, New South Wales)
Corowa Free Press (Corowa, New South Wales)
Daily Advertiser (Wagga Wagga, New South Wales)
Daily Telegraph (Sydney, New South Wales)
Evening News (Sydney, New South Wales)
Express and Telegraph (Adelaide, South Australia)
Goulburn Herald (Goulburn, New South Wales)
Goulburn Herald and Chronicle (Goulburn, New South Wales)
Goulburn Herald and County of Argyle Advertiser (Goulburn, New South Wales)
Gundagai Times (Gundagai, New South Wales)
Gundagai Times and Tumut, Adelong and Murrumbidgee District Advertiser (Gundagai, New South Wales)
Illustrated Sydney News (Sydney, New South Wales)
Limerick Times (Limerick, Ireland)
Maitland Mercury and Hunter River General Advertiser (Maitland, New South Wales)
McIvor Times and Rodney Advertiser (Heathcote, Victoria)
Mildura Cultivator (Mildura, Victoria)
Mining Record and Grenfell General Advertiser (Grenfell, New South Wales)
Molong Argus (Molong, New South Wales)
Muswellbrook Chronicle (Muswellbrook, New South Wales)
Narandera Argus and Riverina Advertiser (Narrandera, New South Wales)
Narrandera Argus (Narrandera, New South Wales)
Ovens and Murray Advertiser (Beechworth, New South Wales)
Pinnaroo and Border Times (Pinnaroo, South Australia)
Port Augusta Dispatch and Flinders Advertiser (Port Augusta, South Australia)
Port Phillip Gazette and Settlers' Journal (Melbourne, Victoria)
Queenslander (Brisbane, Queensland)
Queensland Figaro and Punch (Brisbane, Queensland)

Queensland Times, Ipswich Herald and General Advertiser (Ipswich, Queensland)
Scrutineer and Berrima District Press (Moss Vale, New South Wales)
South Australian Advertiser (Adelaide, South Australia)
South Australian Chronicle and Weekly Mail (Adelaide, South Australia)
South Australian Register (Adelaide, South Australia)
Southern Highland News (Bowral, New South Wales)
Southern Mail (Bowral, New South Wales)
Sydney Gazette and New South Wales Advertiser (Sydney, New South Wales)
Sydney Mail (Sydney, New South Wales)
Sydney Mail and New South Wales Advertiser (Sydney, New South Wales)
Sydney Morning Herald (Sydney, New South Wales)
The Advertiser (South Australia)
The Argus (Melbourne, Victoria)
The Australasian (Melbourne, Victoria)
The Capricornian (Rockhampton, Queensland)
The Chronicle (Adelaide, South Australia)
The Empire (Sydney, New South Wales)
The Guardian (Australian Edition) (Sydney, New South Wales)
The Journal (Adelaide, South Australia)
The Leader (Melbourne, Victoria)
The News (Adelaide, South Australia)
The Telegraph (Brisbane, Queensland)
The Register (Adelaide, South Australia)
The Week (Brisbane, Queensland)
Tumut and Adelong Times (Tumut, New South Wales)
Wagga Wagga Advertiser (Wagga Wagga new South Wales)
Wagga Wagga Express (Wagga Wagga, New South Wales)
Wagga Wagga Express and Murrumbidgee District Advertiser (Wagga Wagga, New South Wales)
Wangaratta Chronicle (Wangaratta, Victoria)
Warwick Examiner and Times (Warwick, Queensland)
Yass Courier (Yass, New South Wales)

Legislation and Subordinate Legislation

Judgment of Death Act 1823 (UK) (4 Geo. 4 c. 48)

Sale of Waste Lands Act 1846 (Imp) (9 Vic. 19 c. 104)

Act for Protecting the Crown Lands of this Colony from Encroachment, Intrusion and Trespass 1833 (1833) (4 Will. 4 No. 10 (NSW))

Act to Restrain the Unauthorised Occupation of Crown Lands 1836 (NSW) (7 Will. 4 No. 4 (NSW))

Crown Lands Alienation Act 1861 (NSW) (25 Vic. No. 1 (NSW))

Crown Lands Occupation Act 1861 (NSW) (25 Vic. No. 2 (NSW))

Lands Acts Amendments Act 1875 (NSW) (39 Vic. No. 13 (NSW))

Crown Lands Act 1884 (NSW) (48 Vic. No. 18 (NSW))

Crown Lands Act 1884 (Qld) (48 Vic. No. 28 (NSW))

Aboriginals Protection and Restriction of the Sale of Opium Act 1897 (Qld) (61 Vic. No. 17 (Qld))

Order of the Queen in Council 1847 (see the *Port Phillip Gazette and Settler's Journal*, Saturday, 14 August 1847)

Court Reports

O'Shanassy v Joachim and Others [1876] UKPC 7

The Queen v Jenkins [1877] Knox's Reports 295

Government Gazettes

New South Wales Government Gazette (No. 80) (Wednesday, 11 September 1833, p. 356)

New South Wales Government Gazette (No. 242) (Wednesday, 5 October 1836, p. 745)

New South Wales Government Gazette (No. 254) (Wednesday, 21 December 1836, p. 376)

Supplement to the New South Wales Government Gazette (No. 109) (Tuesday, 27 September 1848, p. 1315)

Supplement to the New South Wales Government Gazette (No. 73) (Tuesday, 28 April 1863, p. 986)

Supplement to the New South Wales Government Gazette (No 96) (Friday, 16 April 1869, pp. 1047 and 1049)

Queensland Government Gazette (Saturday, 16 April 1904)

Other Government Records

United Kingdom Parliamentary Debates ("Hansard"), House of Commons (Friday, 9 February 1810, cols. 366-374: Sir Samuel Romilly)

Public Records Office, England and Wales ("PRO") (ASSI, 31/23/95518)

PRO (ASSI, 35/260/2, PFF 790)

National Archives (Home Office — England): Convict Prison Hulks: Registers and Letter Books, 1802-1849 — John Jenkins (Microfilm, H09, Roll 5)

Proceedings of the Old Bailey Online — Henry Thomas Williams (Ref. No. t18200217 — 92) (http://tinyurl.com/ydbw9fkn)

New South Wales Votes and Proceedings (1839), Vol. 2, p. 68

New South Wales Votes and Proceedings (1890), Vol. 6, p. 145

New South Wales State Archives and Records (AONSW, Series 1273, Reels 2505 — 2507 and 2551-2552)

New South Wales State Archives and Records (AONSW, Reel 2748)

New South Wales State Archives and Records (AONSW, 4/2348.2)

New South Wales State Archives and Records (AONSW, 4/2393.2)

New South Wales State Archives and Records (AONSW, 4/2438.2)

New South Wales State Archives and Records (AONSW, 4/2565.1)

State Records of New South Wales, Lands Department, Ministerial Branch, Correspondence (Letter from Edward White to Robert Hoddle — 18 December 1850)

New South Wales Register of Births, Deaths and Marriages — Marriages: Thomas Jenkins and Jane Dunsdon (Vol. 25C, No. 467)

New South Wales Register of Births, Deaths and Marriages — Marriages: Francis Jenkins and Bridget Fennell (No. 5305/1878)

New South Wales Register of Births, Deaths and Marriages — Deaths: Elizabeth Williams (No. 2480/1865)

New South Wales Register of Births, Deaths and Marriages — Deaths: Robert James Jenkins (No. 9311/1871)

New South Wales Register of Births, Deaths and Marriages — Deaths: Charlotte Elizabeth Berthon (No. 10597/1880)

New South Wales Register of Births, Deaths and Marriages — Deaths: Mary Ann Garner (No. 6329/1898)

New South Wales Register of Births, Deaths and Marriages — Deaths: John Jenkins (No. 14209/1899)

New South Wales Register of Births, Deaths and Marriages — Deaths: Francis Jenkins (No. 10226/1902)

Parliament of Victoria: *Parliamentary Debates*, Legislative Assembly (Wednesday, 19 September 2007, p. 3982)

Public Records Office of Victoria ("PROV") — Pastoral Runs Files, 1840-1878 (VPRS 5359 and 5920, No. 798, Mildura)

Victorian Deaths Register — Ridley William Jenkins (No. 1866/11390)

Queensland State Archives — Pastoral Holdings Files (Series 218, Item 437408)

Queensland State Archives — Sale of Crown Lands After Auction (Series 14078, Items 78292 and 78293)

NT Place Names Register — Cockroach Waterhole (http://tinyurl.com/y6lfghec)

NT Place Names Register — Wigley Gorge (http://tinyurl.com/yy6xh2bw)

Australians At War Film Archive: Ronald Williams (No. 1232) (2003) (http://tinyurl.com/ya2ofuvh)

National Film and Sound Archive of Australia — The Broken Melody DVD.